# Praise for *AS WE SPEAK*

### A *New York Post* Notable Career Book of 2011

"Whether you are a seasoned speaker or a novice, the advice here will carry you to the next level, helping you make authentic audience connections, deliver relevant messages, and become a better communicator overall. This book truly helps one master the moment in all kinds of speaking situations."

—Jack A. Markell, governor of Delaware

"This career-changing book will enable you to overcome your fears and limitations, making you a far more effective speaker and inspiring leader of your team, your company, or your country. Their high-impact strategies have been transformational for me. Simply put, it's the single best guide to public speaking you'll ever read."

—Jon Cowan, president, Third Way, and former chief of staff of the U.S. Department of Housing and Urban Development

"The key to being a good coach is good communication. For coaches, leaders, teachers, or parents, this book will help motivate people to be the best they can be."

—Ronnie Lott, NFL Hall of Famer and sports announcer

"Effective communication is critical to success in virtually everything we do. *As We Speak* provides a fresh look and unique perspective that will prove valuable to anyone who needs to improve their communications skills, which is to say, basically . . . all of us!"

—Thomas Rowe, CEO, California State Fund Insurance

"This book is a how-to guide for creating a connection with one person or a thousand. Peter and Shann helped shift my interactions from talking to communicating. Their advice can help you transform your message so it will be received and appreciated."

—Mike Latham, global head of iShares

"This is a must-read book for every leader who wants to communicate with deep impact. It can be used as a guide for self-coaching in all situations where leaders need to stand and deliver."

—George A. Kohlrieser, professor of Leadership and Organizational Behavior, IMD Business School, and author of *Hostage at the Table: How Leaders Can Overcome Conflict, Influence Others, and Raise Performance*

"This book engages the reader not only with the written word, but also with suggested exercises, master tips, feedback forms, and many other tools. Anyone seeking the power to engage need look no further."

—Magnus Bocker, chief executive officer, Singapore Exchange

"Drawing from hundreds of years of cumulative knowledge, ranging from great Russian acting teachers to Fortune 500 CEOs and radio show personalities, *As We Speak* is as strikingly modern as it is practical and insightful. There's not a person I know who wouldn't benefit from a close study of Peter and Shann's profound ideas."

—Jack Conte, composer

"I wish I'd had this book twenty years ago when I was first starting out. It is an important work, not just about communication, but about the most effective ways to bring people together. This book has inspired me to become a better leader."

—Doreen Ida, VP, Marketing, Nestlé USA

"In the new global world, your success is defined by your ability to work across multiple cultures, time zones, and boundaries. This book gives you one crystal-clear universal strategy to do the most important thing of all—create trust."

—Yvon LeRoux, vice president, Cisco Systems

# As We Speak

## HOW TO MAKE YOUR POINT

## AND HAVE IT STICK

*Peter Meyers and Shann Nix*

**ATRIA** PAPERBACK

NEW YORK   LONDON   TORONTO   SYDNEY   NEW DELHI

**ATRIA** PAPERBACK
A Division of Simon & Schuster, Inc.
1230 Avenue of the Americas
New York, NY 10020

First Atria Paperback edition August 2012

**ATRIA** PAPERBACK and colophon are trademarks of Simon & Schuster, Inc.

For information about special discounts for bulk purchases,
please contact Simon & Schuster Special Sales at 1-866-506-1949
or business@simonandschuster.com.

The Simon & Schuster Speakers Bureau can bring authors to
your live event. For more information or to book an event contact the
Simon & Schuster Speakers Bureau at 1-866-248-3049 or visit our website
at www.simonspeakers.com.

Designed by Dana Sloan

Manufactured in the United States of America

10   9   8   7   6   5   4   3   2

The Library of Congress has cataloged the hardcover edition as follows:

Meyers, Peter, date.
 As we speak : how to make your point and have it stick / Peter Meyers and Shann Nix.
   p. cm.
 Includes bibliographical references.
1. Interpersonal communication. 2. Communication in management. 3. Public speaking.
I. Nix, Shann. II. Title.
   HM1166.M49 2011
   808.5′1—dc22                                        2011015029

ISBN 978-1-4391-5305-5
ISBN 978-1-4391-5308-6 (pbk)
ISBN 978-1-4391-7139-4 (ebook)

We dedicate this book to our fathers.

*Peter:*

When I was eight years old, my father became the youngest vice president at Fruit of the Loom. He brought home a dark leather-bound book, with gold lettering on the cover, called *Better Letters*. It became his Bible; using it, he taught me that nothing is more important than good communication. He traveled a lot, wrote us letters, and insisted that we write back. He engaged us at the dinner table, made us fight for our ideas, developed in us the ability to have a point of view and be able to defend it. I would like to dedicate this book to my father, Howard A. Meyers—always a true champion of the spoken word.

*Shann:*

My father grew up on a dirt farm in West Texas, with no art anywhere in sight. From this arid beginning, he somehow managed to conjure for our family a lush oasis of creative expression, opera, and literature. I learned the art of good conversation around our dinner table. In his seventies, my father rather spectacularly developed yet another career and became the author of a number of books detailing his inspired perceptions, both mystic and scientific, of the cosmos. With love and respect, I dedicate this book to Don Clinton Nix—the man who taught me to speak up for myself.

# CONTENTS

# As We Speak

# INTRODUCTION

YOU'RE WAITING IN the dark, about to go onstage to give your big presentation. Your palms are wet. You're pacing back and forth, thumbing through your notecards. You should have numbered them. You dropped them coming up the stairs, and now they're completely out of order. What does the first slide say? You can't remember. You should have stayed up longer last night. You should have spent more time preparing. Did you choose the right tie? Is the knot straight? You check it again. The suit that looked fine this morning suddenly feels crumpled and too tight.

Your face feels red and hot. What if you forget what you're going to say? What if they don't like you? What if they ask you tough questions? What if they find out that you're not as smart as they think you are? There are people in that audience who know more about this topic than you do, you're sure of it . . .

You peek out from behind the heavy red velvet curtain again. There are still people coming in and finding their seats. The people who are seated look bored already, and you haven't said a word yet. You spot your boss in the second row, looking worried. He's got high hopes for you. Just this morning, he told you how much is riding on this presentation. Sitting next to your boss is Brad—the guy in the office who's after your job. Brad is leaning back in his chair, arms folded, smirking. He's got a clipboard and a red pen on his lap, ready to take notes and find the holes in your data. He's looking forward to this, you can tell.

You can see nearly all of your colleagues in the audience. If only it were just a customer meeting, where the worst that could happen was that you would lose the account. But these people know you. You will have to face them tomorrow in the elevator, and every morning after that. Whatever you say out there on that stage, you will have to live with for the next few years. It will be talked about, written about, gossiped about. They're already looking at their watches, pulling out their smartphones, poised to text and tweet the results of your efforts around the globe before you leave the stage.

You can feel your heart thumping against your ribs. All you can do is pray that your boss won't recognize the look of terror on your face. You can feel the sweat on your upper lip, and you wipe it off. You notice that your hands are trembling. You shove them in your pockets, then pull them out again.

A sympathetic gray-haired lady introduces you. There is a smattering of applause. You raise your chin, take a deep breath, and walk out onstage. The bright lights hit you like a wall. As you look into the audience, you can feel five hundred sets of eyeballs staring at you. Everything feels surreal, as if you're in a dream. Every nerve in your body is screaming at you to run. Your legs are moving on their own, like some macabre dance step. Why are you here? Why did you ever agree to this? Your hands, despite your best intentions, seem to have wound up in your pockets again. With an effort you pull them out, and grab the podium with white knuckles. Your mouth has gone dry, and you notice, too late, that there is no water glass at the podium. You quickly check the computer screen, and then look up. Your brain is completely blank. You cannot remember your name, much less the first line of your presentation. The silent seconds stretch out like hours. The people in the front row are watching you with an expression that you realize, after a moment, is pity.

Does this sound like your worst nightmare? If you're terrified by the thought of standing up and speaking in front of a group of people, you're not alone. And there's nothing wrong with you. The problem is that as human beings, *we are hardwired to fail* in a situation like this.

Why is that? Well, it's because of two tiny, almond-shaped structures in your brain called the amygdalae. Lodged in the oldest part of the brain, the amygdalae have only one job, and it's not to think—it's to keep you alive. The amygdalae never sleep; they are part of an early-warning system that constantly scans for danger and sends an alert to your body anytime you're under threat. And at the moment, standing on that stage, your DNA tells you that you are in serious trouble. Your mammalian brain, sharpened by millions of years of evolution, knows exactly what it means to feel hundreds of eyes staring at you from out of the darkness. It means you're about to be *lunch*.

Your amygdalae swing into action. They wrest control away from your evolved higher brain, and pass it back to the primitive part of your brain that specializes in survival. The adrenal glands, sitting just over your kidneys, start to pump adrenaline into your system. You breathe more rapidly, oxygenating the blood. Your heartbeat speeds up, preparing you for exertion. You start to sweat, becoming slippery and harder to grab. Your vision sharpens in preparation for battle or escape. Blood flow is redirected toward the large muscle groups in your arms and legs, to help you fight or run. All noncritical functions shut down. Blood is robbed from any organ not immediately necessary for survival.

Unfortunately for you right now, one of these nonessentials is your frontal cortex, where language is processed. The words of your carefully prepared presentation leave your head as the blood drains away from your forebrain. You blank your opening. You feel stupid because, at that moment, your IQ has actually dropped. You are in the middle of what is called an **amygdala hijack.**

Being smart, successful, beautiful, or talented doesn't protect you from falling prey to an amygdala hijack. In fact, lots of Fortune 500

CEOs, global leaders, diplomats, ambassadors, and political candidates experience the same problem. And when they do, many of them call us.

Who are we? We're two people who come from the front lines of high-performance communication. Peter Meyers is the founder and director of Stand & Deliver, a company that travels the world to coach CEOs and top executives in the United States, Western Europe, Scandinavia, Russia, Japan, Latin America, and the Middle East. Shann Nix is an award-winning journalist, novelist, playwright, and former radio talk show host on a number one–rated radio station, speaking to nearly one million listeners a night. Together we have a combined fifty years of experience working in theater, radio, film, television, fiction, and journalism.

And what do we do? Well, when a leader steps into the spotlight, all eyes are on him. Whether it's the president of the United States or the president of the local library fund, the expectations when he opens his mouth are daunting. He's supposed to automatically exhibit certain qualities of insight, clarity, and confidence.

The problem is that being smart doesn't necessarily make someone a good communicator. In fact, the tragedy of many smart people is that their ability to *think* exceeds their ability to *speak*. And that's where we come in.

We are often called into a high-stakes situation twenty-four or forty-eight hours before the event, to avert a potential communication crisis. We've coached leaders in greenrooms just before they step out onstage, and rewritten speeches through the night before the morning of the presentation. We develop the language and content, put them on their feet, rehearse them, and give them the tools they need to rise to the occasion.

Sometimes we come in when the leaders of an organization need to win the hearts and minds of their people, to influence a team to step up to a new challenge or align disparate groups so that they're working more collaboratively.

We are often asked to work with a high-level executive who is intelligent and experienced, but who is undermining her own authority with old habits. We help her translate her ideas into action, and to speak with a level of authority and confidence so that she will finally get the attention she deserves. We might coach the senior vice president who is brilliant at his job, but falls apart when asked to report to the board. We help speakers provide clarity where there is confusion, credibility where there is doubt, and excitement where there is monotony.

We're brought in to make sure that the thinking gets the expression it deserves: that the quality of the ideas is matched by the vitality of the speaker's presence. We work with smart midlevel people who are getting passed over because they are unable to speak up. We help people who want to communicate better in meetings, who are asking questions like: "How do I jump in?" "How do I fight against the extroverts?" "How do I hold my own in the room if I'm more of a reflective thinker, or a numbers guy?" We're often called in to work with financial or analytical people who need to know how to translate data into memorable, compelling narratives. Often we are asked to work with CEOs who are intelligent but emotionally cold, struggling to connect with their people.

People generally call us for one of two reasons. Either they've already had some success in communication and, having had a taste of it, want more; or they've had a painful experience like the one we described in the opening, and don't ever want to suffer like that again. A lot of the people who call us are "getting through" their presentations, but the process of preparation is filled with dread. They want to stop the panic, and start to enjoy the process and get better results. There are a lot of people out there who are already *pretty good* communicators. But in the words of Jim Collins, "good is the enemy of great." We work with people who are committed to raising their standards.

If you're reading this book, congratulations. You've clearly understood that if you want to get things done, you need to communicate well. Regardless of the technology available out there, you know that you still motivate people one presentation or one conversation at a time.

You now have access to the same information and practical techniques as the CEOs and organizational leaders who call us in to work with them, or fly around the world to take our trainings. It's here in your hands. This book and the accompanying Web-based links will provide you with a virtual learning experience that's designed to dramatically raise your impact when speaking.

You don't *get* confidence. It's not something you go out and acquire. And nobody can *give* you confidence. Confidence comes from challenging yourself to do difficult things, and coming out the other side. It comes from accumulating a series of victories, both large and small. Having the right knowledge and the right skills, at the right time, is absolutely essential. But your fears can only be conquered by doing the thing you fear the most, getting it right, and demonstrating to yourself that you can overcome it. This book is designed so that when you do face the fear, you will be victorious—time after time.

We will help you demystify the daunting experience of facing a crowd. Our intention is to move you through the fear, into a position of strength and generosity, so that you can offer your knowledge as a gift to others.

Why bother to think of speaking as an opportunity to give a gift?

There are two kinds of speaking. Sometimes we speak purely for our own benefit, to get something off our chests, or to think through something out loud. We may talk simply in reaction to something that has just happened. We usually talk based on what we want to say.

But there's another kind of speaking, in which you speak with the intention of having an impact on another human being. You are giving something, whether it is knowledge, insight, information, inspiration, an experience, or a feeling.

When someone speaks with the intention to impart something that will change the listener, it becomes an act of leadership. She constructs language designed to create something that doesn't exist yet. She asks the question "How do I make this a better situation?" and then uses her words and ideas to bring this about.

Of course it's good for the listener when the speaker has the intention of giving a gift. *But it's good for the speaker as well.* The fear and the monotony that are the bane of public speaking disappear in the face of a generous spirit. It's a mysterious principle of human communication: when you are giving, you tend to be more interesting, and fear is held at bay. Because you're engaged in a purpose that is larger than yourself, a magical effect occurs. You find the compelling reason to do what you're doing, and it draws you forward. The desire to make a difference is more exciting than being scared. The hope of something greater is stronger than the fear. It's the only thing that takes us through terror.

Well, you might say, that sounds great for people who get to make inspiring speeches. But what about me? All I do is present data for quarterly updates. Will this work for me?

Yes!

Even if what you're doing is sitting in a toll booth and saying thank you after every interaction, it's the **intention** that informs your communication. Performing the most basic routine, including saying "Good morning," with the intention to give a gift will elevate what you're doing. The intention transforms the action.

## PETER

I once sat in a five-star restaurant in Paris, and watched a waiter working. He moved as if he were on skates, gliding so smoothly, with such balance, that it was a pleasure to watch him. As he put the food down on each table, he said something to the people sitting there. Each diner's face would light up as the waiter spoke. I watched the other waiters, and no one seemed to be having the same impact on the people they were serving. I caught this waiter's eye, and he came over to my table at once.

"May I help you, m'sieur?"

"I know this sounds like a strange question," I said, "but I've been watching you, and you seem to be having a huge impact on the people in this room. What are you saying to them?"

He smiled. "As a young man, when I first came to work in a fine restaurant, I was instructed by the headwaiter to say 'Bon appétit' after I served each table. Because I was in such a rush, I would usually just put the plates down, repeat, 'Bon appétit,' and leave quickly. One day I noticed that there was one second, after I put the plate down, when the diners would look up at me. I found that in that moment, I could look into their eyes, say, 'Bon appétit,' and mean it. I could tell them without words, 'I wish that you have a good meal. I want you to be happy.' Through this simplest gesture, I could make them feel wonderful. It took only a moment to do this, to put the plate down in front of them as if I had cooked it myself. I went from serving food to serving a sacrament. I am the most fortunate of men, m'sieur. What an honor it is to host a meal, to bring nourishment to people, to offer things that brought them joy and delight!"

That's where I learned that with the right intention, you can transform anything into the opportunity to give a gift.

---

This is good news for you as a speaker. What it means is that you don't have to be perfect. Your intention to give a gift trumps the necessity to be flawless. Yes, it's nice to get the words right. But it's okay to flub a line, or to make a mistake, because it's the *overall experience* that will linger in their mind.

We've all sat through the presentation of someone who said the right words and showed the right slides, but still left us feeling cold. Remember the now infamous Tiger Words apology? He had every phrase and camera angle perfect—and ended up infuriating everyone even more. We can feel it when someone is aligned with serving our needs, and we can feel it when they're out to save their own backside. You can sense the difference.

Then there's the other end of the spectrum—we've all listened to someone who may have made plenty of mistakes, who was rough or raw or edgy, but who moved us in a way that we never forgot. Perfection is not the answer. You don't need to become slicker, glossier, or more "sales-y" to have more influence on the people around you. You need to be *more authentic.*

Self-consciousness is nothing more than *too much concentration on self.* It's an obsessive concern with questions like: "Do I look good?" "Do I sound smart?" "How do I make sure I don't look like a fool?"

When we relieve ourselves of the compulsive concern with looking good, and put ourselves in the service of the listener, we start asking different questions. We ask questions like: "How can I make a difference to them?" "What knowledge can I share?" "What insights can I offer?" "How can I reassure them, congratulate them, lighten their workload?" "How can I bring them joy, comfort, curiosity, or excitement?"

At this moment, the prospect of facing a crowd stops being paralyzing, and becomes a great honor. Once a person is acting on behalf of another, a different quality shows up. This simple change of focus summons our best intelligence, our best energy. It unleashes expressive powers that were always there, but might have otherwise remained dormant. In the moments when we realize we're living for something larger than ourselves, we become more resourceful. You want more courage when you're speaking? Speak in the service of something larger than yourself. Courage is easy to summon when you're driven by a higher purpose. Any of us can reflect back on moments when we have stood up for something, or stood for something, and found that voice, depth, power, energy, or force of will was there when we needed it.

You engage in hundreds of conversations every week, with people who matter. You might be speaking to one person over the kitchen table, or to five hundred people in an auditorium. Each one of these conversations has the potential to change the course of events in your life, your career, your family, your school, or your organization. It is a bold and audacious act to ask for change.

It is, in fact, an act of leadership. And in order to achieve your desired result, your communication must be effective. It's that simple.

The world is full of brilliant people whose ideas are never heard. This book is designed to make sure that you're not one of them. It's about developing your ability to create change through the power of the spoken word. There has never been a greater need for you to step forward and make your own personal contribution. Now more than ever, we're looking to our parents, teachers, bosses, colleagues, and political leaders for direction, meaning, and trust. If you fall into one of those categories, this book is for you.

No matter what you actually do, you're in the relationship business. Your level of influence is determined by the quality of your relationships. And those relationships are defined by the quality of your communication. Good communication is like good manners: it takes the other person's well-being into account. It's about being clear, relevant, and succinct—crafting your message in a way that's easy for the other person to understand, absorb, and remember.

Once upon a time, information was power. Now that you can get all the data you need in a heartbeat, the information age is over. The Internet ended it, by making information free and equally available to everyone.

Now we are drowning in data, and starved for meaningful connection.

Trying to influence someone by simply offering him information doesn't work. Recent research has revealed the dirty secret of the human brain: decisions are made not on the left side of the brain, which deals with logic, facts, analysis, and sequential process, but on the right side of the brain, which deals with emotions, concepts, metaphors, humor and stories.[1] In other words, we make decisions based not on the facts, but on how we *feel*. We "go with our gut," or "have a hunch." Then we scurry over to the logical side of the brain—the left side—and gather the facts and arguments we need to back up the decision we've already made.

So when you try to influence someone purely by giving him data, you're speaking to the wrong part of the brain. You're wasting your time.

We've been doing it backward. Now we know better. Expert communication these days is no longer about downloading data; it's about creating an emotional experience for the listener. Realistically, you will forget 90 percent of whatever you heard today by the time your head hits the pillow—and so will your listener. As Warren Beatty once said, "They may forget what you said, but they will never forget how you made them feel."

Most of us make our first mistake in communication before we ever open our mouths. We assume that the listener cares about what we want to say.

But they don't.

Not because they're selfish or bad people. It's just that each person's favorite subject is himself. And the question the listener is asking, as soon as you begin to speak, is: "What's in it for me?" Still, most of us will go into a difficult conversation and stubbornly insist on talking about what we want to say.

There's not a shred of evidence that this has any positive impact on the other person.

To truly communicate with another person, you need to think about what *they* need. Not just telling them what they want to hear—but understanding what the other person needs to feel, know, and experience in order to create a shift in their thinking.

***It's not about you. It's all about them.***

A leader's impact is exponential; not just a few, but hundreds or thousands of people are affected by every word he speaks. If you've ever left a job because of your boss's communication skills (or lack of them!) you're not alone; it's the reason most frequently given for leaving a position. And yet most people don't wake up and say, "How can I ruin someone's day with my words today?" The issue is that they wake up and ask, "How can I get across *what I want to say*?" without thinking about how it's going to impact the listener. And in the process they often end up leaving people confused, angry, or overwhelmed.

What does this mean for someone who's about to stand up and give a speech to a tough crowd? What about the parent who's about to have a difficult conversation with a teenager? What does it mean for you when you're about to walk into a situation where emotions are already running high?

This book is about how all the knowledge in the world comes down to one point of contact. It's about your ability to create a bond with the listener so that even in a hostile situation, you begin to shift their experience, overcome the hostility, and instill a sense of trust.

The problem is that the situation itself conspires against us. For hundreds of thousands of years, our amygdalae have thrown us into a relentless scan for danger. We are conditioned to ask the question "How can I get through this without getting hurt?"

We need to recondition ourselves. To overcome this process requires nothing short of rewiring the brain.

So, how do you rewire the brain?

This work begins at the level of **mind-set** and **beliefs.** When you're trying to influence others, the first person you have to influence is yourself. This is the critical part of the process that is neglected in traditional presentation training. Lots of communication coaches will do "trait training," in which they tell you how to use your hands, inflect your voice, where to stand, how to use slides.

We say that speaking is an "inside job." After working with thousands of people across the world, it has become clear to us that generally the problem isn't outside, it's *inside*. Rarely do we come across someone who needs "vocal training." Your voice is fine. Your hands are fine. For decades, you've been using them to communicate effectively with other people. The question is, what are you doing inside your head that makes you behave unnaturally when you're in the spotlight?

Sure, this book will offer you detailed insider information on how professionals use their hands, eyes, body, and voice onstage. But more important, we'll give you the technology to explore and shift your own mind-set and beliefs about speaking, so that you truly begin to experience speaking as an opportunity to give a gift. You will learn to stop worrying about things like "Will they like me?" and look forward to your next presentation as a chance to *connect*.

Real communication can only occur when there is a human connection. Without connection, there is no influence, no rapport, no moving the listener from point A to point B. And this connection is *not* going to be forged during an eye-wateringly boring slide presentation in a darkened room, where someone is repeating text that you've already read on their slides. Connection happens when you show up, shed your armor, and let the listener see the light in your eyes. It's about getting close to the people with whom you're communicating, in such a way that you are able to meet some of their needs. We call this a **bond.**

And this bond can be a powerful and much-needed thing, because we live in frightening times. Many people feel that they are trapped in a downward spiral, in which they have no control over their own fate, and no faith that their leaders can save them. One of the few things you can control is your own ability to communicate clearly. Learning to clarify your outcome, connect with your listener, and make your point in a persuasive, memorable way makes you the master of your own destiny. It's the best possible investment you can make toward your own security. No matter where the future may take you, superior communication skills will give you the greatest possible advantage.

These days, trust is the highest currency. The level of trust that you win or lose is directly proportionate to the quality of your communication. We decide very quickly whether or not we trust someone, based not only on the information they give us but on *the way they say it*. You may have the best data in the world, but if your body language doesn't match your message, your listener will instinctively distrust what you say.

Think about it. During an average week, how much of your time is spent in meetings? And how many of those meetings go on far too long, with people jabbering on meaninglessly until you clutch for any form of caffeine or sugar, desperate just to stay awake?

Well, here's the bad news: those people are *you*. We all use far too many words. We have lost the art of brevity. We have forgotten how to convey our message in vivid, visceral language that makes communication pleasurable. We are draining the lifeblood of our organizations, killing millions of brain cells per hour with sheer boredom.

Look around you the next time you're in a meeting. What do you see? Are people engaged? Are they contributing? Are they discovering and articulating their ideas with passion? Or are they sitting back and passively attending, waiting for the meeting to be over? For those of us in organizations, it's critical that we redefine these times when we are gathered together in a room as an opportunity to wake up our sense of purpose, excitement, and meaning.

People who consistently achieve results in this field have one thing in common: they've raised their standards. In the last century, you could afford to show up and do an average job. After fifty years, you might well be given a gold watch and a pat on the back. Today if you do an average job, you will simply be forgotten. Having good information is no longer good enough. Each person to whom you speak has thousands of bids on their attention every day, from advertising, TV, Internet, radio, digital billboards, texts, cold calls, etc. It is only at the level of outstanding that your voice will rise above the din. To break through the chatter, you need a strategy. We call this strategy **High Performance Communication.**

Think of it this way: **High Performance Communication gets results. Everything else is just talk.**

High Performance Communication is about creating clarity where there's confusion. It's about creating relevance when people feel disconnected. And most important, it's about inspiring people to achieve things they never thought possible.

As a species, we've spent a lot of time improving our machines, and very little improving our communication skills. In fact, communication hasn't changed much in the two thousand years since the Greeks perfected the art of dialectic in the forum. Over the past fifty years, we've actually lost ground in the art of conversation.

Today we exist in a web of connections, and technology gives us the power to extend that web all over the globe. The challenge is that too often technologies like e-mail, phone conferencing, and video communication can actually distance us from the listener, unless we are skillful enough to use these technologies to enhance the bond. The technology on its own won't automatically connect you to your listener—just as a musical instrument won't play itself. You must learn to use the medium so that it projects *you* through time and space, without dulling and deadening the human component.

In today's high-tech environment, the ability to use the spoken word well is becoming increasingly rare. Master it, and you will have an enormous advantage. Nothing will accelerate your career or your ability to create change in the world faster than developing your ability to communicate. And nothing will handicap you more than a failure to do so. Who hasn't seen the loss of an intimate relationship because of an inability to communicate? Who hasn't suffered the frustration of being unable to communicate clearly with their boss, kids, or colleagues?

For organizations, the cost of poor communication is not millions, but billions of dollars left on the table. Poor communication by senior management is the number one employee complaint.[2] Poor communication between medical professionals is the greatest cause of life-threatening medical mistakes.[3] And poor communication in families produces teenagers who are more likely to engage in risk-taking behaviors.[4] While the quantity of information we receive every day has increased exponentially, the quality of face-to-face communication has hit an all-time low.

Most of us spend between 75 and 90 percent of our day communicating—and yet we are never trained to do it well. For you, that's about to change. The good news is that the principles of High Performance Communication are universal. Once you've learned them, the very same rules apply whether you are speaking to one teenager or an audience of five thousand.

## GETTING STARTED

In our work, we've discovered an interesting fact: the higher you go in an organization, the shorter your attention span. CEOs don't have time to waste.

Neither do you.

So, we've gathered materials from many different sources, and distilled them into a handbook of core principles that works immediately to raise your level of confidence and your ability to influence. We have drawn heavily from the works of: Constantin Stanislavski, the great Russian acting teacher; psychologist Abraham Maslow, for his insights on needs analysis; and motivational speaker Anthony Robbins, for his expertise on state and peak performance. We have also taken much information and inspiration from the fields of sports, psychology, Neuro-Linguistic Programming, and the martial and performing arts.

We have kept this book intentionally lean and fast-paced, designed to provide you with practices that will make you Monday morning–ready. But there's a world of wonderful theoretical reading to be done in many fields that connect through the discipline of communication.

For more detailed information on our sources, citations, and favorite books, please see the end notes and bibliography at the end. A note about gender references: to avoid awkward "him or herself" constructions, we have scattered male and female pronouns through the text at random. None of these references is intended to convey anything specific about males or females. We've also used fictional names in examples throughout.

*This book is not about learning to relax.* As Jerry Lewis said, "If you're not nervous, you're either a liar or a fool, but you're not a professional." You're never going to be relaxed in a high-stakes situation— nor should you be. Olympic athletes, martial artists, and Broadway actors are not relaxed before they go on. Everyone experiences a rapid surge in energy before an event.

The difference between performing and choking is determined by *what you do with that energy.* An amateur locks the energy in her throat, and chokes on the fear. A top performer interprets the energy as a sign that she is ready, and releases it with her breath. German psychotherapist Fritz Perls put it this way: "Fear is only excitement without the breath." You will learn a method for turning your fear into excitement.

This method is based on principles of human behavior. They are universal laws like the laws of gravity, which have to do with the ways that human beings in every culture respond to certain stimuli. Like good cooking ingredients, once you know how to apply these principles, you can combine them in any number of ways to suit a specific situation.

This book is not just about ideas; it's about putting ideas into action. We will explain a concept, show you how it works, and give you the techniques that will enable you to master it. The point of this training is not just to make a little improvement in your communication skills. It's about producing *transformational results* that will have an immediate impact on the quality of your relationships.

How can you learn to communicate from a book?

High Performance Communication requires three things:

1. A clear strategy.
2. Practice.
3. Feedback.

This book will give you the strategy. But we can't make you practice—you're going to have to do that yourself. If you want to build muscle, you're going to have to go to the gym and actually lift the weights. Just thinking about it won't do the trick.

You're also going to have to get feedback from your listeners. When you're communicating, the only thing that really counts is *the listener's experience.* Trying to improve your communication skills without getting feedback is like trying to fly a plane without instruments—you don't have the information you need to chart your course. We've provided forms in Appendix One, at the back of the book, to make that process simple and specific. Ask your colleagues, hire a coach, beg your friends, or phone us. But one way or another, get feedback!

Although you can read the book on its own, we've designed it as a multidimensional learning experience, with interactive things for you to see, hear, and do. All of these supplemental items are available for you to download. Before you begin Chapter One, go to http://www.stand anddelivergroup.com, where you'll see a prompt for "As We Speak." Along with the forms you'll find some bonus audio tracks there to supplement the reading.

Your success in this area, as in any other, depends on your commitment. Read this as if you were taking a training with us, and allow us to be your coaches. Lean into the training, grab it, and pull it toward you. Do the activities. Participate in the exercises. Download the forms, and fill them out. Be willing to stretch to your outer limits. That's how you develop new capacities.

## HOW TO USE THIS BOOK

The good news is that there are only three things you have to master in High Performance Communication. They are:

1. **Content.**
2. **Delivery.**
3. **State.**

and they work together, as diagrammed below:

Part One focuses on **Content,** which is the sum total of the information you want to convey. You will learn to rapidly construct a clear and lucid architecture of ideas designed to lead your listener through a memorable emotional experience.

Part Two is all about **Delivery,** or the art of expression. You will learn the principles of performance used by professionals—how to use your body, voice, eyes, and hands in a way that naturally supports your message. You will expand the range and effective use of your voice with the help of vocal techniques that are included in the downloads accompanying this book.

**HIGH PERFORMANCE COMMUNICATION**

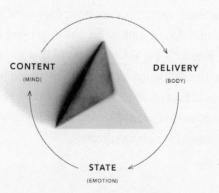

Part Three is about the element that drives both your content and your delivery: your **State.** State is the way you feel when you speak, and it is both the most powerful and most frequently overlooked component of communication. Your state speaks louder than your words. Every professional performer has ways to jumpstart his system into peak performance condition before stepping onto the stage or field, or into the conference room. High performance communicators learn to direct their state to meet the demands of the event.

Part Four applies the principles you've learned to **specific situations.** How do you handle a difficult face-to-face conversation? How about using technology—what's the most effective way to use the different media of phone conference, video, or e-mail? How do you communicate in a crisis, when all eyes are on you and emotions are running high?

Finally, Part Five supplies you with some powerful **tools** that will help you to create a compelling personal vision, organize and clarify your engagements into a relationship dashboard, and enhance your ability to collaborate and innovate with others.

## START WHERE YOU ARE

Chances are, you're reading this book for one of two reasons. Either:

1. You're already getting results from your communication. The success that you've had so far has given you an appetite for greater possibilities. You understand that the ability to speak well is ultimately the deciding factor between who gets the job or promotion, and who stays behind. For you, this book is about moving to the next level of your potential, and creating the conditions for a breakthrough.

or

2. You've had a bad experience, or are afraid of having a bad experience when you stand up to speak. Something might have happened to you that is so painful, you've decided *never again*. The pain has motivated you to gain some expertise. Maybe you've decided that there's something holding you back, and it's the way you talk. You might be undermining your own authority and sabotaging yourself, because you haven't yet learned to communicate your best ideas with power and speed. For you, this book is about identifying ineffective habits, and getting out of your own way.

Either way, in order to move ahead, you need to know two things:

1. Where are you now?
2. Where are you going?

To accomplish this, fill out the self-assessment on pages 22–23. This will give you specific information about what you're already doing well, and what's holding you back. Go through each question and score yourself, assigning yourself the appropriate number value. *Be rigorously honest.*

# Self-Assessment

| CONTENT | |
|---|---|
| **PLEASE RESPOND TO THE FOLLOWING WITH:** | |

5 = *almost always true*

4 = *usually true*

3 = *sometimes true*

2 = *usually not true*

1 = *almost never true*

| | |
|---|---|
| | I bring insightful analysis and relevant detail to my presentations. I support my ideas with evidence and examples to illustrate my points. |
| | I speak to the emotional as well as intellectual needs of my listener. |
| | I use stories and vivid imagery to help people feel and see what I am describing. |
| | I create powerful closings that come full circle with my opening—reinforcing my key point and leaving the audience feeling satisfied. |
| | I create a strong opening by talking about what the listener truly cares about, and rarely begin by talking about myself. |
| | My talk resembles an engaging narrative more than a series of slides, bullet points, and lists of data. |
| | I typically open a conversation or presentation with a central theme or sentence, which I reinforce throughout. |
| | I organize my ideas in an integrated and sequential narrative flow with ideas building upon each other, making it easier for the listener to understand. |
| | I use brevity, and never go on too long. People leave my presentations knowing clearly what I was saying. |
| | I focus on my objective when I'm speaking. I know why I'm speaking and what I want from a particular audience or listener. My listener is consistently moved to new insight, decision, or action. |
| | My language is fresh, active, and easy to understand. I rarely use vague or confusing jargon, acronyms, or clichés. |
| | **< CONTENT** TOTAL SCORE |

## DELIVERY

PLEASE RESPOND TO THE FOLLOWING WITH:

5 = *almost always true*
4 = *usually true*
3 = *sometimes true*
2 = *usually not true*
1 = *almost never true*

| | |
|---|---|
| | I am fully aware of what is happening in the room when I'm speaking to people; I can see and read their responses, and I adjust as needed. |
| | I am comfortable using gestures in front of a group and never feel awkward about using my hands. |
| | I always listen to people and demonstrate that I care about their point of view. |
| | I take time to prepare myself mentally and physically, so that when I speak to one person or one hundred, I am in an optimum performance state. |
| | I begin by gaining rapport with others. I start by creating common ground before jumping into my agenda. |
| | I maintain eye contact while speaking to groups. |
| | My language and tone are generally warm, personable, and conversational. |
| | I use slides, handouts, or media only to support my presentation; I don't let my slides become more important than my presence. |
| | When I speak, I know that I vary my tempo, pitch, and volume to enliven my content with nuance and variety. |
| | < **DELIVERY** TOTAL SCORE |

Now take the following steps:

1. Add up your scores. You will have two separate totals: one for the content, and one for the delivery. For example, you might end up with a score of 30 for content, and 20 for delivery.
2. Take that score, and plot it on the performance grid below. Content is on the vertical axis, delivery on the horizontal. Put a solid dot where you are now.

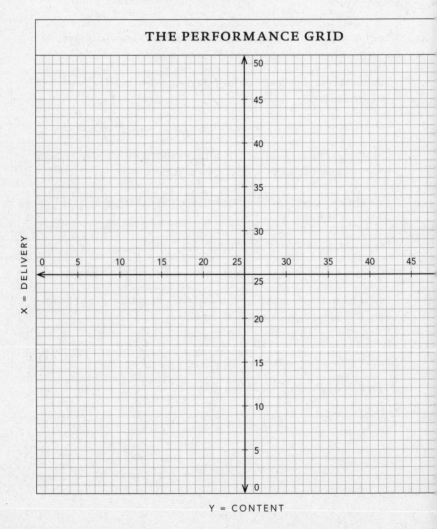

THE PERFORMANCE GRID

## Interpreting Your Score

If you're in the **lower left** box, you're in trouble. You've scored yourself low on both content *and* delivery. Chances are that the listener is having difficulty connecting to your ideas, as well as your style. The result is that they are bored. The danger is that they're disengaging, falling asleep, or getting angry. You need to work on both content and delivery.

If you're in the **lower right** box, you've scored yourself high on delivery, which means that your style—your posture, expression, and voice—are engaging the listener, but the substance is lacking. You may need to work on developing more clarity, relevance, and brevity. People are engaged and maybe even entertained by you, but they're not being nourished intellectually.

If you're in the **upper left,** you've scored yourself high on content, but low on delivery. Most likely your thinking is strong, but your voice and body are not supporting your message in a dynamic way. You are articulating clear points, organizing information well, and targeting your message effectively to the listener—but your delivery is possibly flat and dull, making it difficult for people to stay engaged. The danger here is that the listener wants to hear your good ideas; they are working so hard that they're frustrated. At its worst, there is a level of tedium that produces a negative impact.

If you're in the **upper right,** your ideas are clear, relevant, and organized. Your delivery is dynamic and compelling. You're bringing an appropriate level of energy, passion, and clear thinking that brings value to your listener. You're not only inspiring people, but you're creating results. After listening to you, people are ready to act—to do something. That's High Performance Communication.

See the diagram on the following page for a fuller explanation of the performance grid.

*Note:* The closer you are to the center of any quadrant, the milder the effect you're having on the listener. As you move to the outer edges, the effect becomes more extreme. In other words, if you're in

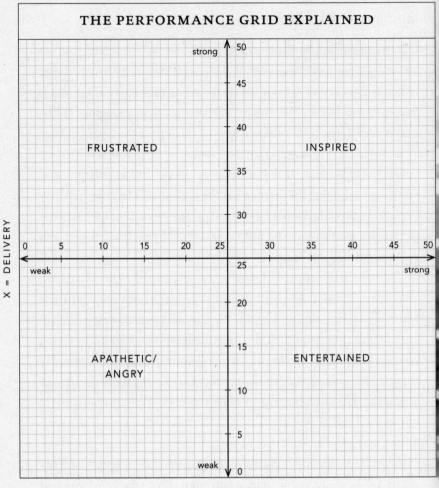

## THE PERFORMANCE GRID EXPLAINED

X = DELIVERY
Y = CONTENT

FRUSTRATED

INSPIRED

APATHETIC/
ANGRY

ENTERTAINED

strong
weak
strong
weak

### THE LISTENER FEELS:

**FRUSTRATED**
- Great Content
- Flat Performance
- Audience is interested in the
  message but has difficulty
  staying focused.

**INSPIRED**
- Great Content
- Engaging Performance
- Audience is stimulated by
  ideas and moved to take
  action.

**APATHETIC**
- Poor Content
- Flat Performance
- Audience daydreams or
  performs tasks while
  pretending to listen.

**ENTERTAINED**
- Poor Content
- Engaging Performance
- Audience is pleasantly
  engaged but dismisses
  event as superficial.

the "frustrated" quadrant, and you're close to the X-Y axis, your listener is mildly frustrated. If you're at the outer edges, they're grinding their teeth when they listen to you!

Notice that the upper right is the **only** quadrant in which you get positive results. Every other quadrant *produces a negative experience for the listener.*

## What Next?

1. If you want to create growth, you need a clear and compelling goal. What are the results you want to create in your relationships at work, at home, and with your friends? In order to achieve that, where does your communication need to appear on the performance grid? Put an X on that spot. (Hint—it should be somewhere in the upper right quadrant!)
2. Draw a line between the solid dot that marks where you are now and the X that marks where you need to be.
3. Note the angle of the line. If the line is vertical, you need to work on content. If it's horizontal, you need to work on delivery. If the line is at an angle, you need work on both content and delivery.

Let this analysis guide you as you go through the book; it will tell you where you need to concentrate your focus first. You become a co-creator in your own curriculum by directing how you want to learn. *We want you to get results.* If you have a limited amount of time, go straight to the place where you need the most work.

But the elements of content, delivery, and state are linked. If you want to achieve a breakthrough in your communication, you need to master all three.

If you want to go deeper and take the assessment process to the next level, we've included an additional tool in Appendix One at the back of the book. This is an assessment survey that you hand out to people you know, so that you can get a 360-degree survey of exactly how listeners are experiencing your communication. The results you get may surprise you! Use the communication feedback data to determine the order in which you pick up the skills.

After two decades of coaching, we know that when you're learning something new, it's essential to acquire one skill at a time. Don't try to focus on everything at once. Keep the book on your desk and use it as a handbook, a guide, and a reference tool. Like any muscle group, the new skill sets that you are developing will be strengthened over time with practice. If you're stepping into the spotlight within forty-eight hours, go straight to delivery and finish with state. If you are facing a presentation that is a week or more away, start with content. Move on to delivery and finish with state.

## OUR COMMITMENT TO YOU

If you're not under a deadline, start by going through the full assessment process. Evaluate yourself, then get the key people around you to complete the assessment in Appendix One. Apply and practice this technology for thirty days. Then hand out the assessments again, to the same people.

Compare the results.

You'll be amazed at the difference—we promise.

Now, let's get to work.

# Part One

CONTENT

CONTENT IS WHAT you say. It's your words, images, stories, statistics, metaphors, messages, pie charts, and data, all arranged in an order that makes sense.

What makes great content?

Let's start by looking at what can go wrong. In twenty-six countries across the world, the people we've spoken to during our trainings all make the same complaints about horrible presentations they've suffered through:

1. Too much information.
2. Not relevant.
3. No point.

When it comes to content, the challenge is that once again, we are hardwired to get it wrong. Here's why: most of the time we are talking about what we want to say. Makes sense, right? We might even talk about our own point of view, as if it actually mattered to our listener. And we may be tempted to add every piece of data we can think of, just to try to impress the listener with how smart we are.

But that's not going to work, because the listener does not automatically care what you want to say, or how many facts you can throw around. Your listener cares about himself. What's in it for him? If you're trying to influence someone, it's not about what you want to say. It's about **what the listener needs to know and feel.** High Performance Communicators ask this question: what does the listener require, in order to make a new decision?

To help you make this subtle but critical shift in how you approach your content, let's look at someone who's getting it wrong. Consider the example of John. John needs to go in and motivate his listeners to raise their performance. How's he doing?

> *Hi, I'm John Stevens, and I'm the senior vice president here. I just want to say how happy I am to be here. I have been with this company for sixteen years, and I have waited for this day for a long time. I'm really passionate about this. I just want to say that I was the guy who said this could never be done. I was the one who never believed it. So today, I want you to know how much I appreciate what we're about to do. What I want from everybody here is a full commitment. I want you to walk out of here today ready to take the hill. I know we can do it. We need to go from 10 to 15 percent this quarter, and with the new technology, and everyone's full involvement, I know we can make this happen.*

How's he doing? Are you feeling motivated? Probably not! And why not? Because all John is talking about is himself. *And no one cares but John.*

In order to influence a listener, you need to speak to his needs. Your content should be focused on what he cares about the most. Now imagine John takes another swing at this speech. This time, he's concentrating not on what he wants to say, but on what the listeners need to know and feel in order to feel motivated:

> *For many of you this has been a tough year. Your perseverance and commitment is borne out by the success this team has demonstrated. Our market share is up, and our products are transforming more lives than ever. This has been made possible by only one thing—your efforts. Thank you. Now, we are still ahead of the competition but they're right behind us, and they're closing in. All of you remember the pride of having them miles behind us. Now we're going to have to push harder than ever, to show that our service to customers is second to none. Now is when we find what we we're made of, as we draw upon the culture*

*we've created, the strategies we've honed, and the reputation that we've earned. We're going to have to go out there every day and demonstrate that our products and our services are still the best in the market. Are you with me?*

Let's make an important distinction—we're not talking about telling your listener what he *wants* to hear, in a flattering or manipulative way. We're talking about starting with your listener first, and shaping a message that will be relevant to him. The question that you ask yourself is not "How much information can I shovel down his throat?" The question is "What does he need to know and feel to move him to action?" Instead of fire-hosing your audience with data, you're going to learn to rapidly develop a lucid structure of ideas that will guide your audience through an experience. Chapter One will take you through the **preparation** process. Chapter Two focuses on constructing the **architecture** of your talk. And Chapter Three will explore some of the specific **techniques** that you can use to flesh out your presentation, including **stories, metaphor, active language, refrain** and **Q&A.**

# 1

# PREPARATION

WHY WASTE TIME with preparation? Because without preparation, you're not communicating intentionally—you're just thinking out loud. That's fine in a social setting, but if you're trying to get something done, you need a strategy.

Sure, there are people out there who roll out of bed in the morning full of brilliant, beautifully formed sentences. They just open their mouths and effortlessly bring clarity and insight to others, all day long.

But the rest of us mortals have to prepare.

Before you know what you're going to say, you need to know *why* you're saying it. If you're in a leadership role, you will touch hundreds of lives every week. In the absence of preparation, you will probably default to talking about what you want to talk about, rather than what the listener needs to know. If you haven't stopped to think about the needs of your listeners, your return on investment is probably a fraction of your potential. This may or may not be contributing to your reputation and your own personal brand—and you might be doing more harm than good. Chances are that out of the seventy thousand words you use on average in a given week, few of them will land with any real impact—because you have no strategy.

Think of it like a dinner party. You wouldn't invite people over for dinner, wait until they arrive, and then fling open the fridge to see what's inside. If you're a good host, you take the time to think about your guests: Who's coming? What's the occasion? What kind of menu would be appropriate? You're not there to just cook a meal—you're there to provide an experience. You design a structure for the evening: How many courses? What kind of wine? How do you end the evening on a high note, with a fabulous dessert? The secret is in the preparation.

And communication is just the same.

The diagram below shows the three steps to preparing any engagement:

1. **Outcome.**
2. **Relevance.**
3. **Point.**

If you're in a rush to put your presentation together, you may think you don't have time to prepare. But this preparation process will *save* you time. Once you've mastered the principles involved, the steps will speed you through the development of your talk.

These three steps are also designed to help you avoid those three common complaints that people make about content: that it's too long, not relevant to the listener, or has no point. If all you do is take thirty seconds to run through this process in your mind before your next phone call, you will create an immediate transformation in your level of impact.

Let's take a closer look at the three steps in the preparation process:

## PREPARATION

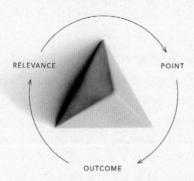

1. Define your **outcome.** What do you want to achieve?
2. Find the **relevance.** Why should they care?
3. Clarify your **point.** What's your message, in one memorable phrase?

## OUTCOME

What do you want to accomplish? Without this knowledge firmly in mind, you will be tempted to simply give information, or worse—try to dump everything you know on the audience.

By the end of the speech or conversation, you want *something to happen.* You need to know what this is, before you begin. If you don't know what you want, it's a sure thing that you won't get it.

In an effective conversation, there are three possible positive outcomes:

1. Your listener has an **insight** that shifts her mind-set. She sees things in a way that she didn't see them before.
2. Your listener makes a new **decision** because of the conversation. The decision may be made in the moment, or the conversation may catalyze a later decision.

3. Your listener takes an **action**. She actually does something in your presence: stamps the form, signs the check, says the word "yes."

So what do you want? Be specific. Write it down. The clearer you are, the better your chances of achieving it. See it, hear it, quantify it.

Remember, the test of success is in the behavior of the other person. So always state your outcome in terms of the listener's behavior: "**By the end of this talk, my listener(s) will** understand / decide / take action on . . ."

For example: "By the end of the conversation, Lisa will agree to join the team." "By the end of the presentation, the board will agree to greenlight our project."

An ideal outcome is **specific.** "Gaining greater buy-in from stakeholders" is too general. "By the end of this talk, the board will agree to fund the first phase of our project" is specific. "Talking to my teenager about drugs" is too general. "By the end of this talk, my son will agree to be honest with me about whether or not he's using drugs" is specific.

Avoid the following constructions when stating your outcome: "They will understand more about . . ." "I will tell them . . ." "They will know . . ." "They will consider . . ." These openers seduce you into vagueness.

Your outcome should also be **achievable,** something you can actually do in the time you have to speak. One conversation can't transform an organization. But one speech *can* rebuild the spirit of a disenchanted team. Look for a way that you can make your outcome **verifiable.** You need to be able to check your progress, and know whether or not you've achieved your goal.

Avoid constructions that begin with "I." "I want to tell them . . ." "I want to share . . ." "I want to demonstrate . . ." These are tactics, not outcomes. These kinds of statements are all about you, and you're not the listener. Anyone in a leadership role is in service to his listeners. Make it all about them. And finally, your outcome should be **compelling.** You need to motivate yourself and your listener with a sense of urgency and passion.

# SHANN

When I was in my junior year of college, I decided that I didn't want to take the classes that were required for me to fulfill my major. Instead, I flipped through the course catalog and picked out all the anthropology, sociology, drama, English, journalism, and media courses that sounded the most interesting. I wrote up a degree description (called "Cultural Belief in Performance") that linked all these classes together. Then I went to see the dean of the humanities department.

"If you will sign this piece of paper, allowing me to take these courses as requirements for my major, I promise to never bother you again. You will never see me. I will never need counseling. This is the last you will ever see of me."

"Do you promise?" he said. "I will never see you again?"

"I swear it," I said.

He signed the paper. Two years later I graduated with that list of courses as my own personal degree program. As a result, I'm one of the few people I know who actually use their college degree; I've found it useful every day of my working life! I learned something else, as well: if you know exactly what you want, your chances of achieving it go way up.

So, you've defined your outcome. You know exactly what you want to happen. Now it's time to make that outcome become reality. To do this, we're going to explode out the idea of outcome.

You want to move the listener from point A to point B. In order for people to make a shift, there are certain things they need to learn from you. This is the basis of your content. Imagine a little drop-down menu underneath your outcome: **What three things does the listener need to know in order for you to achieve your outcome?**

Most of us will fall into the trap of making a long list—a litany of things we want to tell the other person. But if you discipline yourself, you can get it down to three things he *needs* to know. Not seven—not twelve—just **three.** The discipline of three will ensure that you avoid the number one objection people make about presentations: *too much information.*

Now, suppose that you were trying to get a group of people excited and motivated about doing better this year than they did last year—but you don't have any additional money to offer them. What would they need to know?

They might need to know the following three things: (1) The timing is perfect for the new product line; (2) They are going to be equipped with additional tools this year; and (3) You are going to be personally available to help them make introductions, see customers, and close deals.

Great, now you've figured out what they need to know. But do people make decisions based strictly on what they know? Of course not.

Research from the world of neuroscience gives us an insight about how the brain works during the decision-making process. Neurologist Antonio Damasio tells the story of "Elliot," a successful attorney who underwent surgery on the right side of his brain to remove a tumor. While Elliot was able to function normally in many respects after the surgery, he could no longer make even the simplest decisions.[1]

Damasio's work was the first to demonstrate that contrary to what you might expect, decisions are made *not* on the left side of the brain, where we process data and information, but on the right side of the brain, which deals with stories, emotion, color, and humor.

The implications are staggering.

It is not enough, to simply offer someone information—because we don't make decisions based on logic. We make decisions based on the way we *feel*. If you're not speaking to the emotional part of the brain, you're not talking to the decision maker. You may have great data, but if you don't inspire emotion in the other person, you won't get results.

In the words of Alan Weiss, business consulting expert and author, "Logic makes people think, emotion makes them act."[2]

So, in strategic communication, we add one refinement to the drop-down menu under your outcome: **What does the listener need to *feel* in order for you to achieve your outcome?**

This is a critical part of speaking—and one that is rarely addressed. Identifying the emotional experience that you want for your listener forces you to construct an experience that is directed at producing those emotions.

Start with your desired result in mind: "What is the final emotion I want my listener to have?" Do you want to leave them feeling hopeful? Welcomed? Excited? Reassured? Inspired? Fed up? Cared for? Determined? Optimistic? Cautious? Write it down.

Then choose another emotion, one that contrasts with the first. This contrast is important, because monotony comes from sameness. Pavarotti could sing a perfect C-sharp, but if he sang it ceaselessly for sixty seconds, you would want to chew your own ears off. If you want to inspire your listeners, it won't work to be a relentless cheerleader all the way through your talk. They will tire of your obvious efforts, and it will produce a backlash effect. Like colors, one emotion is strengthened by contrast with another.

And like a painter with a full palette in front of him, there are many emotions available to you as a speaker. Explanations that offer clarity can produce feelings of reassurance, calm, trust. Cautionary tales can produce a feeling of motivation, particularly if you are warning of impending danger. Don't back away from the darker emotional tones that come from dangers and threats.

People are motivated by the desires both to seek pleasure and avoid pain. When you're influencing decisions, you need to address both ends of this spectrum. You may want your listeners to end up feeling excited, inspired, confident, and reassured. But you also have a responsibility, as a leader, to talk about the threats and risks. If you're in the lifeguard chair and you see sharks out there, it's your job to speak up! The leader sees what's ahead, defines reality, and gives direction. By talking about potential dangers you produce a sense of urgency that can be a powerful motivator. But don't overuse it; like the boy who cried wolf, if you describe everything as an emergency, your credibility will quickly begin to suffer.

To understand how this works, let's look at one of the finest calls to arms ever uttered: Winston Churchill's first speech as prime minister of Britain on May 13, 1940. In the middle of the speech, he says this: "I have nothing to offer but blood, toil, tears, and sweat. We have before us an ordeal of the most grievous kind. We have before us many, many long months of struggle and of suffering. . . . Without victory, there is no survival." Dark colors indeed!

But Churchill shifts to a very different emotional note at the end. Note the strength of the contrast with his earlier words, which makes his finish even more compelling: "But I take up my task with buoyancy and hope. I feel sure that our cause will not be suffered to fail among men. At this time I feel entitled to claim the aid of all, and I say, 'Come, then, let us go forward together with our united strength.'"

"Hang on a minute," you might be saying. "I'm a numbers guy. Do I really need to mess with this emotional stuff? Aren't the facts and figures enough?" Well, the bottom line is always important, of course. But data only addresses a part of what informs human behavior. If you want to move your listener to action, you must take the emotional side of his brain into account.

Then again, you might be thinking, "Hang on, this sounds too complicated. All I need to do is give them some information about our second-quarter results."

Sure, you can do that. But if you've been asked to update your team, why settle for being just a messenger? Messengers deliver information; leaders generate experience. So raise your brand. Create a meaningful experience.

If we put our newly refined outcome all together on the page, it looks like this:

*Outcome:* By the end of this talk, they will decide to/ agree to . . .

_____

_____

    In order to achieve this, they need to:

*Know:*

1. _____

_____

2. _____

_____

3. _____

_____

*Feel:*

1. _____
2. _____

    Now that we've created a specific outcome, let's turn to the **relevance** of your talk.

## RELEVANCE

One of the biggest mistakes any speaker can make is to jump straight into giving information without first identifying why anyone should care. If no one cares, then no one's going to be listening.

    You find the relevance of your talk by simply asking yourself the question: *why should the listener care?* What's in it for them? This accomplishes three important things:

1. It makes the listener sit up and pay attention.
2. It immediately demonstrates to the listener that you have his best interest at heart.

3. It avoids the complaint: "Not relevant to me!"

Give yourself three good, solid reasons why the listener should care about what you have to say. What's at stake for them? What could be gained, what could be lost? Why does it matter? We sum all these questions up with this shorthand: ***"Where's the heat?"***

*Relevance:* Why should the listener care? What's in it for him?

1. _____

   _____

2. _____

   _____

3. _____

   _____

## POINT

In our desire to give the audience everything we know, we quite often fail to clarify our point! In the absence of knowing what our point is, we can rattle on indefinitely. This can lead to the third core objection that people make to poor presentations—that there is no point.

You may have spent four weeks building up to your big presentation. But the sad reality is that despite all your hard work, your audience will most likely forget 90 percent of what you say by the time their heads hit the pillow that night. So what's the one thing that you want them to remember?

Quite simply, your point is your message, boiled down to one memorable phrase or sentence. If everyone did this, we would all save hours every week. It's not a matter of dumbing down your talk; it is simply a process of distilling and clarifying your thinking to a single sharp point, like an arrow designed to travel a long distance. It doesn't need to be catchy—just clear. Couch it in your most straightforward, muscular language: "If we want to capture this opportunity, we must move in the next thirty days." "We are taking full responsibility." "We need to bring more discipline to spending."

It's a good exercise to get in the habit of refining your point before you open your mouth in conversation as well. It's not uncommon that someone will say, "What's your point?" If you can't answer that question, concisely and clearly, in that moment, your credibility will vanish.

*What's your point, in one sentence?*

_____

_____

_____

## PUTTING IT ALL TOGETHER

You have just walked through a process that will help you prepare for any conversation, presentation, phone call, or e-mail. It's rare that anyone actually stops to prepare before a phone call, but the few moments that it takes to define your **outcome,** find the **relevance,** and clarify your **point** will dramatically raise your level of influence. It will also save you time in the long run. One minute of preparation could transform a potentially painful, hour-long conversation into an efficient, ten-minute exchange. Try it and see.

---

**MASTER TIP:** Take three minutes to prepare before your next phone call. What do you want to accomplish?

---

On the following page is a communication outline that applies to any talk preparation. You can download a fresh copy from our website for future use. There are some additional elements in this outline that will be explained in the next session.

# Communication Outline

**WHO'S LISTENING?**

_____

_____

**STEP 1 – OUTCOME:** *By the end of the conversation, they will . . .*
*decide to/agree to*

_____

*In order to achieve this they need to . . .*
*know:* _____
1. _____
2. _____
3. _____


*feel:* _____
1. _____
2. _____

**STEP 2 – RELEVANCE:** *Why should they care?*

1. _____

2. _____

3. _____

_____

_____

**STEP 3 – POINT:** *What's your message in one sentence?*

_____

**CLASSIC NARRATION STRUCTURE**

| RAMP: *From purpose* | POINTS OF DISCOVERY: *From Know* | DESSERT: *Story* |
|---|---|---|

## Example

Imagine that you are the head of HR (human resources) for a large organization. You need to ask the senior management team for a budget to establish a leadership development program. The following page shows a sample of how you might create a preparation blueprint for your talk:

# Communication Outline

WHO'S LISTENING?

Senior management team

---

**STEP 1 – OUTCOME:** *By the end of the conversation, they will . . . decide to/agree to*

Allocate $200,000 to the proposed leadership development program.

*In order to achieve this they need to . . .*
*know:*

1. Our current managers are unprepared to take senior management roles over the next five years.
2. The benefits of the program.
3. The cost.

*feel:*

1. A sense of urgency about the fact that our organization doesn't have a plan for future leadership.
2. Excited about the new program.

---

**STEP 2 – RELEVANCE:** *Why should they care?*

1. Because if we don't foster the next generation of leaders, the stability of the entire organization is jeopardized.
2. Because they have a sense of pride in the organization and the legacy that they've created, and they want to do what's best for the company.
3. Because the board has specifically requested a comprehensive plan to foster the next generation of leaders and their reputations are on the line, as they are accountable to the board.

---

**STEP 3 – POINT:** *What's your message in one sentence?*

Our future depends on investing in tomorrow's leaders, today.

---

**CLASSIC NARRATION STRUCTURE**

| **RAMP:** *From purpose* | **POINTS OF DISCOVERY:** *From Know* | **DESSERT:** *Story* |
| --- | --- | --- |

# 2

# ARCHITECTURE

WHEW! GREAT WORK. You've completed the preparation stage, ensuring that your speech is outcome-focused, relevant, and on point. If you were building a house, you've now interviewed your client, surveyed the ground, and gotten your planning permissions in order. You're ready to begin.

But you can't just start slapping the bricks together. First, you need to know where they go. You need a design. So now it's time to put together the architecture of ideas. The good news is that the work you've already done on preparation will make crafting the architecture quick and easy.

Like every book, movie, opera, or play ever written, your talk has three parts: a beginning, a middle, and an end. Each part has a job to do. The job of the beginning is to capture the listener's attention and give him a reason to listen. A successful beginning will dilate the listener's brain and cause him to lean forward, intent on hearing what you have to say. The middle provides the meat and potatoes of the presentation; it's there to supply the knowledge that the listener needs. And the function of the ending is to create a feeling. Because we make decisions based on our emotions, rather than our logic, it's important to leave the listener with the emotions needed to move them to action.

When we ask people in our trainings if they think beginnings, middles, or endings are the most important, we always get the same response. About half say they think the beginning is the most important. Half of them vote for endings. Hardly anyone ever thinks the middle is the most important section. And yet for the vast majority of us, *the middle is where we spend most of our time.*

The truth, of course, is that beginnings, middles, and endings are all important. Like a triangle, if you remove one leg, the entire structure will collapse. But you neglect the beginning and ending at your own peril. Without an attention-grabbing opening, there is no presentation. Audiences decide almost immediately whether they are going to pay attention to what you have to say. If your opening isn't dynamic, the audience will tune you out long before you ever reach the middle. And if the ending is disappointing, they will quickly forget all the good work that you put in earlier.

So with those concerns in mind, here's our suggestion for a quick and effective way to create the architecture of your talk:

1. **Ramp** (the beginning).
2. **Discovery** (the middle).
3. **Dessert** (the end).

as shown in the diagram below. We'll walk through these sections one at a time.

CONTENT

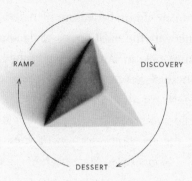

RAMP · DISCOVERY · DESSERT

## RAMP

Most speakers make their first mistake before they ever open their mouth. It's a crucial one, and it will render everything you say meaningless. It is this: *you assume that your listeners are listening to you. But they're not.*

You cannot assume that the presence of bodies in seats means that they are paying attention to you. Chances are, they're thinking about what they're going to do on the weekend, planning what they're going to cook for supper, or worrying about something that happened at the office that day. Remember, the audience doesn't care about your message until you give them a reason to listen. They care about themselves. Your opening needs to be compelling enough to make them look up from their smartphones. And they won't look up unless you get them interested in what you're about to say. What's in it for them?

Imagine that each person in your audience is sitting back, legs crossed, arms folded. There is no point in starting in on the information section of your speech until you have them sitting on the edge of their chair, eager and anxious to hear what you have to say. You have to make them care. And the way you do this is to construct what we call a **ramp.**

A ramp is the first few sentences that come out of your mouth. It should immediately engage the listener's attention, and set the stakes high enough that whatever comes next is of interest to him. Like a ski jump, a ramp alters the angle of attack and sends you to a higher level. It elevates the importance of what you're going to say to a higher priority in the listener's brain. Once your audience cares about what you're going to say, then you can go on with the rest of your talk. Now they're listening—they're with you.

How do you go about constructing a ramp? It's very simple. Go back and reread the **relevance** section of your preparation. Why should they care? The answer to that question is a perfect opening to your talk.

Let's revisit the **relevance** section in our previous example, to see how this works. We decided that the senior management team at your company cares about funding a leadership development program because: (1) If they don't foster the next generation of leaders, the stability of the entire organization will be jeopardized; (2) They have a sense of pride in the organization and the legacy that they've created, and they want to do what's best for the company; (3) The board has asked for a plan to foster the next generation of leaders, and senior management is accountable to the board—their jobs are on the line.

Take the three reasons that the listener should care, and string them together like pearls on a necklace. This guarantees that you demonstrate to the listener, as soon as you open your mouth, that you care about his needs. So, you might construct an opening, or **ramp,** that goes like this:

> *Each and every one of you has made profound contributions to the success of this organization. Many of you are founders. Together you've built this company up to become a leader in the industry. But, ladies and gentlemen, we are facing a challenge. Thirty-five percent of you will be retiring in the next seven years. And we do not have another group of leaders prepared to navigate into the future.*
>
> *It's as if we've set out on a voyage with enough supplies to get us to*

*the destination, but not enough to bring us home. The future success of this organization is at stake if we don't take action now.*

*Over the next forty-five minutes, I'm going to share with you some studies we've made that demonstrate where the gap is, what we need to do about it, and what it's going to cost. By the end of this talk, I'd like your approval to proceed with phase one of the legacy project.*

You can see how **relevance** leads to the **ramp** in the outline on page 46.

Contrast this example with the following opening, which is a more typical approach. Monitor your own reactions as you read:

*Good morning, everyone. I'm really excited about today's presentation. I want to thank all of you for coming here today, as I know you're all busy. Before I start, I'd like to specifically thank Mark Conti for his contribution to organizing today's event. A few housekeeping details before we start. The bathrooms are down the hall to the left. I've asked Elaine to pass out handouts detailing the plan. She'll be coming around in a minute.*

*I'm pretty passionate about leadership, and I've prepared sixty-six slides that outline how the team and I have developed a clear plan and process for creating what I think is a great leadership development program. I'll be walking through the slides over the next forty-five minutes, but feel free to interrupt me at any time with any questions, and I'll be glad to answer them.*

Notice anything? What's the most commonly used word in that opening? "I." Who does the listener care about? Himself. This is mostly about the speaker, and not about the listener. How do we know? Because the word "I" shows up twelve times, while the word "you" appears only twice.

Other problems? The speaker has wasted precious time on unnecessary housekeeping details, losing ground in the critical first few seconds of the talk. The person coming around to pass out handouts will pull focus away from the speaker. Asking to be interrupted immediately undermines your status and says to the listener that none of this is so important that it can't be derailed. The real overall issue or challenge, which gives urgency to the talk, has not yet been mentioned. And the speaker has let us know that this is going to be a long, boring presentation. Watch the heads go down, and the smartphones come out.

You need to shift your attention away from yourself, and focus it on your audience. Abraham Lincoln, one of the most accomplished speakers in history, said, "When I am getting ready to reason with a man, I spend one-third of my time thinking about myself and what I am going to say and two-thirds about him and what he is going to say."

A simple technique to ensure that your focus is on the other person is the I:You ratio, as defined by executive speech coach Patricia Fripp.[1] How many times do you use the word "I," and how many times do you use the word "you"?

---

**MASTER TIP:** *Get the I:You ratio right.* Use ten "You"s . . . for every "I"!

---

In most talks, it's the other way around. The first word out of most people's mouths is "I." It's generally the first word of any sentence, and the most frequently used pronoun after "that." People generally use the word "I" roughly ten times for every time they use the word "you." Doubt it? Open your e-mail in-box and check any e-mail—either the ones you've received or the ones you've sent! Unless you're a movie star or telling a compelling personal story (more on this technique later), limit your use of the word "I." Who does the listener care about? Herself. Open with the word "you," and you're off to a good start; you're talking about her favorite subject.

When you design your opening, make it sharp, clean, and fast. Hit the ground running. There is no time to waste. You make conscious and unconscious decisions all day long about how much focus you choose to give anything—and so does your listener. It takes incredible discipline and a strong will to pull someone's focus, and get his exclusive attention. When you get up in front of a group of people to speak, how much time do you think they give you before they make their first decision about you? One minute? Two? Studies tell us that you have *seven seconds* before a listener forms his first crucial decision about whether or not he's going to listen to you.[2]

---

**MASTER TIP:** *The Seven Second Rule:* You have only seven seconds in which the audience decides whether or not they're going to pay attention.

---

Here's what's really unfair: most of the time, your seven seconds are up before you get to your second sentence. Half of it is used just by walking up to the podium. If you've got just one sentence left before those seven seconds are up, don't waste it saying good morning for the fifth time, or thanking everyone again for coming. Demonstrate immediately that you're there to bring value. Open with something meaningful and nourishing: something that shows the listener that (1) you understand their situation, and (2) you're there to help.

If you need to do housekeeping, introduce yourself, or go through the agenda, do it after the opening. An agenda is not an opening. "Good morning, thank you all for coming" is not an opening. Telling people how happy you are to be there is not an opening. It's noncaloric blab. And when people hear it, they immediately get a signal that nothing important is going on.

Most speakers do quite well after the first five or ten minutes, once they get warmed up. The problem is that they're warming up on the audience's time. After five or ten minutes, when you've hit your stride, your audience is long gone. They may still be sitting there, but they're not listening to you. You've lost them. And now, it's either too late to get them back, or you're going to have to work doubly hard.

Go for what we call "the clean open." No names, no introductions, no greetings. Go straight in, and get straight to the point.

Have another look at our sample open:

*Each and every one of you has made profound contributions to the success of this organization. Many of you are founders. Together you've built this company up to become a leader in the industry. But, ladies and gentlemen, we are facing a challenge. Thirty-five percent of you will be retiring in the next seven years. And we do not have another group of leaders prepared to navigate into the future.*

*It's as if we've set out on a voyage with enough supplies to get us to the destination, but not enough to bring us home. The future success of this organization is at stake if we don't take action now.*

Notice: no "good morning," no "thank you for coming." Instead of being polite by mouthing meaningless pleasantries, show respect for your listeners by not wasting their time, and immediately engaging their attention.

If you need to introduce yourself, do it later on, after you've already captured their attention:

*I'm Jane Green, head of HR. Over the next forty-five minutes, I'm going to share with you some studies we've made that demonstrate where the gap is, what we need to do about it, and what it's going to cost. By the end of this talk, I'd like your approval to proceed with phase one of the legacy project.*

And for goodness' sake, don't waste your first precious seven seconds talking about the location of the bathrooms!

The traditional advice says always open with a joke. We say be wary of opening with a joke, unless (1) you know you're funny—*really* funny; (2) the joke is fresh and new; and (3) most important, it's relevant to your topic.

---

**MASTER TIP:** *Beware of opening with a joke.*

---

If the joke's not funny, and you open with a thud, you might as well pack up and go home. You're going to have to spend the next thirty minutes trying to get your credibility back, and what's worse, the audience now feels sorry for you. If the joke's not fresh or original, and they've already heard it two weeks ago, they're going to suspect that everything else you have to say is yesterday's news as well. And if the joke's not relevant to your topic, especially in a formal environment, it signals the audience that the rest of your talk may be equally irrelevant.

Sometimes people say, "I want to save my best bit for the end." Don't bother. If you haven't put your best stuff up front and hooked the audience, they won't be listening by the end anyway. In journalism, we call the opening the "lede." "Never bury the lede" is what they teach in journalism school. This is because journalists understand that very few readers will actually read all the way to the end of a newspaper story. Give them your best stuff first.

---

**MASTER TIP:** *Don't bury the lede.* If you don't hook them right up front, you've lost them forever. There are no second chances.

---

Here is a brief list of some powerful opening strategies for your ramp:

1. **OPEN WITH THE WORD "YOU."** This gives you an immediate advantage; you're talking about the audience's favorite topic—themselves. Be direct and clear. Demonstrate that you know their situation, you appreciate what they're feeling, and you care.
2. **USE A POWERFUL STATISTIC,** or what we call a "sexy number." A sexy number contains an element of surprise for the listener; it makes them sit up and take notice. If you're in the telecom industry, you might open with: "Half the world's population has never made a telephone call. Imagine the opportunity for us." A few more examples of sexy numbers: "About 20 percent of all U.S.

heads of household have never sent an e-mail." "The market for smartphones is expected to be $400 million by 2012—quadruple what it was four years before that." "Only 4 percent of Arab women use the Internet." "In ten years, e-waste from old computers is set to increase by 400 percent in China and South Africa from 2007 levels, and by 500 percent in India."

3. **ASK A QUESTION.** "How many of you spend more than half your time in meetings?" "Does anybody know what the population of polar bears was in 1959? Anybody know what it is today?" "How many of you feel that your children's school could be doing a better job?"

4. **SHOCK THEM.** Governor Jerry Brown of California opened his State of the State address on January 31, 2011, this way: "California faces a crisis that is real and unprecedented. Each of us will have to struggle with our conscience and our constituencies as we hammer out a sensible plan to put our state on a sound fiscal footing, honestly balance our budget and position California to regain its historic momentum."

5. **MAKE A CONFESSION.** Be vulnerable. "I've always been afraid of spiders. And the other day, in the boardroom, the CEO asked me to get rid of a spider he saw in the corner. Well . . ."

6. **USE THE WORD "IMAGINE."** "Imagine this. It's three years from now, the new gymnasium has been built, and our kids have just won their first basketball championship . . ." "Imagine" is an incredibly powerful word, because it makes the communication interactive. The listener moves from being passive to becoming an active participant in the process, co-creating an idea or vision.

7. **TELL A HISTORICAL ANECDOTE.** "Once when General Dwight D. Eisenhower was under siege, he sent a sergeant out to do some reconnaissance. When he returned, General Eisenhower said, 'Sergeant, give me a brief assessment of our position.' The sergeant replied, 'Sir, imagine a doughnut. We're the hole.' That's a little what it feels like for us today . . ."

8. **TELL A STORY.** Find the human interest in your data, and lead with it. Put a human face on your material. "Luis is a client of mine. He called me up and told me that if we couldn't find a solution to his problem within the next two weeks, he'd be out on the street."

For more examples of ramps, see Appendix Two.

## ROAD MAP

Once you've hooked your audience's attention with the **ramp,** you add the second element of your opening. We call this the **road map.** Imagine that you're going on a road trip. To keep your passengers happy, you need to tell them where they're going, what route you're going to use, and how long it's going to take to get there. Similarly, the road map for your talk should do three things:

1. **IT TELLS PEOPLE HOW LONG YOU'RE GOING TO BE SPEAKING.** People need to know the duration of the commitment. So, tell them. "I'm going to be speaking for fifteen minutes. Then we have fifteen minutes for an open discussion, during which I can answer some of your questions. We will end promptly at three o'clock." What a relief!

2. **IT GIVES THEM A PREVIEW OF YOUR STRUCTURE** (and reassures them that you have one)! "We're going to look at developing leadership in terms of where we are today, where we need to be five years from now, and what we need to do in order to get there."

3. **IT SETS UP THE RULES OF ENGAGEMENT.** People want to participate. Do you want them to ask questions as you go along, or would you prefer them to wait until the **Q&A**? If you say nothing, one of two things will happen: (1) you get nothing, or (2) you will be interrupted. It's your speech; take control. It doesn't guarantee that they won't interrupt you, but you stand a much better chance of

controlling the discussion if you say either "I'm going to be speaking for fifteen minutes, and then we'll have fifteen minutes of Q&A, so please hold your questions until then," or "I'd like this to be an open discussion, so please ask questions as we go along."

Traditionally, speakers make two mistakes with the road map. Either they (1) Avoid it altogether, or (2) Completely overwhelm the audience.

Consider the following road map, noticing your reaction as you go: "Today I'll be talking to you about seven new areas of product development. I'll discuss how the new additions fit into our strategic focus, marketing for the new products, and sales strategies. We'll also be looking at impacting organizational structure. I'll be introducing four new members of the team, and then finally I'd like to talk to you about the new leadership legacy program developed by our new HR team. Okay, let's get started."

Doesn't it make your heart sink? We're already exhausted! This speaker has just run a conveyor belt of information past us, and we have no desire to keep up. Keep the road map brief—no more than three items. Which three items? The three items you want in your road map will be your three **Points of Discovery.** To determine what they are, read on to learn about the section we call . . .

## DISCOVERY

So, you've captured the audience's attention with the ramp, and told them where you're taking them with the road map. You've completed your opening. Now it's time to enter the middle of the speech. As we said earlier, the middle of your speech is there to provide knowledge. This knowledge may be new information that you are going to offer, or it may be knowledge they already have that needs to be reinforced. But it's not just any old data on a slide that you happen to have downloaded, and it's not just about whatever you want to say. It's about what the audience needs to know, or discover, in order for you to achieve your outcome.

We call this the **discovery** section. Why discovery? Because ideally, you are going to provide insights that stimulate your listener to make discoveries, rather than forcing information down his throat. Discovery can be as simple as someone realizing that he can finally make sense of a confusing topic. It's an exciting activity for the brain—people enjoy the "Aha!" sensation of working things out for themselves.

We organize the discovery section into three Points of Discovery— or PoDs, for short. And we ask you to be rigorously disciplined about narrowing it down to three, even if you're sure that you have at least seventeen points to make.

Why three? Three is a universal number. A triangle is the strongest structure in the world. And frankly, three items are about as many as most people want to deal with. Three things are easy to learn, and easy to remember. Research tells us that the brain doesn't record data in an unbroken stream, like a videocassette recorder. Instead, it handles information by dividing it into meaningful chunks, or categories. Chunking your data into three categories means that you are offering the information already sliced up, in the way the listener's brain wants to process it. No matter what you need to say, or how complex it is, create a structure of three. People simply cannot follow structures of seven or twelve in a short fifteen-minute talk. Creating a triad serves the listener as well as yourself. They know where you are, and so do you.

Think how your heart would sink if you heard a speaker say, "I'm now going to discuss each of these sixteen developments in our company's history. . . ." More coffee, please! Now imagine that the speaker says, "I'm going to walk you through three eras of leadership in this company: our past, our present, and our future." See? Simple, easy, brings a sense of relief. You know where you're headed and it's not too overwhelming. A leader doesn't dumb things down; he takes complex things and makes them clear.

Franklin Delano Roosevelt gave a classic example of this in his first radio "Fireside Chat," which he delivered to an anxious nation on Sunday, March 12, 1933, during the Great Depression:

> *My friends, I want to talk for a few minutes with the people of the United States about banking—to talk with the comparatively few who understand the mechanics of banking, but more particularly with the overwhelming majority of you who use banks for the making of deposits and the drawing of checks. I want to tell you what has been done in the last few days, and why it was done, and what the next steps are going to be.*

Note his three-part road map: (1) What has been done in the last few days; (2) Why it was done; (3) What the next steps are going to be.

Think of the PoDs as baskets that will help you organize your ideas. All of your content—data, information, stories, anecdotes, statistics, quotes, graphs, etc.—can be sorted into these three baskets. The three PoDs simply provide a structure.

For example, if you're about to roll out a new system to a group of salespeople, they probably need to know: (1) How it works, (2) Ways in which it can help them; and (3) What they're going to need to do in order to use it. If you're talking to a teenager about drinking and driving, she might need to know: (1) The dangers involved; (2) Your expectations of her; and (3) Your commitment to be available for rides.

---

**MASTER TIP:** No matter how many items you have to discuss, chunk them into no more than three categories, or Points of Discovery.

---

How do you know which three PoDs you should use? The good news is that you've already done the work necessary to figure it out. Remember back in the preparation process, when you identified the **three things the audience needs to know** in order for you to achieve your outcome? Well, those three things are your three PoDs. Simple!

To see how the three "need-to-know" items are connected to your three PoD's, glance back at the outline on page 46.

Go back and insert your three PoDs into your road map. For example, "For the next fifteen minutes, we'll be discussing the new system. I'll walk you through how it works, the ways in which it can help you, and what you're going to need to do in order to implement it."

Now you've got your three categories. You can design the middle of your presentation by fleshing out each PoD with stories, metaphors, active language, statistics, etc. For more information on these techniques, please see the **Techniques** section of the book.

## SUMMARIZE

If you've been speaking for more than five minutes, after you have completed the **discovery** section, the listener needs a summary; he needs you to remind him of the big picture. Summarize succinctly, with an emphasis on how the related parts all fit together. Ideally you summarize just before the Q&A segment (explored in further detail below), because the summary will stimulate conversation by reminding people of what they wanted to ask about. The summary should be crisp, clear, and brief—but not rushed. If there is a request in your presentation, summarize and then make the request. This is a good place to make a request, because if you've done your job effectively, you've brought the listener to a high point.

*Today, we've examined the question of whether or not to put more money into the arts program in our schools.* [There's your point.] *We've looked at the potential benefits, the investment costs, and we've explained our five-year plan to bring an integrated arts program into this district.* [Those are your three PoDs.] *Ladies and gentlemen, you have an important decision to make. I'd like to ensure that we have plenty of time to answer any questions that you might have, before you put this matter to a vote.*

## NEVER END ON Q&A

Most formal presentations include a Q&A period, and we think it's a good idea. People want to engage with you as a speaker; they want to have a dialogue.

*However.*

Most people also get it wrong by putting the Q&A at the very end of the presentation. Bad idea! We say *never* end on Q&A—it's too risky. Here's why:

You've worked hard to bring your listener to a high point at the end of your speech. You've done a good job. You finish triumphantly, then say, "Okay, we've got fifteen minutes left. Are there any questions?" There's a dead silence. "Anyone? Not even one question?" Nothing. You're looking around with increasing desperation. "Are you sure?" Everyone squirms, avoiding your eye. "Okay, then," you mumble. "I guess I'll just wrap it up, then. Um, thank you for your time. . . ." You look incredibly foolish and slink off after collecting your laptop, completely spoiling the effect of all your good work.

Or even worse: Things have gone well in your speech. Now it's time for Q&A—and you have an aggressive questioner. You remember him—he's that well-dressed guy in the pinstriped suit, with the goatee and the red pen. He sat through your entire presentation, patiently waiting for the question period to start. In fact, he doesn't have questions; he has an *agenda*. And his agenda is to demonstrate that he's smarter than you by finding flaws in your work. He might ask you something like this: "Where did you get your numbers? You said that we've got a 12.6 increase in the third quarter. But I happen to know it's only 11.9." No matter how skillfully you deal with his questions, your credibility has been attacked. (For information on how to handle Q&A like a pro, please see Chapter Three: Techniques.) The audience is watching it all happen. And all the work that you've put in up to this point to move your audience emotionally has been compromised. If you were taking your listeners on an emotional journey, you're losing altitude fast.

Despite the risk, we recommend that you include Q&A whenever possible. It's a great way to bond with the audience and build trust. But you must build in a way that **ensures a strong finish** afterward, because the ending pays disproportionate dividends. People remember what they heard and experienced last. In a movie, the ending needs to be terrific. In a book, the final chapter has to be the best. In a conversation or presentation, the last three minutes must tie it all together and leave your listener on a high note. You wouldn't invite people over to your house, feed them a lovely salad, a delicate soup, and then shove them out the door right after the roast beef, would you? Of course not. You offer them a little crème brûlée or chocolate cake to round off the evening. It's the same with your talk. After the Q&A is over, you wow them with the grand finale. We call this the . . .

## DESSERT

**Dessert** is the part where you take back control of the presentation, and ensure that you finish on a high note. No matter what heavy losses you may have sustained during the Q&A, the dessert is the ace up your sleeve that ensures your victory in the end.

Remember when we said that each part of the presentation has a job to do? Well, the job of the ending, or dessert, is to create an **emotion** in the listener. You're going to produce a feeling. The ending is not the place to give the audience any new information, or unload another thing that they need to know. The listener's brain is packed up—they're waiting for the train. This is not the time to force them to open up their bags so that you can shovel in one more piece of data. You've already given them all the facts. This is the time to address the emotions.

Strong emotion makes things "sticky," or memorable. If you do a good job with your dessert, your listeners will remember it forever, long after they've forgotten your data. The best dessert is a story, anecdote, metaphor, or image. It should touch the emotions of the listener in some way. This creates a feeling that they will associate with listening to you.

You might introduce your dessert by saying something like, "Before we close, I'd like to leave you with this thought. . . ." Then give it to them. It might be an example of what your idea might look like in the real world. You could tell the story of someone else in a similar situation. You might look to the past, showing an example of your product or initiative as it was demonstrated successfully. Or you might try drawing a future picture for your listeners. "Imagine this . . ."

There are an infinite variety of possible desserts; it can be anything that leaves the audience with a powerful emotional sensation or image that reinforces your point.

For example:

Tim Tebow "The Promise" (after losing to Ole Miss, he went on to lead the Gators to a national championship victory):

> *To the fans and everybody in Gator Nation, I'm sorry. I'm extremely sorry. We were hoping for an undefeated season. That was my goal, something Florida has never done here.*
>
> *I promise you one thing, a lot of good will come out of this. You will never see any player in the entire country play as hard as I will play the rest of the season. You will never see someone push the rest of the team as hard as I will push everybody the rest of the season.*
>
> *You will never see a team play harder than we will the rest of the season. God bless.*
>
> *(http://www.youtube.com/watch?v=96vAbtpakLg)*

For more examples of desserts, please see Appendix Two.

The very best desserts will circle back to echo something that you mentioned in the ramp. Using this full-circle technique gives a subtle elegance to your finish; returning to the original image creates a powerful sense of satisfaction and closure in the listener's mind. The following are two examples of connected ramps and desserts:

Mary Fisher, "1992 Republican National Convention Address":

**Ramp:** *Less than three months ago at platform hearings in Salt Lake City, I asked the Republican Party to lift the shroud of silence which has been draped over the issue of HIV and AIDS. I have come tonight to bring our silence to an end. I bear a message of challenge, not self-congratulation. I want your attention, not your applause.*

**The speech ends with this dessert:** *To my children, I make this pledge: I will not give in, Zachary, because I draw my courage from you. Your silly giggle gives me hope; your gentle prayers give me strength; and you, my child, give me the reason to say to America, "You are at risk." And I will not rest, Max, until I have done all I can to make your world safe. I will seek a place where intimacy is not the prelude to suffering. I will not hurry to leave you, my children, but when I go, I pray that you will not suffer shame on my account.*

*To all within the sound of my voice, I appeal: Learn with me the lessons of history and of grace, so my children will not be afraid to say the word "AIDS" when I am gone. Then, their children and yours may not need to whisper it at all."*

*(http://www.americanrhetoric.com/speeches/maryfisher1992rnc.html)*

Elie Wiesel, "The Perils of Indifference":

**Ramp:** *Fifty-four years ago to the day, a young Jewish boy from a small town in the Carpathian Mountains woke up, not far from Goethe's beloved Weimar, in a place of eternal infamy called Buchenwald. He was finally free, but there was no joy in his heart. He thought there never would be again. Liberated a day earlier by American soldiers,* *he remembers their rage at what they saw. And even if he lives to be a very old man, he will always be grateful to them for that rage, and also for their compassion. Though he did not understand their language, their eyes told him what he needed to know—that they, too, would remember, and bear witness.*

**The speech comes full circle with this:** *And so, once again, I think of the young Jewish boy from the Carpathian Mountains. He has accompanied the old man I have become throughout these years of quest and struggle. And together we walk towards the new millennium, carried by profound fear and extraordinary hope.*

*(http://www.americanrhetoric.com/speeches/ewieselperilsofindifference.html)*

For more information on how to tell a story that would make a good dessert, please see Chapter Three: Techniques.

## ADJUSTING YOUR DESIGN

If you've got tomatoes, garlic, and olive oil, you can combine them to make any number of Italian dishes. Similarly, once you've mastered the core ingredients of **preparation** and **architecture,** you can combine them in an infinite variety of ways to create your own recipes. Think of them as plug-and-play modules that can be rearranged to meet your communication needs in any situation.

For example, every important communication that you make, including e-mails, voice mails, and audio conferences, should begin with the elements of **preparation:** a clear outcome, relevance, and point. You must know what you're trying to accomplish, why the listener should care, and what your message is in one sentence. If you don't know these things before you pick up the phone, you're wasting both your time and hers.

In a formal presentation, the structure becomes more refined, and the elements of **architecture** come into play. Let's look at a few situations that require different combinations of the core principles.

In a situation where you're communicating with your peers, and you want to get through the entire narrative before being interrupted, the classical structure is most powerful:

1. Ramp.
2. Road map.
3. Three PoDs.
4. Q&A.
5. Dessert.

This allows you to make it clear in your road map that there will be time for questions, and increases the chances that you make it all the way through your talk.

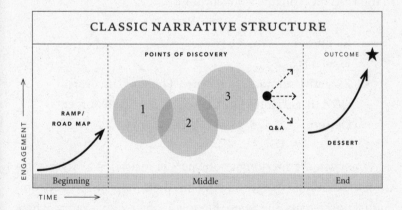

When you're speaking to an audience that is senior to you, it helps to remember: *senior managers like to interrupt.* The more senior they are, the more they like to get their hands on the interaction. They want to control and direct how they're getting the information. They generally do it through questions. In practice, this means that you have very little chance of actually making it through your presentation without being interrupted. In the military they say, "No plan survives the enemy." In communication we say, "No outline survives the CEO." This means that your lovely, organized schematic is likely to be shattered by people throwing questions to you outside your given order.

The most effective response to this is NOT to look annoyed and snap, "I'll get to that point in a minute . . . or in the next slide. . . ." You need to respond to most questions *in that very moment.* So, plan for it. The best structure for an executive presentation is to offer them a quick, clean ramp and road map, engaging their interest and letting them know the areas you're prepared to explore. Give them a five-minute executive summary. And then open it up for questions. The majority of your knowledge and information will come out as you answer their queries. *Let the listeners' questions drive your narrative.* This establishes you as responsive, interactive, and someone who doesn't want to waste their time. Of course, as always, you finish with dessert. In this case, the structure would be this:

1. Ramp.
2. Road map.
3. Executive summary of the three Points of Discovery.
4. Q&A that explores the three PoDs, in a flexible order.
5. Dessert.

When you are speaking to one person instead of a larger audience, the method changes slightly but the core principles of communication remain the same. First, you open with a ramp, where the bond with your listener is created. This is where you demonstrate an understanding of their needs. "When you joined the organization six months ago, you told us you wanted the opportunity to grow and develop your career. You also said you wanted feedback on anything that might be getting in your way. I'd like to share some thoughts about what you need to do to move to the next level. Is that okay?"

Then you create a road map: "We have an hour. I'd like to share three suggestions with you, hear what you think about each one, and then create a plan for going forward. How does that sound?" Most likely he'll say, "Good," satisfied that there will be no surprises in the conversation. You're off and running. Because this is a dialogue, the questions will be sprinkled throughout the body of the communication, instead of being held until the end. The diagram below shows the form of this narrative structure.

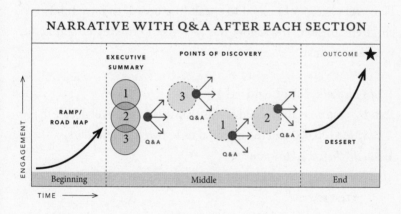

At the end of your conversation, you offer dessert. Just as in a larger presentation, you need to close the communication on an emotional high note. Plan ahead—what are you going to say at the very end of the talk that will send him out the door with a feeling of renewed clarity, confidence, and dedication? For example: "By the way, I got an e-mail from one of your customers the other day. He took the time to say how much he appreciated the personal attention that you gave him during a crisis. It's that kind of dedication that's inspiring to all of us. Thank you."

For more information on one-on-one interactions, see Chapter Ten: Courageous Conversations.

## PUTTING IT ALL TOGETHER

So, we've pulled apart the engine, taken off the tires, and shown you how it all works. Now let's put the car back together and watch how it performs in the real world, when you actually put it on the road. Here are two examples of presentations constructed according to the principles of High Performance Communication. One speech was given by Peter, one by a client.

### Example Number One: Peter

Five years ago, I was asked to speak to a board, to raise funds for a children's theater. The school was at a major crossroads, and its survival was at stake.

*Who's Listening?* The board.

*Step 1—Outcome:* By the end of this talk, this funder will decide to provide $120,000 and recommend us to two other funders.

*What do they need to know?*
 1. Theater helps kids with language arts performance, and raises test scores.
 2. Theater helps kids socially, teaching them to understand other cultures and work in teams.
 3. Theater helps kids to get attention in a positive way, which keeps them out of jail.

*What do they need to feel?*
 1. Urgency about helping kids at risk.
 2. Confidence in our plan.

*Step 2—Relevance: Why should they care?*
 1. They're frustrated with rising juvenile delinquency and lower test scores in schools.
 2. They want to make a difference.
 3. They need to find a worthwhile, reliable project to fund.

*Step 3—Point:* "Theater helps kids succeed in school."

Here's the **ramp** I created, based on **relevance:** "Each and every one of you is here because you care about kids. You know that hundreds of thousands of children in California today are at risk of falling through the cracks in the educational system because they cannot read, write, or speak English at grade level. You're aware that test scores are going down, juvenile crime is going up, and more and more kids are at risk of being disenfranchised." (Note the strong **I:You ratio,** and high angle of the ramp, created by a sense of urgency: children's lives are at stake.)

My three **Points of Discovery,** based on the three things they needed to know, were: (1) Theater helps kids by improving their language skills; (2) Theater helps kids by developing their social skills; (3) Theater helps kids by keeping them out of jail—giving them the spotlight in a positive way and keeping them out of trouble caused by attention seeking. I **supported each PoD** with stories, anecdotes, and statistics.

Then I summarized, moved into **Q&A** and took questions, some of which were aggressive. One listener asked: "Why are your programs so expensive?" I **acknowledged** the listener: "That's an important question, and it needs to be addressed." Because the question was aggressive, I didn't **embed** the question in the answer. Instead, I **reframed:** "This is a question about quality. We're sending artists into some of the toughest schools in California. And when we send them in, we send in only the very best people we can find. The work is difficult. Trying to save money on teachers by paying them the minimum is not the answer. This is an investment in our children. We find the most talented people available, and we pay them fairly." (For more details on **embedding, acknowledgment, reframing,** and other techniques for handling Q&A, please see Chapter Three: Techniques.)

After the Q&A, I took back the floor for **dessert.** I said, "Before we close, I'd like to leave you with a story about one of these programs in action. Recently I went to watch auditions in the auditorium of one of the schools. Kids were running everywhere—it was chaos. Suddenly this one little girl stood up. She had two long black pigtails, shiny patent leather shoes, and a purple lace dress—the kind you would wear to Sunday school. She began to walk very slowly toward the stage. The kids saw this and gathered in amazement as they began to sit down. You could hear them whispering, 'Shhh . . . Maria's going, Maria's going. It's Maria.'

"Soon they were all sitting there, motionless. Maria walked to the front of the stage and stood with her toes exactly placed on the edge. She lifted her head high enough so that you could just barely see her eyes, and recited a poem by Dr. Seuss. You could hardly hear what she was saying. But every kid in that room sat there and listened in complete silence. As I stood in the back of the room with the teacher, I saw that the teacher's eyes were wet, and her chin was quivering. I leaned over and whispered, 'What in the world is going on?' She said, *'That's the first time we've ever heard that little girl speak.'*

"And that is why we teach theater in schools."

Outcome of the presentation? The board signed the check for $120,000, and the school was saved.

## David

All his life, David had wanted to be a VP. He had watched his father's life fall apart after he was laid off following a merger, and David was determined to climb the corporate ladder and win, for his dad's sake. David enrolled in business school, got his MBA, and began a long apprenticeship at a large, high-tech firm in Silicon Valley. After five years working in sales, his hard work and long hours paid off when he became the youngest manager in the history of the company. He was given a region with 120 people in it, and life looked good. But eight months after he stepped into his new role, the bottom dropped out of the market. The competition became increasingly aggressive, offering similar products at cheaper prices and winning customers who had been loyal to David's company for years. Members of David's team started defecting at an alarming rate, lured by the success of the competition and the promise of better salaries. David's boss called him in, and said that he had three months to raise his employee retention rate, or he would be moving back down to a sales role. He needed to begin a series of face-to-face meetings with the team, designed to get them back on board. Here's how he organized his first speech.

## Example Number Two: Hal

*Step 1—Who's Listening?* The team.
*Outcome:* By the end of this presentation, anyone thinking of leaving will have renewed their commitment at least six months.
*What do they need to know?*
1. The current market trends point to a growing opportunity in our area of expertise.
2. How we're going to take advantage of the opportunity ahead.
3. The ways I will support them in the field.

*What do they need to feel?*
1. Determination to avoid missing out on a big opportunity;
2. Confidence about the future.

*Step 2—Relevance: Why should they care?*
1. They've felt what it's like to be part of a high-performing team in the past, and they want it back.
2. They've already struggled through the hardest part, and it would be a waste of their efforts to quit right before the rewards come due.
3. They want to get their bonuses back.

*Step 3—Point:* The rewards for our hard work are just ahead.

Here's David's **ramp,** based on **relevance:** "Three years ago we were number one in the market. We were right up on top of the mountain, and our competitors were way down in the foothills. They didn't even have a base camp. Each and every one of you has tasted that kind of success, and you remember how it feels. Three years later, we've slipped from that summit. In the past eight months you've all seen a lot of changes—some of them not so good. But one benefit of the struggle is this: our company has demonstrated its ability to adapt, to innovate, and invest in our products and marketing. We are still on our feet, still moving forward. The tough times have made us lean and mean. Our skills have been honed under blizzard conditions. And after three tough years, we are just a few miles away from what could be our greatest success yet. These efforts are about to come to fruition. That number one spot can be ours again. [David's **road map:**] In the next forty-five minutes, I'd like to show you how we're going to accomplish this, by walking you through (1) current market trends that point to a growing opportunity in our area of expertise; (2) how we're going to take advantage of the new opportunity; and (3) my commitment to supporting you out in the field." (Note the 3 **Points of Discovery.** David then moves through each PoD, elaborating on each with stories, statistics, anecdotes, graphs, etc.)

*Dessert:* "Ladies and gentlemen, it's been a long journey, and it's not over yet. The hardest part of climbing to the summit of a mountain is the last mile. The oxygen gets thinner, and your muscles start to get tired. Along the way, we've lost some people. Some have gone gracefully, some not so gracefully. You may feel that you're never going to make it all the way up to the top. That's the time when you may feel the most like giving up. But folks—we can see the summit from where we are. We've done this together. We've come this far. Let me say to you what I believe with all my heart: this is not the time to let go of the rope. This is the time to dig deep, push forward, and follow the team. Reach down and grab the guy who's behind you and pull him up. Reach up and accept the hand above you when it is offered. Keep your eye on the goal. And imagine, when we reach that summit, how it's going to feel to look around, and own the top of the mountain again."

# PETER

This architecture works equally well in formal and informal settings. One of the toughest talks that I ever gave was to my teenage son. When Tyler was a senior in high school, he came downstairs one day with his electric guitar slung over his shoulder, and announced that he had decided not to go to college. Instead, he planned to live at home with us for the next few years while he pursued his interest in heavy metal music. My wife turned to me and said, "Okay, Mr. Communication, you go upstairs and have a talk with Tyler. Do your thing."

I knew that I could give him twenty-five good reasons to go to college. But I also knew that by reason number five, he would have tuned me out. Time for a strategy. So, I defined my outcome: By the end of this conversation, Tyler will reconsider his decision about college. What did he need to know? (1) That I am committed to his success no matter how he defines it; (2) That his heroes, like Jimi Hendrix, Eric Clapton, and Carlos Santana, all became hugely successful not by playing other people's music, but by composing their own; and (3) That in college, he would learn how to compose his own music. What did Tyler need to feel? (1) Concern that he may be missing out on opportunities if he doesn't go to college; (2) Excitement about new possibilities. Then I found the relevance. Why did Tyler care? Because he wants to be a successful musician, and he wants to make money, and he wants an active social life. I clarified my point, which was this: If you want to be successful as a musician, you need to learn to compose your own music.

My dessert? "By the way, at any midsize university, there are between ten and twenty thousand girls without boyfriends who have just left home."

The talk went well. The end of the story? Today Tyler is a senior in college with a 4.0 average—and he's applying to medical school.

# 3

# TECHNIQUES

**Y**OU SPEAK AN average of seven thousand words a day. (Men average around six thousand, women average around eight thousand!)[1] But with all those words spoken, the sad fact is that most of what you say will be forgotten by the time the listener's head hits the pillow.

Still, you get up every day and communicate things that you hope people will remember. If you're a leader, or somebody who must create influence with your board, your children or your team, you have to figure out how to make your message stick in people's memory. The shorthand we use for this quality is **stickiness,** a term popularized by Chip and Dan Heath in their great book on the topic, *Made to Stick.*[2]

So, what makes something sticky?

It should be:

1. Simple.
2. Emotional.
3. Vivid.

Sounds straightforward, right? But simplicity has to do with mastery. Watch a master do anything, and it looks easy. That's because they're literally using fewer muscles than a beginner. Beginners are tense; if you look at a scan of their brain when they're doing something for the first time, every neural pathway is lit up. They're sticking out their tongue and hunching their shoulders, in an effort to move their leg. Mastery is a process of subtraction—the better you get at something, the fewer neurons you require to make the movement, and the easier it looks.

So we'd like to share with you some techniques that will help move you down the road toward mastery. We've chosen what we believe to be the key elements of good communication. And like a good carpenter with sharp tools, you should have them available to you whenever you need them.

These are classical techniques, based on good old common sense, and used by great speakers, writers, and thinkers since the time of Cicero.

**Stories** put a human face on your data. **Metaphors** make things memorable. **Active language** is more compelling than business jargon. A **refrain** becomes a way of reinforcing your key point. Sharpening your **Q&A** skills will give you a chance to engage with your listeners.

Like any technique, the goal is that once you master it, it will ultimately disappear. The ultimate focus will be on your audience, and the connection you have with them.

## STORIES

Your listeners may not remember a string of numbers. But they will remember a story. Because of the way that our brains are wired, we will listen with absorbed attention to almost any story, no matter how strange it seems. It can be quite minimal: "I had a colleague named Ralph, who discovered one day that his computer had crashed, right before an important meeting. And suddenly, he had an idea . . ." We will sit forward and listen with rapt attention to what comes next, because that's the way our brains are wired.

Use it. *Tell stories.*

## Principles of Storytelling

A story can be used in any part of your speech, from the ramp to the dessert. A story shows cause and effect over time. It puts flesh on an idea, relates the idea back to the listener, and shows how it affects him with real opportunities and costs. A story is the ideal place to illustrate your values, without listing them up front. Stories create a bond; they produce a sense of identification that causes the listener to say, "Me, too!" Stories accelerate understanding, because a story *shows,* instead of *tells.* Stories have been used to teach since the beginning of time. A story also demonstrates empathy and allows you to evoke emotion, without becoming sentimental.

A good story starts with three coordinates: (1) Where; (2) When; (3) Who.

Thus the classical formation "Once upon a time, there was a handsome prince who lived in a castle all alone . . ." can be easily adapted: "Last summer, I took my nine-year-old son up the Amazon in a canoe . . ." Now we're in the movie. Every listener has visual images of a father, a son, and a rain forest. The stage is set, and the story can begin.

A successful story starts with a **platform,** according to international improvisation expert Keith Johnstone, founder of Theatersports.[3] The platform is a stable, ordinary circumstance. Then you **tilt** the platform. The tilt is the unexpected element that throws the main character into a struggle to regain balance. It can be as simple as a clown whose umbrella turns inside out, or as complex as Hamlet. (*Note:* the story of *The Lion King* is the same story as Hamlet. Classical story formulations appear over and over.)

The *struggle* is what defines the story. No struggle, no story. The struggle is what makes it exciting, funny, inspiring, and emotional. It's what makes us cheer when the hero overcomes an obstacle.

There comes a point in the story where the main character has to make a decision; a fork in the road. Again, the more difficult the decision, the more interesting the story. Work in an element of mystery; create surprise and delight your audience by doing something unexpected. Use **reincorporation**—allow elements to appear in the story, and then reappear. If there's a surprise, it's satisfying when it is linked to something that appeared earlier. When the prince meets the old hag in the forest, she hands him a goblet; later in the story, the goblet will fit in nicely when he needs to drink the magic potion.

**Show, don't tell.** Listeners are naturally rebellious; if you tell them what to feel, they'll do the opposite. If you say to a kid, "I'm going to tell you a scary story," nine times out of ten, they will say afterward, "That wasn't scary." Tell an audience that you're about to say something funny, and watch them sit back and fold their arms with a scowl on their faces, determined not to laugh. So, don't tell the listener what to feel. Just describe the scene, and let him draw his own conclusions. Instead of saying, "He was nervous," say, "His palms were sweaty." Instead of "It was a beautiful day," say, "The sun was shining through the palm trees, and there was a soft breeze." Instead of "The mother felt really sad as she watched her son drive off to join the army," say, "As she watched her son drive away, she turned her face away, and wiped her eyes on her sleeve." Imagine that you're creating a movie for the listener to watch. Allow people to experience their own emotions, based on the story you're telling.

Where can you find a good story? Consider these sources:

1. **History**—either the history of your organization, or world history.
2. **Your own life,** or the lives of people you know, particularly in difficult situations where obstacles have been overcome.

3. **Newspapers**—current events provide a gold mine of topical stories.

4. **Literature** or the arts—classic stories lend great power and dignity to a talk.

5. **Your children**—kids are always a great source of stories that everyone can understand.

There are different types of stories. Two of the most useful are *cautionary tales,* which warn us of danger ahead, and *inspirational tales,* which talk about someone overcoming an obstacle. There is a simple mathematical formula to building an inspirational tale: the bigger the dragon, and the smaller the hero, the more compelling the story will be. When an ordinary person perseveres through great difficulty and comes out the other side, we feel inspired. To add more inspiration, create more difficulty and a longer path in order for the person to succeed. If Superman breaks down a door, it's no big deal. But if he's encased in kryptonite, it suddenly becomes more interesting.

The best stories are true ones. Authenticity has a ring that you simply can't fake. Sometimes if you look more closely, your personal experience may furnish a perfect story for your topic.

## PETER

We were working with a senior executive, a charismatic Asian American man named Stan, at a global technology firm that was hosting a conference on collaboration. We kept rehearsing and rewriting his keynote address, but it felt uninspired—he could talk endlessly about collaboration, but only in the abstract. There was something missing—his presentation lacked soul.

I prodded him for a personal story that might breathe some life into his talk. I remembered him mentioning that he was a marathon runner and then saying something cryptic about the fact that he hadn't always been able to run. When I pressed him, he said he'd actually had polio as a child and was confined to a wheelchair until he was twelve. It sounded like a potentially very powerful personal story about overcoming tremendous odds.

"But it's got nothing to do with collaboration," Stan said. "And besides, I don't want to talk about myself."

I pressed further. It turns out that Stan's parents and his five siblings refused to accept the prognosis that polio would prevent him from walking. They worked tirelessly with him and with a team of physical therapists. Finally, one day, at age twelve, Stan stood up from the wheelchair and walked on his own.

After that, he ran. And today, he's an accomplished marathoner.

I convinced Stan that he had an inspiring story about collaboration—his doctors, therapists, and family had all worked together toward a common goal. But Stan was still uneasy about sharing his plight. It went against his cultural upbringing, he said, to put the spotlight on himself.

It's true, the story was about Stan—but only on the surface. In fact, it was because of the heroic efforts of the team around him that he was able to leave that wheelchair behind. This was really a story about collaboration, not about isolated, individual effort. Stan was telling a story about himself, but he was giving all the credit to others.

On the day of the conference, when Stan started talking about his journey from the wheelchair to the marathon, the audience was rapt. Five years later, people who heard that story still remember it, and Stan's message about the value of collaboration.

## METAPHOR

Using a metaphor is like shining a spotlight on a darkened stage. It focuses your listener's attention where you want it.

As you think about that, notice what happens in your brain—you can see the picture of a spotlight in your head, making the idea easier to grasp and remember than a lot of words that jostle around meaninglessly.

This is the power of a metaphor; it creates a word picture. It makes you able to *see* the idea. It makes your words concrete. The brain processes images sixty thousand times faster than words alone.[4] So a picture is really worth sixty thousand words. Imagine how much time you save by bringing up a picture in your listener's mind.

Remember the quote from Dwight D. Eisenhower's sergeant, when asked to provide an instant assessment of the battlefield? "Sir, imagine a doughnut. We're the hole." Chances are that you do remember that metaphor, even though you've read a lot of words in the meantime.

Because of their power, metaphors are one of the oldest literary devices known to mankind.[5] Why? Well, metaphors make your language sticky, because they're processed on the right side of the brain, along with color, stories, and emotion. In a time when brevity is a virtue, metaphors accelerate the speed of understanding. Metaphors also create feeling, and can simplify complex ideas.

We use metaphors all the time: "My computer crashed." "We had runaway inflation." "I hit the jackpot." "We're holding our ground." "We're losing altitude." "She's in a bumpy period." "We're coming up to the finish line." "He knocked it out of the park."

Every time you say the words "e-mail" or "in-box," you're using a metaphor. We've made a complex, hard-to-grasp idea comprehensible by giving it a physical shape that we understand.

If you're trying to describe a complicated new delivery system to someone who doesn't understand it, you might say, "We're like the veins of the body; we carry vital components from the brain out to the arms and legs, so the work can get done."

To create a metaphor, write down the thing you're trying to describe. For example, let's use the delivery system. Write a list of qualities describing that object. Example: it moves things from place to place, connects pieces together, it provides a critical function without which everything breaks down.

Now, pick one of those descriptors. Example: moves objects from place to place. What else moves objects from place to place? Make a list: plumbing pipes, roads, veins, train tracks. Look at the list and evaluate the possibilities of each one as a usable metaphor. Plumbing pipes may not be a good choice, for example, because the connotations are sewage, rats, and waste. *Not* associations that you want to create in the listener's mind. Roads have potential as a metaphor in this case; without roadways, transportation locks down and commerce is crippled.

But veins provide an even more fertile image. It's organic, everyone instinctively understands it, and without veins the organism will obviously die. Healthy veins mean a healthy organization. They take things from the central intelligence system, the brain, out to the limbs where work is accomplished.

A good metaphor will spin out even more implications than you originally spotted; an excellent metaphor will actually supercharge your presentation by suggesting additional possibilities.

Two cautions when dealing with metaphor: be careful to avoid dead metaphors, or clichés. "Like apples and oranges" is not a metaphor, but a cliché. This will hurt you instead of helping you. (For more on avoiding clichés, see the section on active language.) Also beware of mixing your metaphors or packing more than one into your presentation. Ideally you should have one overarching metaphor that creates a memorable visual picture, and then you can tease it out through the rest of your presentation. "If the delivery system components are the veins of the company, the people in the depots are the hands and feet. To keep them working well, we need to . . ."

Metaphors can be used as a powerful tool in the workplace. For example: Sylvia was a manager in a large organization. She was happily doing her job until her boss added another manager to her region, doing the exact same job.

Sylvia complained that there was too much duplication going on. Her boss responded that by putting more resources in the region, they would gain a greater market share. They were in deadlock.

Finally, Sylvia used this metaphor to clinch her business case: "Imagine we're in a race. It's a race we can win. We're ahead. But at the moment we've got a racecar with two steering wheels, and two drivers." Her boss, who was a big NASCAR fan, laughed. The next day Sylvia got an e-mail that said, "The region is all yours."

## SHANN

I was once in a situation where my boss wasn't giving me the resources I needed to do my job. I sent him an e-mail that read, *"Hey, Cap'n— Quick dispatch from your foot soldier on the front lines. It's getting a little scary out here under fire, and we're undersupplied—how about sending us some ammunition?"* My metaphor essentially created a story line for my boss to enter, like a little movie. In this minidrama, my boss was cast as the captain—and a good captain would never send his foot soldiers out onto the front lines without equipping them with the necessary supplies. There is only one happy ending to this story— the captain gives the foot soldier what's needed. And that's exactly what my boss did.

## ACTIVE LANGUAGE

Words have power.

High Performance Communication is all about saying the right words, in the right way, when the pressure is on. There are infinite ways of saying things, and your choice of words can have far-reaching consequences. The most powerful language is **fresh, concrete,** and set at the **appropriate level of intensity.**

## PETER

About five years ago, I was asked to give a speech to raise money for a theater company, at an evening event in San Francisco.

At about 11:30 p.m., I got a call from my wife, Marcia. She said, "Don't forget the cat food."

I said, "Honey, I'm in the middle of a fund-raiser."

She said, "That's fine. Just don't come home without the cat food."

Turns out the cat had just had kittens, and Marcia couldn't leave the house because our son was asleep. "Fine," I said. "I'll get the cat food."

The event finished at one o'clock in the morning. Now, San Francisco is a pretty nice place, except for one area. It's called the Tenderloin, and it happens to be the one place where the shops stay open all night. So I got on my motorcycle and drove into the Tenderloin, where I found a twenty-four-hour liquor store that also sold groceries.

As I pulled my motorcycle up onto its center stand, I looked around. On one corner there were prostitutes. Across the street were a couple of shady-looking guys wearing big hooded coats and sunglasses, staring at me and whispering to each other. I thought, Hey, I'm from New York. They're not going to mess with me. But I took my helmet and keys in with me, just in case.

I bought the cat food, along with some eggs and juice for the morning. As I walked out of the shop, I saw one of the shady-looking guys point two fingers straight at my eyes, like he was marking me. Then they both started to move toward me, fast. My first instinct was to run—but I knew they would catch me. My second instinct was to fight—but there were two of them, and only one of me. I just stood there, completely paralyzed. The next second, they were on me.

The first guy hit me in the face, and my bag of groceries went flying. Then the second guy hit me in the stomach, and I bent double. I could feel someone punching me in the ribs, and other hands in my pocket, trying to get my wallet.

I had a sudden vision of myself lying in the gutter unconscious, blood trickling out of my mouth. I thought of my wife and my son waiting for me at home, and knew I had to do something. Without thinking I grabbed the inside lapel of my coat, as if it had a microphone in it, and started yelling at the top of my lungs, "VECTOR FIVE, VECTOR FIVE, ALL UNITS MOVE IN. RED ALERT, RED ALERT, TARGETS AT MISSION AND 13th. DEPLOY ALL UNITS, I NEED FULL BACKUP NOW, MOVE, MOVE, MOVE!"

There was a long pause. I looked up. The guys who had been attacking me were gone. The hookers were gone. In fact, the entire street was empty. I picked up my juice, and the cat food. The eggs were past rescuing. As I raced my bike out of there, as fast as I could go, it occurred to me that the right words, spoken in the right way, at the right time, had probably just saved my life.

---

It's always tempting to slide into the tar pit of trendy business clichés, especially in the corporate world. George Orwell, author and famous chronicler of English culture, says that modern language "at its worst does not consist in picking out words for the sake of their meaning and inventing images in order to make the meaning clearer. It consists in gumming together long strips of words which have already been set in order by someone else . . ."[6]

You know this "prefab" language, or business-speak, when you hear it. It sounds something like this: "At the end of the day, going forward, we need to be team players—to drill down, do a deep dive, and find a silver bullet vis-à-vis the low-hanging fruit that will leverage the value proposition for our stakeholders so we can achieve critical mass when the rubber meets the road."[7]

Sound familiar? Avoid it. Use *real* words that are simple, direct, and muscular. Effective communication avoids clichés and insider jargon. Listeners will judge the freshness of your ideas by the freshness of your language. There's a game called Bullsh*t Bingo, in which players download a bingo card with overused jargon words and phrases, and check off the words to keep themselves awake during boring presentations. When a player gets bingo, she's supposed to stand up and shout, "Bullsh*t!" To be fair, we've never heard of anyone actually standing up and shouting during a presentation. But you never know. Don't let it happen to you.

Here's a list (not exhaustive, by any means!) of phrases that make the Bullsh*t Bingo list. Scrub them from your vocabulary! They will make your talk sound dated and stale.

- Synergy
- Out of the box
- Bottom line
- Revisit
- 24/7
- Out of the loop
- Benchmark
- Value-added
- Proactive
- Win-win
- Think outside the box
- Fast track
- Result-driven
- Empower (or empowerment)
- Knowledge base
- At the end of the day
- Touch base
- Ballpark
- Game plan
- Leverage

No matter how big and ambitious your vision may be, the language you use to convey that vision still needs to be *specific* and *detailed*. Let's look at a few famous examples that use concrete images to support an overarching goal or vision.

Gray language is the enemy. Imagine that you are a movie director. Choose images, and create scenes in the mind's eye of the listener.

Different words also have different temperatures. It's important to pitch your language at the appropriate level of intensity. How much voltage do you want to send through the wires? Saying, *"He let me down,"* is very different from saying, *"He stabbed me in the back."* The difference will affect both you and your listener.

Notice the increasing degrees of intensity in the following three statements: (1) "I'm *concerned* about the budget." (2) "I'm *worried* about the costs. (3) "I'm *fearful* that this will put us into bankruptcy."

Match your word choice to your intentions. Choose the amount of heat you want your words to convey. Sometimes it's important to be diplomatic; other times, you need to phrase things in the most direct or dramatic way. Do you mean to *attract your listener's attention,* do you mean to *alarm* him, or do you mean to *frighten* him?

If a project didn't turn out as you planned, saying, "We failed," may kill the hope and optimism in the team. If you want to bring their attention to the fact, but not terrify them, you might want to put it this way: "We didn't meet all of our goals."

On the other hand, if you're the head of the fire department, and your guys are in a building that's about to explode, it's not the time to say, "You gentlemen might want to consider being more expeditious in your exit strategy." The phrase you're looking for is "Get out now!"

When you are choosing your words, there is no choice that is always right or wrong. The only wrong choice is to *fail to make a choice*. Be intentional with your language.

THE FIRST IS FROM JOHN F. KENNEDY'S "MAN ON THE MOON" SPEECH IN 1961:

| THE VISION | THE SPECIFIC, COMPELLING IMAGE |
|---|---|
| *"to win the battle that is now going on around the world between freedom and tyranny."* | "First, I believe that this nation should commit itself to achieving the goal, before this decade is out, of landing a man on the moon and returning him safely to the earth. No single space project in this period will be more impressive to mankind, or more important for the long-range exploration of space; and none will be so difficult or expensive to accomplish. We propose to accelerate the development of the appropriate lunar space craft. We propose to develop alternate liquid and solid fuel boosters, much larger than any now being developed, until certain which is superior." |

NOTES

The vision is the overarching objective—here, freedom (and scientific knowledge). Notice that the man-on-the-moon image is *supporting evidence* for that broader vision (which is actually, in the context of this speech, to defeat the Soviet Union in the hearts and minds of the world).

And notice the specifics in Kennedy's image—landing a man on the moon and returning him safely to the earth ... alternate liquid and solid fuel boosters!

Imagine this same speech with business jargon: "No single space project in this period will do more to maximize the value proposition for the American stakeholder ..."

HERE'S ANOTHER ONE YOU KNOW: CHURCHILL'S SPEECH TO BRITISH PARLIAMENT IN 1940:

| THE VISION | THE SPECIFIC, COMPELLING IMAGE |
|---|---|
| *"we shall not flag or fail"* [i.e., we're going to win this war]. | "... we shall fight with growing confidence and growing strength in the air, we shall defend our Island, whatever the cost may be, we shall fight on the beaches, we shall fight on the landing grounds, we shall fight in the fields and in the streets, we shall fight in the hills: we shall never surrender." |

NOTES

Notice the list of clear and simple nouns: beaches, grounds, fields, streets, hills. Four of the five are single-syllable words: clear, forceful, concrete.

*Here's how it might sound in business-speak:* "We need to come out of our silos and create new synergies with increased enthusiasm, while leveraging our existing aviation to its fullest extent. We're going to fortify all of our existing resources to cover the territory, regardless of the investment. We will be continuing those efforts with the kind of commitment that we've always been known for, for as long as it takes to be successful. I'm absolutely confident that this team can achieve those kinds of results, and I look forward to our continued success in the future."

AND FINALLY, FROM MARTIN LUTHER KING'S FAMOUS 1963 SPEECH:

| THE VISION | THE SPECIFIC, COMPELLING IMAGE |
| --- | --- |
| *"that all men—yes, black men as well as white men—would be guaranteed the inalienable rights of life, liberty, and the pursuit of happiness."* | "I have a dream that one day, on the red hills of Georgia, the sons of former slaves and the sons of former slave owners will be able to sit down together at the table of brotherhood. <br><br> I have a dream that one day even the state of Mississippi, a state sweltering with the heat of injustice, sweltering with the heat of oppression, will be transformed into an oasis of freedom and justice. <br><br> I have a dream that my four little children will one day live in a nation where they will not be judged by the color of their skin but by the content of their character." |

| NOTES |
| --- |
| Again, specifics: red hills of Georgia … table of brotherhood … sweltering heat … four little children. These are concrete pictures that are immediately clear in our minds. <br><br> For a reminder of just how vivid King's images are—and, by contrast, how bland and uninspiring corporate jargon can be—try putting King's ideas into business clichés: "Going forward, we need to think out of the box to find a scalable solution to racial inequality. We need an impactful solution that will break down silos between black and white people …" |

# REFRAIN

We've said it before, and we'll say it again: one of your biggest challenges as a speaker is that your listeners will immediately forget 90 percent of what you say. So what's a speaker to do?

To help solve this problem, we turn to the group of people who create memorable word patterns better than anyone else—songwriters. Ever notice when you leave the theater after a good musical, everyone is humming the same tune? That's no accident. In any given song, there is a chorus, or refrain. The refrain is repeated, not just once, but many times through the song. If it's compelling enough, it will stick in your head for years—or forever. Think, ". . . and she's buying a stairway to heaven." Very few people know all the words to that Led Zeppelin classic, but almost all of us can all hum the refrain.

There is a sense of inevitability about a great refrain—a way in which you can hear it coming. When it arrives, there is an uncontrollable impulse to sing along, because everything has been building up to it. The lyrics all lead to the chorus, giving a sense of satisfaction and closure.

Like a good song, any good speech will have one memorable "red thread" that weaves through it. Powerful political campaigns and speeches nearly always feature a refrain of some kind. Think Obama and "Yes we can." Or Ronald Reagan's famous "Tear down this wall" speech. John F. Kennedy's speech in West Berlin on June 26, 1963, was a classic example of the powerful use of refrain:

> *There are many people in the world who really don't understand, or say they don't, what is the great issue between the free world and the Communist world. Let them come to Berlin. There are some who say that communism is the wave of the future. Let them come to Berlin. And there are some who say in Europe and elsewhere we can work with the Communists. Let them come to Berlin. And there are even a few who say that it is true that communism is an evil system, but it permits us to make economic progress. Lass' sie nach Berlin kommen. Let them come to Berlin.*

One of the most famous uses of refrain comes from Martin Luther King Jr.'s "I Have a Dream" speech, in which he repeats the phrase no fewer than nine times. He ends the speech this way: (Note that there are actually two *additional* repeated elements in the finish, on top of the original "I have a dream" refrain!)

> *Let freedom ring from Stone Mountain of Georgia.*
> *Let freedom ring from Lookout Mountain of Tennessee.*
> *Let freedom ring from every hill and molehill of Mississippi.*
> *From every mountainside, let freedom ring.*
>
> *And when this happens, when we allow freedom to ring, when we let it ring from every village and every hamlet, from every state and every city, we will be able to speed up that day when all of God's children, black men and white men, Jews and Gentiles, Protestants and Catholics, will be able to join hands and sing in the words of the old Negro spiritual, "Free at last! Free at last! Thank God Almighty, we are free at last!"*

These are all pretty lofty and poetic examples of the use of refrain. But a refrain can be simple and pragmatic as well: "And that's why we need to move quickly." Or "We all need to work together." Or ". . . because we know that you'll make the right decision."

Although the use of a refrain has the effect of a sophisticated rhetorical tool, it's actually quite simple: pick an element and repeat it. Keep returning to it. Anytime you repeat something, you create a pattern, and the brain loves patterns. Coming back to something familiar helps you regroup, and ensures that everything relates back to your central point. Using a refrain can also help you build your argument, by pulling the content forward.

What should you use as a refrain? More good news—you've already done the hard work of finding your refrain, when you clarified your **point.** When you repeat your point more than once, it becomes your **refrain.**

> *Three years ago this team suffered massive cuts. We had no training, and we faced huge challenges. We overcame them. Six months ago, people were leaving, we had a lot of chaos, people didn't know to whom they were reporting. We faced those challenges, and we overcame them.*

*Now our fiercest competitor has created a beachhead in a territory that has always been ours. Once again, we are facing enormous challenges. And once again, we will overcome them.*

Using a refrain in this way not only organizes the information for the listener, but also for the speaker. In a prepared speech, you can carefully choose the spots where you return to your refrain. But in an improvised talk, a refrain is even more useful; it becomes a great springboard for the speaker. Whenever you find yourself beginning to lose momentum, you can return to your refrain like a touchstone. It will reorganize your thoughts, and send you out again with a fresh bounce, while helping you to stay on point. "I opened by saying that *everything we've done has prepared us for this moment* [refrain]. So, what does that mean when it comes to new products?"

## Q&A

No matter how good your speech is, it is during the question and answer period that people find out what you're made of. Listeners make key decisions about you and your material, by seeing how you think and relate in the moment; they want to watch the way your mind works. It is through dialogue that people develop a greater level of trust, rapport, and clarity. It is also during the Q&A that you demonstrate your real ability to respond to the listeners' needs and create a bond. Most speakers dread Q&As, and simply hope that the audience won't ask too many difficult questions. We suggest that you welcome the opportunity to interact with your listeners.

Don't try to dodge the uncomfortable issues. Answer the unanswered questions early in the presentation. If last year the program cost you $25,000, and everyone in the committee knows that this year it's going to cost $35,000, everyone will be preoccupied until you've addressed this issue.

The key to success in a Q&A is in the preparation. Failing to prepare for Q&A is like spending months getting ready to run a marathon, and then forgetting your shoes on the day of the race. Here are some techniques to help you prepare for and master the Q&A process: Write down and answer for yourself: (1) the ten questions they are most likely to ask; (2) the ten questions you most dread. Rehearse your answers with other people who can give you feedback. Remember the Horror Scenario we described back in the **Architecture** section, where there were no questions during Q&A, and you ended up slinking offstage, feeling like a fool? Well, here's a technique that will prevent this from ever happening to you: if there are no questions, ask yourself a question that you have prepared ahead of time. Pause for a beat or two, and say something like, "One question that you might have is . . . ," or "Something I'm often asked is . . . ," or "You might be wondering . . ." Then answer your own question. This breaks the awkwardness of the moment, and will often serve to prime the pump, so that listeners begin to ask their own questions. If they don't, you can proceed gracefully on to your **dessert.**

---

**MASTER TIP:** If there are no questions, ask yourself one that you have prepared ahead of time. Then answer it.

---

In a formal event, **repeat** your prepared question out loud before you answer it. This accomplishes several things:

1. It ensures that you heard it properly. There's nothing worse than spending five minutes answering a question, only to hear the listener say, "That's not what I asked."
2. It enables everyone in the room to hear the question.
3. It buys you a precious two or three extra seconds—and that's all the time your brain needs to formulate your answer.

In a less formal environment, where it might seem odd to repeat the question, **embed** the question in the answer. This means that you *repeat part of the question as you answer it.* For example, if the question is, "What are you hearing from our customers?" you answer: "What we're hearing is that customers are hungry for something new. They're saying, 'When is the new version going to appear?' and they're getting antsy." When you embed, you accomplish the following things:

1. You restate the question so that everyone can hear it, without sounding too stuffy.
2. You ensure that you heard the question properly.
3. Most important, embedding forces you to respond to the listener in their own preferred brain language: visual, auditory, feeling/sensory, or logical/numbers.[8]

Everyone has their own preferred "brain language," or **modality**. Some people are visual; they will say, "How does this **look** to you?" Others tend to be auditory. They might say, "It **sounds** to me as though . . ." Digital brain types use numbers: "This happens in **37 percent** of the cases." And feeling/sensory speakers will say something like, "I just **feel** that we're off track here." If someone asks you, "How do you **see** this happening?" (visual) and you respond, "Well, it **feels** to me as though we have a rough road ahead" (feeling/sensory), there will be a *disconnect* in the conversation. They've asked the question in one brain language, or modality, and you've answered in another. This immediately disrupts your connection with the listener. Like a sax player entering a group improvisation in the wrong key, it will jar the harmony of the communication.

Embedding prevents this from happening, by ensuring that you answer in the modality of the questioner. For example, if he asks, "What's your **feeling** on how things are going?" (feeling/sensory) you answer, "My **feeling** is . . ." By using his modality, you ensure rapport. This will make the listener feel heard, understood, and satisfied at a deep level. Embedding the question guarantees that you are **playing in the key of the other person.**

For more details on language modality, see the following chart:

| SPEAK THE LANGUAGE OF YOUR LISTENER | | |
| --- | --- | --- |
| Style | Audience Says | You Say |
| AUDITORY | Did I hear you right?<br>Sounds exciting.<br>That's music to my ears.<br>Your message rings true to me.<br>Talk me through this … | Use auditory metaphors:<br>    "music to my ears"<br>Respond with words like "hear,"<br>    "sounds," "rings true"…<br>Focus on what people said and what it<br>    sounds like. |
| VISUAL | We are seeing eye-to-eye.<br>I'm not sure I see your point.<br>The future looks bright.<br>It appears as if we have a long road<br>    ahead of us. | Draw a picture or use an image to make<br>    a point.<br>Respond with words like "see,"<br>    "looks," "catch sight of"…<br>Use visual metaphors.<br>In stories, describe what you see in the<br>    environment. |
| KINESTHETIC | I feel like we are getting somewhere.<br>It seems like a rough road ahead.<br>He's carrying a heavy load.<br>Let's get a handle on this.<br>Can we smooth this out? | Use feeling metaphors:<br>Respond with words like "feel,"<br>    "sense," "intuit"…<br>In stories, describe texture.<br>Get them on their feet and use an<br>    active exercise. |
| DIGITAL | Let me show you how we came to this …<br>We have three options.<br>This makes sense because …<br>We can double our returns with<br>    10 percent more resources. | Show a graph.<br>Give numbers and facts.<br>Use language that quantifies.<br>Go in chronological order; use sequence<br>    and logic to organize thoughts. |

Another useful technique in Q&A is the **paraphrase.** Sometimes you'll get a question that isn't clear. The questioner is rambling on and on, and by the end of the question, everyone is completely confused. It's your job to create clarity here. You do this by hearing them out, and then paraphrasing the question: "So, what you're asking here is whether or not we have the funds. Is that right?" Generally, the questioner will sigh with relief, and say, "Yes, that's right." They may even thank you!

## In the Case of an Aggressive Question

Take the teeth out of an aggressive question by **acknowledging** the listener. Find something in the question with which you can agree. This is a powerful aikido principle of defense that teaches us to meet the aggressor not with opposing force, but by redirecting the oncoming energy in a way that protects both you and the opponent.[9] Your impulse may be to attack back. Don't do it. Your audience will not forgive you. Remember that they identify with the questioner, and not with you. If you take advantage of your superior position to bully a member of the audience, they will all resent you. Avoid getting defensive. You're in the spotlight; you're expected to take the high road. An example of acknowledgment might be, "That's an important question, and I'm glad you asked it."

Avoid getting into a one-on-one with the questioner. Do not square off with him. If you turn your body full-on to face him and look directly at him, it can be perceived either as an act of aggression, or a signal that he has succeeded in taking you hostage and forcing you to leave the group. After acknowledging the questioner, move your eyes and body away to include the rest of the group in a polite way. This keeps the questioner from getting too much power in the room, and prevents the two of you from getting locked into an "alpha dance" of superiority. Remember that *you must preserve both his dignity and your own*. If you don't, he'll keep coming after you. In the case of an aggressive question, DO NOT EMBED the question in the answer. For example, if he asks, "Why is this project wasting so much money?" you DO NOT reply, "We're wasting money because . . ." All you're doing there is reinforcing the hostile message of the questioner in the other listeners' minds! Richard Nixon ended his career the day he said, "I am not a crook." Famed linguist George Lakoff, in his book *Don't Think of an Elephant!*, explores the concept of "framing."[10] The idea is that you evoke the thought patterns associated with something as soon as you bring it into existence with language. In other words, if you say, "Don't think of an elephant," the listener can think of nothing else. If you don't want them to think of an elephant, **don't say the word.** If you do, you're accepting the negative frame, or presupposition, in the question (for example, that the project is *wasting* money) and reinforcing it in the minds of the listener.

Instead, **reframe.** The reframe takes the question to higher ground by identifying the real core issue behind the question. You might say something like this: "*This is a question about the additional investment* needed to complete the project. As we investigated this project, we found that there were problems in the foundation of the building that would have cost us three times more had we not dealt with it up front." If the aggressive question is, "Why is this so overpriced?" You might reframe it this way: "This is a question *about quality . . .*"

A few examples of useful reframing phrases: "This is a question about value / about long-term investment / about credibility / about personal ethics / feasibility / timing / leadership / resources."

*Note:* Reframing is not about trying to evade the question. What you're doing is lifting the discussion out of the level of personal attack. This allows you to address the issue that listener was *actually raising,* without taking his emotional bait.

Sometimes you will come across a seriously hostile questioner who is trying to entrap you. We call these people "sharks." Generally the shark in the audience will ask a question that is loaded with a presupposition. Like a mine in a minefield, if you step on it, you will unleash it. Questions like this might be: "Why are you lying to us?" "Does it bother you that you're not a good parent?" or "How do you deal with the fact that you don't spend enough time with your team?" Here are some tips for dealing with a shark:

1. Don't repeat their language.
2. Set the record straight. Asked, "Do you still cheat on your taxes?" you might respond this way: "Let me set the record

straight. I take my fiscal responsibility very seriously, I have a perfect record with the IRS, and I intend to keep it that way."

3. Move on. Turn away from the questioner firmly but politely, and make it clear that you are not going to engage with him any further. As Peter's father used to say, "Never wrestle with a pig. You both get dirty—but the pig *likes* it."

Barack Obama offered a masterful example of reframing during the 2008 presidential election, when he came under fire for his association with Rev. Jeremiah Wright. While delivering a speech on race, he was asked this question: "How do you defend your association with this man and his 'anti-American' sentiments?" Obama turned the question into an opportunity to talk about bigger American ideas—the ideal of striving for a "more perfect union" and continuing "the long march of those who came before us, a march for a more just, more equal, more free, more caring, and more prosperous America."

**Always tell the truth** in a Q&A (and everywhere else, for that matter!). The listeners can tell when you're trying to baffle them with BS—don't do it. If you don't know the answer, say so. "I should have that information in front of me, and I'm afraid I don't. If you'd like to give me your card after the talk, I'll find the data and get it to you before Monday." Not knowing every answer is human, and admitting it will earn you respect and credibility. But nothing makes an entire audience single-mindedly loathe a speaker more than listening to someone squirm and try to avoid admitting their ignorance.

And finally, keep circling back to your refrain. "And that's why we're asking for approval for the project today." "And that's why going to college is probably the best choice if you want to make money in music." Each question offers an opportunity to reinforce your initial point.

# Part Two

DELIVERY

## DELIVERY

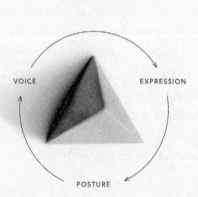

VOICE     EXPRESSION

POSTURE

THE WORLD IS filled with smart people whose ideas will never be heard. Why? They lack delivery skills.

How many times have you watched an intelligent, talented person, with great content and insight, take a well-prepared presentation and turn it into a disaster because *he fell apart when he stood up to speak*? Your ability to create impact with your words is primarily determined by the way you deliver them.

Watch any election. You can generally predict the winner based on one thing: not their ideas, or their party, or their positions, or their home state—but their ability to deliver a message. Your good ideas are not good enough. The facts will not speak for themselves. It's your job to make the facts come alive. Think of the words as notes on the page. It's only sheet music—until you play the instrument. What people see and hear is just as important as what you say. In fact, at the beginning of a speech, the sound of your voice, the look in your eyes, the expression on your face, and the tone of your voice will trump content every time, because that's when the listener decides whether or not he's going to listen. We advocate using *both*—combining your great ideas with the ability to bring them alive through warm, personal delivery.

In today's environment, all bets are off. The rules have changed. Technology and the pace at which audiences are viewing and experiencing things in their everyday lives have accelerated everything. The attention span of the listener has contracted dramatically.[1] The forty-minute presentation showing slides in a logical order is dead. There are infinite ways to get your message across. Burying people with sixty-six text-heavy slides is no longer the best option.

If you've been through the content preparation section, you should have a message that is lucid, relevant, and the right length for your listener. Now you've got to get your message across. The instruments you have available to deliver your message are your **voice,** your **posture and movement,** and your **face and eyes**.

# 4

# VOICE

**M**OST PEOPLE TELL us that they hate their own voices, particularly when they hear recordings of themselves. One reason for this may be that our voice reveals what we're *not* saying. Our voice reveals our inner state.

In an organization setting, this can be uncomfortable. In an effort to be more opaque, we flatten out the sound, hoping that people won't be able to tell how we really feel. The problem is that we have to absorb a huge amount of information from one another. This becomes much more difficult when the speaker's delivery is flat.

We're not suggesting that you start singing and turn the whole thing into a theater performance. What we are suggesting is that you learn to use the basic nuances of voice to your advantage.

You might think you don't have a "good" voice. But that's like someone who never exercises complaining that they don't have a "good" body. Your voice is what you make it. When you use your voice intentionally, you are making it easy for your ideas to be understood.

You need to be conscious about how you are formulating the sound. Think of it as sculpting the sound to hold up the meaning.

Sound too much like hard work?

We've spent many years studying voice, because as actors and radio hosts, we have to. That's how we make a living. But here's an interesting thought—it's the same for you. *You also make your living with your voice.* Your voice is the vehicle through which your thoughts are made visible.

Great actors spend years working on their voices, and then applying the techniques to text to make it sound real. But most people have never spent a single hour developing the one instrument through which we communicate our thoughts and feelings every day. We're born, we start screaming, and we're off. We rarely think of being intentional with our voice, and shaping it, the way we do with other muscles in our body.

The voice responds to conscious development just as any part of your body does. You can *craft* it. Consider famed CEO Jack Welch, who was a serious stutterer, but became a master presenter through hard work and determination.[1] Actor James Earl Jones, who provided the rich bass voice for Darth Vader, also struggled with a stutter so painful that it rendered him nearly mute for eight years. Grammy Award–winning singer Carly Simon overcame a speech impediment with the help of rhythm and music.

Imagine the return on investment if you were to spend a little time and energy working on your voice, the same way that you would work on your muscles in the gym. Your effort will be repaid many times over.

## BREATH

When we work on voice, we begin with breath. Your voice is carried by your breath. Put one hand on your chest, and one hand on your belly. When you breathe, notice which part pushes out. If, when you inhale, your chest goes out and your belly goes in, you are doing what we call "chest breathing."

Now practice breathing so that when you inhale, your belly pushes out against your hand as it fills with air. When you do this, a powerful muscle called the diaphragm flexes down, allowing the oxygen to reach the lower capillaries in your lungs. When you breathe out, the diaphragm flexes up, emptying your lungs. This is called **abdominal breathing,** and it is the type of breathing that professional singers and actors use to support their voice.

When some people get nervous, their chest and throat tighten up like the neck of a balloon. This will impede your airflow. As you breathe, consciously relax your chest and throat. You can drop your volume, speak very quietly, and still have a round, fat sound that is easily heard.

You don't have to speak louder; you just have to be more generous. Focus on taking in more air and releasing your breath with the sound. The opposite of generous is stingy, and it comes from holding your breath, as if you were keeping the idea to yourself. The tension in your breathing creates tension in the audience. Release your breath fully, and it will carry the idea.

## VOCAL VARIETY

The most important thing you can cultivate in your voice is *variety*.

Boredom comes from sameness. The number one complaint that we hear people make about listening to a speaker is **monotone.** When you speak to someone you know, chances are that you don't speak in a monotone. But when you give information or data, which comes from the left side of the brain, the delivery tends to become monotonous. It's *gray*. You doubt it? Listen carefully in the next meeting you attend.

Whether you're talking on the phone, face-to-face, or before a group, the sense of what you're saying comes through the sound. No matter what note you play, you must vary it. Does this mean you have to become a different person or change your personality? Is your voice broken? Do you have a *bad* voice? Absolutely not. The good news is that you already possess everything you need. Your instrument is fine, as shown by the beautiful way you use it when you're not even thinking about it.

If you tell a friend about your river rafting trip, or your daughter's flute recital, your voice will sound all the notes and express your feelings as beautifully as any professional singer. Unfortunately it is when you most need your voice, when you're under the spotlight and the pressure is on, that it tends to go flat.

So, how do we bring color and interest to the voice? The opposite of sameness is **variety.** Imagine that your voice is like a PA system with different sliders and knobs, including

1. volume
2. pitch
3. tempo

(See the illustration below.) They can all be changed up or down, independently. The trick is to learn to work with each slider, one at a time, and then use them all to create vocal variety. We will discuss staccato, legato, and pause on page 114.

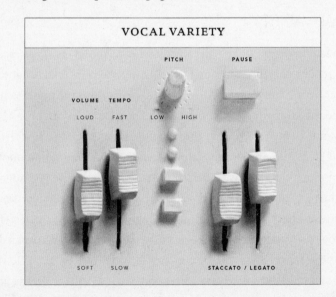

Vocal variety is not about making your voice pretty. It's about taking care of the listener. Here's a quick overview of the vocal qualities that you can use to introduce variety. On the audio track called "Vocal Variety" (available for free download at www.standanddelivergroup.com), we've given you some suggestions on how to develop your voice and expand your vocal range. These are techniques drawn from professional theater, developed for the executives who take our training.

**Volume** means how softly or loudly you're speaking. Where are the places where you can drop the volume down? Contrary to popular opinion, getting louder is not the only way to bring emphasis to a point. When you lower your volume, you are signaling that what comes next is important.

Imagine that you are doing yoga with your voice—go to the extreme. See what happens when you get unpredictable. How soft can you go and still be clearly heard and understood?

Practice speaking very softly, and then increasing your volume until you are speaking very loudly. This is called a *crescendo,* and it is used to build to a climax.

Now start at a high volume, and bring the volume down until it is very quiet. This is a *decrescendo.* It can be very effective to use a *decrescendo,* and make your most important point in a voice so soft that it is almost a whisper. Be aware that volume tends to flatten out over the phone. Cultivate the ability to use variations in volume to demonstrate levels of passion. Be unpredictable.

**Pitch** is how high or low the tone of your voice is. Pitch is one of the key indicators of the emotions of the speaker.

When the voice goes up, it signifies the more tender emotions: joy, compassion and sympathy. Imagine talking to a baby; your pitch will automatically rise. We naturally drop the pitch down to demonstrate confidence, certainty, power, and strength. Most men commonly use a low D in terms of pitch, and tend not to vary much. This means they tend to be automatically perceived as authoritative.[2]

A raise in pitch is the way we signal empathy and excitement. This is a particularly good technique for men in management who need to express empathy or concern in dealing with an emotional topic. Women tend to use the higher register, or what we call the "head voice," meaning that they tend to be automatically perceived as empathetic. To signal authority, women should develop the ability to drop their pitch when needed.

The idea is to be flexible, and able to vary your pitch to match your meaning. There is no right pitch or wrong pitch; the only mistake is to fail to vary your pitch. A constant high note will lose its impact and become annoying. A constant low note will signal a lack of warmth and emotion. It's not a question of which note to play, but of whether you can create a variety in your range that paints a rainbow of emotion. Think of changing your tone to create distinctions between different ideas.

Give yourself permission to go further up and down the scale than you normally would. How high can you go up, and how low can you drop down? For women, cultivate the chest voice—these are the darker vocal tones: the burgundies and chocolates. For men, it's important to develop the lighter tones: the blues, pinks, and yellows.

**Tempo** is the speed at which you speak. Again, the only way to get tempo wrong is to fall into one single speed.

The speed at which you speak conveys levels of excitement or emphasis. If you're speaking at a good pace, the places where you slow down convey to the listener that what you're about to say is important. If you speak slowly the entire time, however, the listener will check out after about eight seconds. We believe that nobody speaks too fast. The brain can process auditory information much faster than you can speak. What we often call "too fast" is actually a problem of rhythm. If you don't find the natural pauses in your thoughts, they won't have a chance to absorb the meaning. And if we mash our ideas and words together into one ongoing running sound, the result is monotony.

We shape the thoughts with our rhythm. As long as you create blocks of meaning so that the listener can absorb and digest an idea, you can talk very quickly and still be understood. To direct focus in a sen-

tence, slow down. You can speed through the parts that are less important, and slow down to make your most critical point. Fast is not bad;
slow is not good. What's important is to *vary* the speed. There are times
to speak quickly, and times to slow it down. It's the extremes that are interesting. To hold the listener's attention over a long period of time,
imagine that you're a cabdriver in Rome—go fast, go slow, slam on the
brakes. Experiment with your speed to avoid predictability.

The **pause** is not just the absence of speech—it's an intentional part
of your vocabulary. It's like a powerful secret weapon that almost no one
dares to use. Why? Most people are afraid that if they pause, either (1)
they will look like they don't know what they're going to say next; (2)
someone will interrupt them; or (3) they will lose momentum. But an
effective pause actually creates more momentum. It is created by building to a point, like the moment of stillness before a high dive.

You lead up to the pause with tempo, pitch, and volume. Bring the
listener to the edge of what you're going to say—and hold for a moment. You're essentially teasing the listener in such a way that they
become interested in what you're going to say next. "There's one thing
I'd like to share with you guys" . . . PAUSE. It creates a quality of curiosity. The pause is where you create space for the other person to have
an experience. That's where discoveries are made.

---

**MASTER TIP:** Communication occurs in the silence. *Use the pause.*

---

In singing, *phrasing* refers to the breaths or "stops" between notes.
Phrasing helps a singer make sense of a song, and avoid awkward pauses
for breath. It's the same when you're speaking. When we *phrase*, we clus-
ter a group of words together because they make more sense together
than apart. Sometimes in phrasing, we deliberately separate some words
to emphasize them. This creates a kind of musicality of ideas, without
which it is difficult for the listener to understand what we're saying.
When you're phrasing effectively, you finish an idea all the way to the

end, allowing your voice to put together the ideas in clusters. When you separate a word or two out for emphasis, do it deliberately. (You can download examples of phrasing at standanddelivergroup.com.)

Meet our two Italian cousins, **staccato** and **legato.** These are musical descriptions that indicate how long you hold on to the sound. Staccato is short and quick; legato is long and fluid. In staccato, each note gets its own emphasis, or value. It can be used to punch out key words in the phrase: "Yes we can." Staccato can be very powerful, but will drive your listener crazy if you carry on too long. In legato, one word flows into the next, instead of each word standing on its own, like, "I have a dream . . ." Generally legato is easier to listen to, but will lull a listener into a stupor after a while. Again, the key: VARIETY. Never get stuck doing one thing all the time. Try to make the words *sing.*

An **operative word** is the word in any phrase that gets emphasis, and allows the listener to understand what you're trying to say. Like using a highlighter to pick out the most important word, you can alter the entire meaning of a sentence by changing the operative word. "***Do*** you want to go to the dance with me?" is a different sentence from "Do you want to go to the dance with **me?**"

Pick a phrase and experiment with altering the operative word. The nuance of the sentence shifts when you change the stress on the words. The only wrong choice is making no choice at all. In the beginning, this may feel forced and unnatural. Eventually, like all techniques, it will fade into habit as you use it. Once you become aware of operative words, you will naturally hit the ones that are important. The critical thing is to become conscious of which words you are stressing.

You can practice vocal variety in the following ways:

**READ BEDTIME STORIES TO YOUR KIDS.** Isolate the vocal qualities of volume, pitch, and tempo, and practice using them one at a time as you read to your children. Tonight, try varying only your volume as you read: up and down, *crescendo* and *decrescendo.* Pick out certain words and make them very loud, or very soft. Pay attention to the way you can change the meaning by changing the volume. Tomorrow, try working only with pitch. Vary your pitch, running up and down the scale. The next night, work only with tempo, practicing staccato, legato, and pauses. Then start combining the three. Bedtime will never be the same!

**READ A BOOK OUT LOUD TO YOURSELF.** Pick a favorite book by some wonderful thinker, like Ralph Waldo Emerson, and read it out loud for a half hour per week. Ask yourself how you can give life to the thoughts. Imagine that you are playing classical music with your voice; find pleasure in the sound of the words. Linger on the notes.

**TRAIL AN AUDIO CD.** Trailing is a learning technique in which you learn by following an expert. On the tennis court, the fastest way to improve is to play with a pro. Most of what we learn, we learn by seeing someone else do it, and then we make it our own. Imitation is the best way to learn. So, while you're driving in your car, put in an audio CD of some speaker whose voice you particularly admire. Talk along with it, mirroring the sounds a split second after you hear them. If you feel crazy doing this, put an earpiece in, and pretend you're talking on the phone. Any CD that you enjoy will do; the content is less important than the voice of the person reading it. This exercise is not about adopting someone else's accent, or imitating someone; the point here is to jump-start your vocal technique by stretching yourself as you mirror a master.

A few suggested audiobooks to try:

- *The Immortal Life of Henrietta Lacks,* by Rebecca Skloot, read by Cassandra Campbell. Riveting nonfiction about the history of genetics, medicine, and racial politics, told through the story of the woman who unknowingly donated her genes to science. Chosen by the *New York Times* as one of the best books of 2010.

- *The Reader,* by Bernhard Schlink, read by Campbell Scott. Beautifully written and moving best-selling fiction: a May-September romance, mystery, suspense, and World War II.
- *Four Blondes,* by Candace Bushnell, read by Cynthia Nixon. Guilty-pleasure chick lit, read with wry sophistication by Nixon.
- *The Harry Potter series,* by J. K. Rowling, read by Stephen Fry. A not-to-be-missed rendition of this children's classic, read by that British master of all voices, Stephen Fry.

**READ POETRY TO YOUR PARTNER.** On the way home from work tonight, stop off and buy a copy of *Twenty Poems of Love* by Pablo Neruda. Poetry is candy for the voice, and you'll have the added benefit of creating some serious romance!

## PETER

When I was at the University of Southern California, the famous John Houseman was running the drama department. I went to see him, and said, "Mr. Houseman, I want to be a director. Where should I go to study?"

"My dear boy," he said in his English accent, straightening his bow tie, "if you want to be a director, whatever you do, don't go to graduate school."

"But how will I learn?" I said.

"The same way everyone else has learned," Houseman said. "Go and watch a master. That is how painters learn to paint, how sculptors learn to sculpt. You won't learn in a classroom. Great artists have always found someone to follow. Find someone to watch and build on his wisdom."

So, that's exactly what I did. If it was good enough for John Houseman, it was good enough for me.

# 5

# POSTURE AND MOVEMENT

THE ART OF delivery is learning to use your body in a way that is *congruent* with your message.

Congruence is defined as "the state achieved by coming together; the state of agreement." In communication, this means that your words, face, body, and eyes are all in a state of agreement—they're saying the same thing at the same time. When human beings act with integrity, we look congruent. Congruence equals trust.

When suspects tell lies under questioning, the police look for a *lack of congruence*: something in their voice, eyes, and body that doesn't match up. Our brains subliminally record these tiny incongruent movements and register them as a general sensation of mistrust. "There was just something about his eyes—I don't know why, but I just had a funny feeling about him," victims will report afterward.

Here's the problem: when you're onstage, in the grip of an amygdala hijack, the fear ripping through your body can *make* you incongruent. When you say, "I'm confident that we can do this," you may believe wholeheartedly in what you're saying—but your chin is wrinkled up because you're terrified. The audience is going to register a lack of authenticity in what you're saying, because your words and your face don't match. If you say, "I'm really excited to be sharing this with you today," and your arms are folded across your chest, your words and your body are saying two different things—and the audience will distrust you, without knowing why. How do you solve this problem? We will offer you some long-term solutions to conquering your fear in Part Three of this book, which is all about mastering your **state.** But for the moment, let's focus on some immediate recommendations for working with body language.

Some presentation trainers will teach you to make a certain gesture at a certain time. We don't. We believe that your body has been accompanying your words with appropriate gestures for nearly as long as you've been alive—it's perfectly capable of doing a great job. All you have to do is to get out of your own way and allow your body to line up with the meaning of your words. As Shakespeare said, "Suit the action to the word, the word to the action."

---

**MASTER TIP:** Make your body congruent with your words.

---

The good news is that no special equipment or training is needed. You've been doing this right since you were a baby. You simply have to allow your natural impulses to come through, joined to an awareness of technique. Culture informs nuances of distance, gesture, and style. But there are universal core principles of stagecraft that you can learn to use to your advantage.

## SPEAKING TO A CROWD

Speaking from a stage is the most powerful—and for most people, the most terrifying!—position for a speaker. This is the place from which elections are won, and history is made. Here are a few techniques that will help you master the format, and make you look at ease onstage.

**Plan your entrance.** When you can control your entrance, enter from stage right, and cross down on a diagonal. Stage right is the speaker's right, as shown in the diagram below. "Upstage" is the area farthest from the audience. "Downstage" is the closest to the audience.

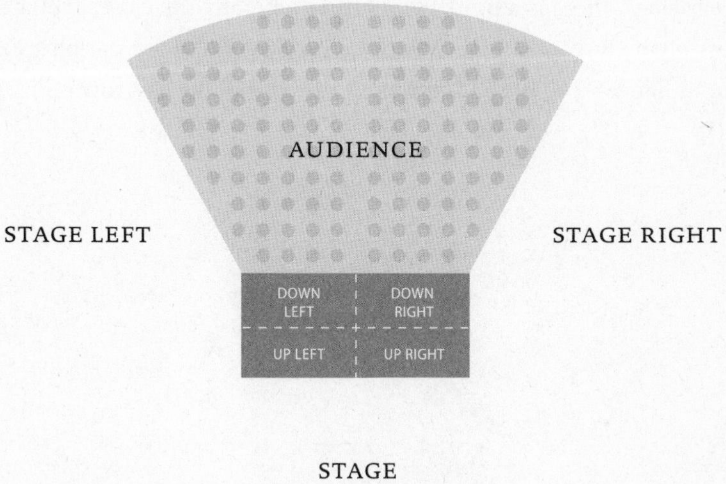

STAGE LEFT

AUDIENCE

STAGE RIGHT

DOWN LEFT | DOWN RIGHT

UP LEFT | UP RIGHT

STAGE

In Western culture, since we read from left to right, entering from the audience's left and moving to their right gives you a positive association. In movies, you will often notice that the good guy enters from the audience's left, while the bad guy comes in from the audience's right. If you can arrange to be standing in the corner before you come on, you will have a valuable moment to adjust to the lights and eyes of the audience. Find a reason to smile slightly, and begin to make eye connections with the audience as you are walking on, before you reach the podium. This way, by the time that you begin to speak, you're already engaged with the listeners. An exception to the enter stage right principle: **If you have to shake someone's hand, it's an advantage to enter from stage left.** When you shake, your body will be open to the audience, and the guy standing stage right will have to turn his back on them.

If possible, try to **avoid entering from the audience.** This is the toughest entrance to make—for the first few seconds, the audience has nothing to focus on but your back and rear end. When you turn around, the impact of the lights and the audience's eyes will hit you abruptly, triggering an amygdala hijack.

**Find the power point.** (And we don't mean the slide program!) Be strategic about where you're going to stand, if you have a choice. On every stage, there is a power point. It is generally the closest you can possibly be to your listeners, without losing sight of the periphery of the audience—i.e., the last person on the edge of the first row.

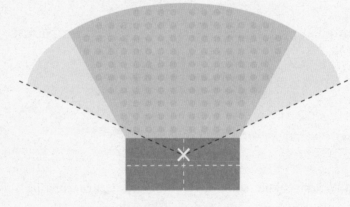

POWER POINT &
FIELD OF VISION

There are three basic things you *must do* before you speak to any-body:

1. **STOP.** After you've entered, hit your mark and stop. Stand still, in heroic neutral (explained on page 123) for one beat. It will feel like an eternity. But in that second of stillness, you focus the audience's attention like a spotlight. More important, it allows you to settle

in. You only need one second. But in the absence of that moment, people walk right through their openings without ever really connecting with themselves or their listeners.

2. **BREATHE.** It's the thing that every athlete does right before an event—they breathe. As you breathe in, you bring life, energy and intention to your body. This one little move brings brightness to your eyes and prepares your voice to speak.

3. **SEE.** In the stillness, during the breath, see your listeners and allow them to see you. You are using one of your first seven seconds to send the most important message your listener needs to hear before you begin: "Boy, am I glad to see you." If you can't see your audience because of the spotlight, then pretend that you can. Imagine their faces as clearly as possible.

Here are a few of the most **common physical symptoms of nervousness**—and what you can do about them:

1. **SHAKING HANDS.** Hold one of the following props: a clicker, pen, book, notebook, or magic marker. This gives your hands something to do. Avoid putting your hands in your pocket or grasping them in front of you, and don't come out onstage holding a coffee cup or bottle of water—it makes you look too casual. Don't use a laser pointer. And whatever you do, don't hold loose papers—that will amplify the shaking effect.

2. **SHAKING LEGS.** Wear baggy trousers. Really! Avoid wearing skirts or tight-fitting trousers that will accentuate the shaking. Move around; get some circulation going. Your body is being infused with energy for good reason. Find reasons to get out there and burn it up.

3. **SWEATING.** If you sweat excessively, keep your jacket on and make sure that you have a 100 percent cotton handkerchief handy. No one wants to watch you wait for that drop of sweat to fall off your forehead—so just wipe your forehead when needed.

4. **DRY MOUTH.** This one is simple: drink water. Make sure there's water near where you'll be speaking, and don't feel self-conscious about pausing for a sip when needed.

5. **WAVERING/CRACKING VOICE.** To get a steady, consistent sound, you need a certain volume of air moving at a certain velocity over your vocal cords. If your voice sounds strange, it's a problem with your breath. It's natural to hold your breath or breathe shallowly as a response to fear. To counter this effect, take deep, full abdominal breaths; this will both sort out the problem with your voice and steady your nerves. For more on abdominal breathing, see Chapter Four: Voice.

6. **TURNING BRIGHT RED.** There are people—generally with fair coloring—who consistently go bright red onstage. If this happens to you, don't worry about it! Even though you may feel like you're glowing, chances are that the audience won't notice a thing. Just breathe and carry on. If you don't suffer over it, the audience won't, either.

## Hands

It is instinctive to bring your hands up in front of your body to protect your core when facing a perceived threat, which can lead to speakers adopting some strange body postures onstage.

The problem occurs when you begin your presentation with your hands in one of the following positions. Your hands will nearly always remain trapped there for the whole talk:

1. *T. rex*—both arms up in front of your chest, hands dangling down, like a dinosaur.
2. *Fig leaf*—hands cover genitals. Is that really where you want your audience to focus?
3. *Hands behind back*—makes you look like a soldier.
4. *Arms crossed*—you may feel more comfortable because you're protected, but this posture is not congruent with the emotions of generosity or sharing.

5. *One hand in pocket, jiggling change*—people are going to wonder what you're *doing* in there.

If you're there to give a gift, make sure that your body shows that.
When we give, our hands are open. Begin your talk in **heroic neutral.**
Heroic neutral is a relaxed stance, sternum lifted, arms loosely down
at your sides. This position may feel awkward to you at first, as you're
going to have to fight the impulse to cover your core. But from the audience, it looks terrific! If you start in heroic neutral, then your hands
are free to move easily as you begin to speak, naturally accompanying
your words the same way they've done your whole life. You don't have
to stay in this stance; just start there.

**Use the open palm.** Gestures are all about the direction your palm
is facing. The back of the hand conveys very little meaning. When we
give and receive, we almost always gesture with the palm turned up. To
see the power of this gesture, look at Renaissance paintings—the open
palm is frequently emphasized. A downturned palm signifies power,
strength, dominance, and certainty. The open palm is generosity, sharing, openness. When you invite questions during Q&A, always use the
inviting open palm instead of the accusatory pointing finger.

## Standing at the Podium

The general principle is that the less stuff—and distance—between
you and your listener, the better. Podiums have advantages and disad-
vantages: they do provide a secure base, which is tempting when
you're feeling nervous. But a podium also traps you in one position,
and blocks most of your body from the audience, so that your expressive tools are limited to your upper body. If you're standing at a podium, remember that it's there to support your script, *not your body.*
Don't clutch or lean on the podium. It makes you look weak, as if
you're not able to support yourself. Your shoulders hunch, and your
neck disappears—not a good look! If you're gripping the sides of the

podium, the audience can see your white knuckles, and the message it sends is one of fear. Instead, allow your hands to float freely. Then you can use them for emphasis.

As you will see in the Remembering Your Content section of the next chapter, we don't recommend reading a speech from a prepared script. Sometimes, however, it's necessary. If you have to walk to the podium and read a speech, here are the basic techniques: Glance down at the script, take in the words, and glance back up to deliver them. Connect with one person at a time, and strive for a sense of openness and transparency, as if you are opening the curtains in front of your face. The idea is to let people see your thoughts. Avoid the bobblehead dog effect; don't look up and down in a predictable, bouncy way. Mentally divide the audience into quadrants: front, back, left, right. When you look up, randomly connect with one person on the left, then one person on the right, one person in the front, etc. Try to share your time equally between the quadrants, making sure that you don't forget the people in the back.

If things are going well in the speech, after you've found your sea legs, consider leaving the podium and walking forward. Yes, scary, we know! But it's an incredibly powerful act—a master move. The walk forward will be meaningful, all by itself. When you come closer to other human beings, it's a demonstration of openness, and the audience will appreciate it. You generally want to cross on a diagonal line, down to the center of the stage. And remember to take your notes with you!

When do you move? Think of it this way: in your speech, there are what we call *linking phrases* and *landing phrases*. A **linking phrase** is like connective tissue; it links one point to another. Phrases like "So, how are we going to do this?" or "Why are we so confident?" or "Let's take a look at the numbers in relation to last year" are linking phrases. They're not terrifically important in and of themselves, and they're not your main point. They're there to connect one idea to the next. A linking phrase is a great place to move. You're signaling with your body that you're moving on to a new concept.

A **landing phrase** is a phrase that you want to *land* with special emphasis. You come to a point; the light bulb goes on. "We're going to fight, using the facts!" To emphasize a landing phrase, you stand still. Never walk through a landing phrase; it diminishes the importance of what you're saying.

So, how does this look onstage? Cross while you're saying your *linking phrase*: "So how are we going to do this?" Then stop, for your *landing phrase*: "We're going to fight, using the facts!"

Congratulations, you've been brave enough to leave the safety of the podium. Where do you go next? There are three basic positions onstage: stage left, stage right, and center stage. Think of these positions as three bases, and share your time between them in a random fashion. Spend roughly 60 percent of your time center stage, 20 percent stage right, and 20 percent stage left. Vary your movement pattern; don't always go right-center-left. Break it up.

When you move, don't float, and don't wander. You need a reason to move. We call this a **motivation.** Your motivation for moving from place to place onstage should be a desire to *get closer* to the audience. You've been stage right for a while—what about the people onstage left? You move stage left with the intention of gently gathering those poor forgotten souls back into the circle of your regard, like a good shepherd. Note—make sure that the lighting designer knows that you're going to be leaving the podium. You don't want to disappear off into the shadows.

If you need to get back to the podium, give yourself some time to get there. Don't stick yourself in the situation of delivering your key message with your back to the audience! When you make what we call an **upstage cross** (crossing away from the audience) you can either tack like a sailboat, slowly working your way back by alternately addressing stage right and stage left, or you can walk in one long line. If you walk on one long line, make sure it's on a diagonal. This ensures that you are still available to the audience in profile, rather than just showing them your back. Never walk backward! It looks silly, and it's dangerous—you might trip.

If you need to cross upstage, it's okay to take your eyes off the audience for about seven seconds—but no longer. Seven seconds should give you time to get upstage on nearly any stage or platform. Just keep the time that you are disconnected from the audience to a minimum. You are their guide; don't abandon them in the darkness.

## SHANN

After college I trained as a massage therapist at Esalen Institute, the home of the human potential movement in Big Sur, California. Massages were done on an open-air redwood balcony overlooking the ocean, and the massage crew was one of the best in the world. One of the lessons they taught us was this: never take your hands off the client. You must remain in contact with the body you're working on at all times. It's your job to make the client feel safe and protected.

Engaging with the audience during a presentation is much the same. The important thing is the continuity of your contact. They're relying on you to stay in relationship with them, and guide them through the experience. Think in terms of always keeping your hands on the body—it's your job to keep the connection intact.

If you're giving a formal speech that must be read out loud, one of the most powerful things you can do is find a place where you can walk away from the podium, talk to the audience heart to heart, and then return to the podium for the finish. This gives you the chance to engage them in a very personal way, and the contrast with the scripted part of the speech makes the intimacy even stronger.

When you have to show slides, but still want to make a closer connection with the audience, here's a technique that works to combine both elements: enter and walk directly downstage center. Have the house lights (that's the lights that are shining on the audience) up, and the lights onstage up as well, so that you can see the audience and connect with them easily. Deliver your ramp and road map from there. At the end of your road map, ask a question like, "How does that sound to everyone?" in order to get group agreement. Then you can cross back to the podium, have the house lights dim, and begin the slide portion of the presentation. After your three PoDs and summary, bring the house lights back up, and leave the podium for Q&A. This allows you to be approachable, and to walk toward the questioners in a way that invites conversation. Stay downstage to deliver your dessert—it's the most powerful place for your big finish.

## TABLE TECHNIQUE

Whether you are seated at a conference table, boardroom table, or dining room table, many of the same delivery principles apply, with a few variations. Before you begin to speak, **stop, breathe,** and **see.** (see p. 120) Leaning forward right before you speak will gather the room's attention. **Heroic neutral** when seated means that your shoulders are squared to your hips, and your torso is supported by your spine in a way that allows hands to float freely. Just as at the podium, don't lean on your elbows—for the same reasons. It makes you look weak, and it makes your neck disappear. **Keep your hands visible.** Avoid having them under the table. They should be available to you to gesture as needed. Don't pound the table, wear jewelry that's going to clash noisily on the tabletop, or fiddle with your hair. Minimize distractions, and cultivate **stillness** at strategic moments when you want to land a point. Low-status players twitch and fidget; high-status players use stillness to create a sense of presence. Which one are you? **Lean in** to create intimacy or emphasis. **Pull back** to create space for someone else to speak. At a table, the subtlest shift in your position sends a powerful but often unconscious set of messages. Be aware of the messages your body posture is sending. Use your eyes for **connected conversations** (for more on connected conversations, see p. 133). Speak to everyone in the room. Include all the listeners, even if the decision will ultimately be made by one single person. The decision maker doesn't want you looking at her the whole time—it's exhausting for her.

When a latecomer comes in, don't look at him reprovingly; take a moment to acknowledge and welcome him warmly. Shake his hand if possible. Say something like, "Glad you could make it. There's a chair for you right over here." Then carry on. If it's a large audience and you can't reach him to shake his hand, make some welcoming comment. If you just glance over at him, or ignore him, he's going to feel rebuked. The general rule is this: *never humiliate anyone in front of an audience.* It creates hostility in the person, and makes everyone in the room feel bad. Never forget that the audience identifies with the latecomer, not with you. If you're welcoming to the latecomer, everyone relaxes and a warm feeling pervades the room. Pausing to do this is not a waste of time; it strengthens the bond not only between you and the latecomer, but between you and the entire audience.

## PETER

At Stand & Deliver we don't do any advertising. We depend completely on word of mouth, so the response of our clients is of the utmost importance to us. To minutely track how we're doing, we ask clients to fill out evaluation sheets at the end of every training. The scores are usually universally high. But every so often, there would be one outlying score that was noticeably low. This attracted my attention, and as I investigated, I began to realize that the low score seemed to always come from the one person who had arrived late. Why was this? After giving the matter some thought, it occurred to me that if a person comes in late, there are two possible reasons: One, there has been a genuine emergency. The car really did break down, or the child at home really is sick, in which case the person is going to be seriously stressed. The other reason for someone to be late is an internal one; he's the rebellious type, who always shows up late as a matter of course. At the time, when latecomers arrived, I was just glancing over at them, and then carrying on with the training. My residual annoyance at being interrupted was no doubt showing up in my glance, and the latecomer was feeling rebuked. So, I reframed the way I was thinking about latecomers. A latecomer, whether he has had problems that morning or is just rebellious, is someone who needs some extra attention. I began to experiment with giving them that extra attention. I would walk over to the person, shake his hand, say, "Glad you could make it," and find him a chair. There would be a collective sigh of relief in the room, as everyone relaxed. And the outlying low score vanished.

---

What if people start whispering to one another during your presentation or meeting? Well, if you're onstage in an auditorium and you can't reach the person because she is in the eighteenth row, or you're all seated at a table, there's not much you can do. You just need to get more interesting.

If you're in a situation where you can move around, gently take a few steps toward the people who are talking—*but don't look at them*. Moving toward them will pull focus away from the whisperer and back to yourself, and they will generally stop.

If they continue to whisper, then do look at them. Try not to interrupt the flow of what you're saying. Keep speaking as if you're offering what you're saying as a treat designed just for them—your intention is not to humiliate them but to give them special attention. If they carry on after that, find a place in the presentation where you can stop and say, "Let me stop here to take some of your questions."

# 6

# FACE AND EYES

*Of all the things you wear, your expression is the most important.*

—UNKNOWN

CHANGING YOUR EXPRESSION is cheaper and easier than buying an entire new wardrobe—and a lot more powerful!

Your mind functions like a supercomputer that picks up millions of pieces of subtle data from the faces of people around you. Your subconscious is constantly organizing and synthesizing this data.[1] A tightening of the muscles around the eyes, dilated pupils, a trickle of sweat coming down from the hairline—you're perceiving and interpreting these cues all the time, and so is your listener.

This interpretation process is what provides you with the "sense" that someone is lying. Just as with your body, if your words are saying one thing and your expression is saying another, the listener will become confused or mistrustful. So—make sure that you connect to what you're saying, in a way that shows up on your face. If you open with "It's

good to see you," and they don't see you registering some level of pleasure on your face, you've discredited yourself in the first seven seconds.
If you tell a team that you're proud of their accomplishments, they're
looking at your eyes. Whether or not you mean it, it's going to show up
there first, so you'd better pull back the curtains and let them see the
light in your eyes. No special equipment needed—just authenticity.

## FACIAL MUSCLES

Generally we spend a lot of energy repressing our natural expression,
especially in business situations. You must *reverse this process* to communicate effectively. We're not talking about grinning like you're in a
toothpaste commercial. But many people are grimacing while telling
their team, "It's a joy to work with you."

In order to find out what message your face is sending, make a
short video of yourself. Watch yourself as you speak for a minute or
two. What do you notice? What is the habitual expression on your
face? Is your face accurately reflecting your feelings? Sometimes it
comes as a shock to realize how disapproving or grumpy your face can
appear. If the muscles of the face are not energized, they tend to slump
into a disagreeable expression. You may not feel this way at all, but this
becomes your default. How many people are seeing this expression
from you during meetings?

There are forty-three muscles in the human face.[2] Most of us use
only three. Look in the mirror and try activating your facial muscles,
just short of a smile. Lift the muscles slightly just above your eyebrows,
and notice how it opens the eyes and pulls the other facial muscles up.
What would your face look like if you were genuinely interested and
concerned about another person?

Unless you're talking about something sad or distressing, one of
the best things you can do before you walk out onstage is to think of
something that brings a slight smile to your face. Not a smug smile,

but a smile that shows your general state as being one of enjoyment. The smile should reflect your pleasure in being there. If you can find a private place to prepare, get a big, goofy grin on your face and hold it there for a few moments. Smiling has a powerful residual effect, and much of it will linger as you make your entrance.

Before you go onstage, wake your face up. Do yoga with it. Stretch it around. By the time we get to middle age, most of us have lost a lot of flexibility in our faces, because we only use a few stock expressions over and over. Like an athlete before a marathon, warm your face up. Make everything in your face—eyes, mouth, etc.—as big and wide as possible, while you make an "Ahhhhhh" sound. Now scrunch up everything in your face as small as possible, like a prune, while you say, "Ooooooh." Grab your chin and massage it. Use both forefingers to massage the two muscles on either side of your face, just below your temples, that connect your upper and lower jaw. Practice moving your eyebrows all the way up toward your hairline and all the way down toward your nose. Put your palms flat on your cheeks and move your cheeks around in a circle. Concentrate on getting energy and circulation back into your face.

## EYES AND CONNECTED CONVERSATIONS

Your eyes are your most crucial communication tools. We have a tendency to mistrust people if we can't see their eyes.[3] We pick up a lot of information from the other person both through their eyes, and the micromovements that occur in the muscles around the eyes.

Communication manuals often advise that you "make eye contact" with your audience. This can result in you moving your eyes rapidly over the audience, or **scanning.** Scanning is one of those reactions provided courtesy of your time-honed survival brain. When you're surrounded by people, just as if you were surrounded by animals in a jungle, you *scan for danger.* One of the reasons that people suffer an amygdala hijack is that their eyes do the same thing they would do under threat—scan. Rapid eye movements are associated with the feeling of being hunted, paranoia, anxiety, and panic.[4] On the other hand, when we truly connect with someone, our eyes land on them, and linger. We look at the other person with genuine curiosity. Watch a child. Their eyes open and they look *deeply*.

We're not biologically designed to talk to more than one human being at a time. You can't even look at two eyes at the same time. Check yourself next time you're standing close and speaking to someone. You'll notice that you have to shift your focus from one eye to another. So, when you have an audience of five hundred in front of you, what do you do? Talk to one person at a time. Instead of scanning and making "eye contact," we suggest that you have **connected conversations.**

For a connected conversation, you look at one person, and speak directly to them. You stay with one person until the first comma, pause, or phrase in the thought ends, and then shift to another person for the next thought. This should amount to roughly three seconds per person.

---

**MASTER TIP:** Forget about eye contact. Have *connected conversations* instead.

---

If you're speaking to a large audience, mentally divide them into four quadrants.

If you pick out one person in the rear left quadrant of a large crowd, the ten people around him will perceive that you are looking at them as well. Land on that one person and hold him in the focus of your attention as if the whole presentation were designed specifically for him. Find your point of stillness. Watch the tendency for your eyes to roam and scan. And then move on to the next person. Make sure that you're moving randomly from quadrant to quadrant, including the entire community to whom you're speaking. Don't make the com-

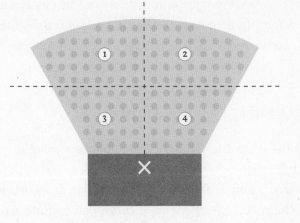

ADDRESSING ALL FOUR
QUADRANTS

mon mistake of giving 90 percent of your talk to 5 percent of the audience. The person you need to convince may be in the back row. But if you've never looked at them, they will never feel totally included.

If you've used your eyes correctly in front of an audience, even as large as a thousand people, most listeners should leave the room feeling as though you took the time to speak directly to them. The other thing you do with your eyes is to direct the audience's focus. The audience looks where you look. If you want to direct their attention to media, slides, or another person, you must turn your body and look at the object in question yourself. When it's time to reconnect, step forward and draw their attention back to you again.

---

**MASTER TIP:** The audience looks where you look.

---

An audience creates a bond with a speaker, and that bond is often broken by a speaker who sends her audience off to look at slides, and then disappears into the darkness.

Your eyes reveal your presence in the room. Don't waste it by staring at the podium, the floor, or your own slides the entire time. The podium doesn't need to feel a sense of connection with you—the listeners do.

## REMEMBERING YOUR CONTENT

One of the biggest fears people have about speaking in public is: "What if I forget what I'm supposed to say?"

This one is simple: **use notes.** Let's dispel a myth about using notes onstage right here. *Notes are not a crutch that indicates weakness— notes are a smart tool.* Consider Barack Obama. Most people around the world would agree that he is a top-notch communicator. Obama often uses a deck of index cards. If notes are good enough for Obama, they're good enough for you!

Notes are actually desirable for a number of reasons. First, they dispel anxiety and allow you to relax and focus on your presentation. Second, notes prevent the "memorization effect." This is when the speaker is putting so much time and energy into memory retrieval that he fails to connect with the audience. Under this heavy and unnecessary burden, his voice flattens, his eyes droop, his body goes limp, and he becomes difficult to hear. Sometimes you can even see the speaker's eyes move to the upper left or upper right, as if he's reading his words from the inside of his forehead. An effect best avoided!

Finally, we believe that the use of notes on a pad or on cards says that the speaker cares enough to come prepared. It also says that she actually has a job to do during the day. It takes an inordinate amount of time to actually memorize even a brief speech. Most of us would prefer the speaker was spending that time doing her job—especially if she's a CEO or the president of the United States!

So, having notes available is perfectly acceptable, as long as you spend most of your time in relationship with the audience, letting them see your eyes. What we're recommending here is that you shift back and forth between your notes and the audience. Glance down at your notes, capture the information, and take a moment to internalize it. This is the moment where you filter the information through your brain, infuse it with your own personal meaning and expression, and allow it to come bubbling back up. We want to see the words emerge through your experience. This is the magic moment where the value is added, and the data is transformed from an anonymous PDF into *your* unique presentation. Then look up, and share the information with the audience. The principle is **capture, internalize, and reconnect.**

There are various ways to access your notes onstage. You can use:

1. An outline on a notepad
2. Notecards
3. Slides
4. A monitor
5. Flip charts

They're all fine, and the choice you make really depends on your personal preference, and the setting in which you will be presenting.

There are two methods, however, that we urge you to avoid when giving informal speeches and presentations. One is that you write out a script word for word, and then memorize every word. As previously discussed, this can actually produce a negative effect. We've rarely heard someone deliver a memorized script in a natural way; it almost always sounds mechanical. It also takes an incredible amount of time and energy, and if you forget one line or phrase, it can often derail your entire presentation. Unless a formal written speech is required, try to stay away from memorized scripts.

Another method we've yet to see work well is writing down the entire script of your talk, word for word, and simply reading it out loud to the audience. Unless you're an Academy Award–winning actor, reading a script will always sound like . . . well, like reading a script. What happens is that you end up just reporting your data. It flows from your eyes to your voice on a monotonous conveyor belt, without much added nuance or emotion. If you insist on this method, be aware that what great speakers do is develop a way of making a scripted speech seem *live,* as if it's being spoken for the first time. They sometimes use the performance technique of seeming to stop at times and search for the words, as if they're putting the concepts together right in front of your eyes. Beware—it's harder than it looks. But whatever you do, don't just read out the speech as if you're serving yesterday's warmed-up leftovers. Great communication is about you and the listener thinking together, and making discoveries. Don't bring in stale, prepackaged ideas—serve up something that looks and sounds fresh.

The exceptions to these recommendations, naturally, are when you find yourself in a legal, diplomatic, or press conference situation where precise wording is extremely important. In these cases, by all means, read from or memorize a prepared script—but let the audience see your eyes.

Our own personal favorite method is to create an **outline** of key points on a notepad. Remember when you learned to make an outline in fifth grade, complete with Roman numerals and supporting points? Our outlines look just like that, written in a discreet black notebook. Have the outline with you at the podium or desk, and refer to it when you need to. This way, you'll never get lost. You can remind yourself of your key points, but it's up to your brain in the moment to find the right words—which will keep it sounding fresh and natural. Like a batter in a baseball game, this method allows you to focus on one thing at a time. After you've hit the ball, all you have to concentrate on is getting to first base—delivering your first Point of Discovery. Once you round first base, then you start looking to second. And once you're on second, you head toward third. You don't have to think about each little step along the way—you're just hitting key points, one large objective at a time.

A lot of speakers choose to use **notecards** onstage—a good option, as they're easy to carry and hold. When you're preparing your cards, put the key point in bold letters at the top, with any supporting points underneath it. Use a black felt pen; it will show up more clearly. Remember that lighting can be dim onstage—use big, bold, clean letters, easy to see at a glance and capture quickly. Write clearly, and *always* number the cards. If you ever drop them, you'll be glad you took the trouble to number them first!

A word of caution: if you do use notecards onstage, don't try to hide them. Don't get all weird and furtive about it. Just pull out the notecard, glance down, capture the information, then look up, reconnect, with the audience, and deliver the message.

The main principle when it comes to notes, whether it's cards or a notebook, is this: don't cover yourself up. Don't use your notes as a blanket, or as a shield.

---

**MASTER TIP:** Do not hold notes in front of you with both hands.

---

This is the most common mistake most speakers make when using notes. It creates a barrier between you and the audience, and the body language it conveys is that you feel the need to protect yourself. Holding notes in front of you also has the effect of cutting off a percentage of the audience—from certain points of view, it's going to look as if someone dropped a shade in front of you, and they won't be able to see you.

Instead, put the notes down on the podium or in an inner pocket, so that your hands are free to gesture. If you find that it's necessary to hold the notes, hold them with one hand, and make sure that the other hand is free. Don't allow the free hand to drift into a pocket. If you do put your notes in your pocket, practice reaching in and pulling them out before you go onstage. Wear a jacket with an appropriate inside pocket. Some pockets are so deep that it will look like you're digging down into your shirt to get hold of the cards. Actors know this: rehearse your props. A prop needs to come smoothly into your hand the moment it is needed, without fumbling or falling.

Don't read the notecard out loud—you're using it as a memory prompt, a springboard. If you're not traveling around a lot onstage, try holding the notecards in one position. Your eyes will create an internal map of where you were on the page last time you looked. When you look back, your eyes will go automatically to the exact spot where you left off. If you are moving around the stage, try leaving one finger on the place where you left off, so that you don't lose your place. A final word about notes: always use notecards or a notepad with a back, *never* just loose paper. When you're nervous, your hands will shake—and loose paper exaggerates this movement, flapping like a noisy sail and drawing everyone's attention.

It's also perfectly acceptable to use your **slides** as a series of prompts, to remind you of your material. Unfortunately the most common mistake people make is to fall into the habit of simply reading the text to your listeners off your sides. Please, we beg you, *don't do this*. If all you're going to do is read out loud, send them the slide deck and stay home. Anyone who has a second-grade education can read faster than you can talk, so you're telling them something for the second time. Boring!

If you do have a few words of text or a compelling image on your slide as a memory prompt, upon which you can then elaborate, try to work with the **monitor** in front of you, rather than turning your back to the audience and reading the text off the wall. Monitors in this situation can be easily placed on the floor. Again, like the notecards, don't try to hide the fact that you're looking at the monitor. There's nothing wrong with needing some support to remember your text. There is, however, something terribly wrong with trying to hide it from the audience!

Don't get seduced into staring at the screen the whole time. The audience didn't come to look at your back; they came to connect with you. Look at the monitor, internalize the information, then reconnect with the audience and deliver it. Steve Jobs, who gives presentations accompanied by massive screens that could dwarf him, finds moments to ensure that he is personally connecting with the audience, and not being upstaged by his own slides.

Embrace the technology, but make sure that you also pick out moments where you can come back in and drive the personal relationship. You are the bridge between the listener and your ideas. No matter how cool the technology may be, nothing will replace that human connection.

And finally, you have the option of using **flip charts.** We think these simple and effective tools are widely underrated as presentation aids—we use them in trainings all the time! Flip charts are reliable and low-tech, will not break down, and give you the ability to spontaneously write down things that the audience says, which provides a high level of interactivity. You can write your cues on a flip chart ahead of time, and then flip the paper up over the top, so that it can't be seen by the audience until you're ready. (You don't want them distracted by looking at what's on the chart ahead of time.) At the appropriate time, you bring down the page in question. You can then add to it in the moment, giving your presentation a feel of up-to-date spontaneity.

## WHEN YOU BLANK

We've all had it happen. You prepare, you're ready, you walk out, and you freeze. Even though you may have your notes in your pocket, you can't remember the first thing you were going to say. In fact, you can't remember your middle name. All you can hear is a voice in your head screaming, "Red alert! Red alert!" It's hard not to panic in this situation. But it's like quicksand—the more you panic, the more you sink. You've got to *roll* out. Here are a few tips to keep in mind for those times when you blank:

1. **REBOOT.** What's happening to you is very similar to what happens to your computer when the hard drive gets stuck. The information is still there—it's just frozen. Just like the computer, you have to do a re-boot. The good news is that for a human being, rebooting only takes a fraction of a second. You're not going to be able to solve the problem in your brain—you to have to use your body. Change your physical pattern. Do something different. Take a drink of water. Adjust the microphone. Take a step back, and step forward again.

2. **BREATHE.** When you blank out, it may be because you have stopped breathing. Stop. Take a slow, deep breath. Look up. Try again.

3. **NOTES.** Your notes are there to get you going again. Use them. Give yourself some insurance against blanking by writing your opening on an index card, and stashing it in your breast coat pocket.

4. **VAMP.** In music, vamping is when the band keeps playing the same two or three introductory bars until the diva is ready to make an entrance. In this case, the diva is your brain—it just hasn't come into the room yet! You just need to keep the band playing until it does. Make small talk. Say, "Good morning . . . Hi . . . Good to see you." It's not your first choice for an opener, but it's better than standing there like a statue.

5. **DON'T SUFFER.** If you blank during your talk, don't suffer over it. The audience will stay with you, as long as you don't make it obvi-ous that you're in pain. Audiences naturally take on the attitude of the speaker; if you're in pain, we will be, too. And this may sound strange—but it could actually be a good thing for your presenta-tion. Practiced speakers sometimes actually *pretend* that they've forgotten their next line, just to keep it feeling fresh. Look up, take a moment, take a breath, let the idea come back, and carry on. A tightrope walker in the circus doesn't just stride straight across the wire without pausing or wobbling—although he probably could. That would make his show incredibly dull. Instead, he stops, he backs up, he wobbles, he *almost* falls—but then he saves himself. Whew! We go to the circus to see the close escape, the miraculous

rebound. That's what makes it exciting. It's the same onstage; it's fascinating to watch people think. The inward glances where you search the files of your mind, find the idea, and bring it back out are part of the excitement of being live. We didn't come to watch a robot perform a smoothly automated routine. We came to see a vulnerable, authentic human being.

## SHANN

When I joined KGO Radio in San Francisco as a fledgling talk show host, management explained that I would have to develop myself into a larger-than-life "personality" in order to do the job properly. It's not too hard to make a radio show mildly interesting, so that people will sit and listen. It's more difficult to become so compelling that people will get up off the couch, pick up the phone, call in, and hang on the line for an hour, waiting to talk to you. But that was my challenge. I was given this advice: "Don't get too slick. Don't try to sound like a newscaster. Most newscasters are much too smooth and perfect to do successful talk shows. It's like a rock—if the rock is too polished, no moss can cling to it. People want you to have craggy edges and rough bits. That's what makes you real. Those are the vulnerabilities that make you seem accessible—and that's where they will attach and cling to you."

## REHEARSAL

A word about rehearsing:

Do.

Theater professionals spend five weeks rehearsing a performance, with the help of a producer, director, lighting designer, costume designer, prop designer, and set designer. You're up there all alone. Don't you think you should at least do yourself the favor of being well prepared?

Some people say that they're afraid rehearsing their presentation will make it sound stale; they claim they're better when they don't rehearse. This is ridiculous—a bit like saying that Roger Federer plays better tennis when he hasn't practiced. Rehearsal is not about preplanning every gesture and movement. It's about practicing. When a soccer player goes out to prepare, he doesn't say, "Thirteen minutes into the game, I will kick the ball at a 67-degree angle, when I am exactly halfway down the field." Instead, he hones his skills—the kicking, the passing, the dribbling. That way, by game day he has the techniques at his command, ready to adapt to the requirements of the moment.

In the professional theater, rehearsal generally has three distinct phases: (1) Actors read the script out loud, often sitting down around a table. This is called, logically enough, "table work"; (2) They get up onstage and add movement, with the script still in hand; and (3) They rehearse "off book," meaning that they know their lines. No professional actor would ever be seen holding a script a week before opening night. By that point, everyone is "off book."

There's a good neurological reason for this: your long-term memory is much more powerful than your short-term memory. If you are storing your script in your short-term memory, most of your mental RAM will be used with the retrieval process, leaving very little bandwidth for you to dedicate to meaningful expression. Received wisdom in the theater states that if you can get your lines memorized a week before performance, you have time to move from focusing on the content to focusing on the delivery. You have to assimilate the content in a way that you can start to move, think, and speak while saying it—and connect with the audience at the same time.

As we mentioned earlier, we don't recommend that you actually *memorize* every word of your content. But you do need to be familiar enough with what you plan to say that you can then turn your full attention to delivery. And this process should happen ideally at least a week before your presentation, so that the content has time to sink into your long-term memory.

This may feel challenging, because the number of nips, tucks, and edits that can be done on your script is endless. You could go on fixing and changing forever. But there comes a time—and it happens a week or so before your presentation—when you must call it finished. Leave the content alone from this point on, and move to working on your delivery.

---

**MASTER TIP:** Rehearsal time is for practicing your delivery—not for endlessly tweaking your content.

---

So here's a rehearsal process for you, based on the one used by professionals in the theater:

1. First, practice just the **words,** concentrating on sense and meaning. You can do this sitting down, or if you're more comfortable moving around, you can get up on your feet. But the emphasis is working with the language, and exploring the narrative. Get your mouth used to the ideas. You can bump through the text, stop and go, think about where you want to land your points, what the operative words are. Practice your transitions. Familiarize yourself with the ideas. Think of it like learning a song.
2. Now you bring in the **movement.** What are you going to do with your body? How will you handle the slides? It's generally not a good idea to plan every gesture and every single move. You want to be yourself, spontaneous and appropriate in each moment. Don't be overly analytical, or try to choreograph each angle of your arm. What you want to do is **block** specific sections. Blocking is theater terminology for the process of

planning where, when, and how actors will move around the stage during a performance. You're going to design blocks of movement—a large-scale plan of action. For example, do you want to be sitting or standing for the first section? Will you begin at the podium, or downstage? Which direction do you want to move for certain key sections after that? Do you want to land this point on the right side of the auditorium, or to the left? Plan ahead of time when you will draw the audience's attention to a slide, or when you want to come downstage and connect with them again. When do you want them looking at the slide, and when do you want them looking at you? Creating a large-scale action plan like this ensures that you will hit all the key moments in a smooth manner—but leaves the details to be improvised and fresh.

When you have finished making these decisions, you can hold a **tech rehearsal.** Whether you're in a theater or a conference room, a tech rehearsal is the time for you to practice all the technical aspects of your performance: plan your entrance, run through the lighting cues, check the slide-change cues, and rehearse any handoffs or transitions that are going to occur. Who's going to introduce you? Will you shake hands? Where do they go after the introduction is over—do they cross upstage or downstage from you? Practicing these things ahead of time allays anxiety and avoids the awkward do-si-dos that can occur onstage if you haven't polished the details in advance.

A tech rehearsal is performed "cue to cue," meaning that you don't have to go through every single word of the presentation. You're just practicing the important cues and transitions—anything involving light, sound, video, or another person entering, exiting, or handing you something. There are a million things that can go wrong with the technical aspects of your presentation—simple bloopers that can easily be avoided by holding a tech rehearsal. Leaving these things to chance is almost always a mistake.

3. Now you're ready to bring the meaning and the movement together for a **dress rehearsal.** No actor would ever step on-stage for opening night without having first done a dress re-hearsal, and neither should you. A dress rehearsal is intended to be as much like the real thing as possible. The key to a dress rehearsal is that if something goes wrong, you *do not stop.* The show must go on. You do the entire presentation from begin-ning to end without pausing, dealing with bumps in the road as you will on the big night itself. This way you're actually practicing what to do if something goes wrong: what will you do if you stumble, for example, or forget your words, or the laptop doesn't work? And make no mistake, it's not a question of *if* something will go wrong; it's a question of *when.* So, dur-ing your dress rehearsal, as long as there's not an earthquake or a fire in the theater, you persevere. There's a good reason for this: by creating the experience of going through the whole thing without stopping, you're literally forging a neural path-way in your brain that gives you confidence. When you get up onstage, you'll have the feeling, "I can do this." How do you know? Because you've done it before.

A note about dress rehearsals: tradition in the theater says that a poor dress rehearsal will always result in a great perfor-mance on opening night—and vice versa. Why that is, no one can explain, but it's marvelously consistent. Maybe it's because a good dress rehearsal makes performers overconfident, while a disastrous one makes them work harder. In any case, don't get discouraged if you have a lousy dress rehearsal—it's actu-ally a good sign!

It's ideal, obviously, to hold these rehearsals in the actual location where you'll be presenting. Sometimes it's possible, sometimes not.

But even if you can't hold a full rehearsal in the space, do your very best to visit the room where you're going to be speaking in advance—preferably at the same time of day that your presentation is scheduled. If you're in a conference room with windows, check the direction of the sun. Make sure that you're standing so that the light is shining on you, and not in the audience's eyes. Use your voice in the room. If you're using a microphone, practice with it. If not, practice filling the room with your voice. Ask a colleague to stand in the back, and tell you if you can be heard. If there's a view out the window, decide whether it would make a nice background, or if it will be distracting for the audience. Are there boats that will come by behind you, or bicyclists? (You won't be able to compete with that—every single eye in the audience will be drawn to the bicycle!) Are there curtains that can be opened or closed? Can this be done ahead of time? Ensure that you're not standing in silhouette against the window. How's the general level of lighting in the room? Too dark, too light, just right? Are there controls on the wall that you can access? Often there will be dimmer switches or even an extra bank of lights available, if you check. What is the temperature like? You don't want your audience to freeze, but an overly warm room will send people to sleep. Is there a screen or a table near where you're going to stand? Do you like it there, or would you prefer that it's removed? Is there a garbage pail standing right next to the place where you'll be presenting? (You'd be amazed how often there is!) Move it! Garbage is not a positive association. Make friends with the person who has the power to change these things—often a technician or hotel employee, depending on where you're presenting—and ask for what you want in terms of temperature, light, furniture, and media to be preset. They are generally happy to help.

If you're presenting in an auditorium and there's a stage, walk onto it. Stand where you're going to stand. Imagine the audience in front of you. Note the distance across which you're going to need to project your energy, eyes, and voice. **Grid** the space—this is where you mark the coordinates of the edges in your mind, all the way to the four corners of the audience, so that you have a mental map and feel for the area you'll have to cover. Where is the screen going to be? Where are you going to stand? Remember, using the podium is only one option. And if you do start there, you don't have to stay there. You're not locked into it. Move around on the stage, and find the place where you feel the most comfortable. Practice your entrance. Can you get onto the stage easily? Go up and down the steps. Are they carpeted or slippery? Is there a loose corner where you're likely to trip? Ask colleagues to sit in different places in the auditorium—some in the back, some along the sides. Have them raise their hands when they feel that you're not reaching them with your voice.

Check your lighting. Remember the last line from *Sunset Boulevard*, when Norma Desmond says: "All right, Mr. DeMille, I'm ready for my close-up." Are you ready for yours? We cringe to think of how many times we've watched a great speech ruined by the fact that the speaker was standing with the light falling oddly across her face, and didn't realize it. Don't get caught looking like the Phantom of the Opera, with half your face in shadow. To avoid this effect, use this old photographer's trick: while standing onstage, turn your back to the audience and hold your hand up in front of your face, at roughly eye level. Move around the stage, watching the way the light hits your hand. This approximates the way the audience will see your face in the light. There will usually be a **dead spot** on the stage, where the lighting is shadowy. Mark it and remember it—and stay out of it! There may also be a **hot spot** on the stage, where the light has a concentrated glare. Avoid this one, as well.

If you have any control over the lighting, or a chance to talk to the lighting technician before the event, ask for **amber gels;** these are filters that can be put over the lights. They warm the light in a flattering way, without making the stage look like a disco. And even if the technician won't put them on for you, he'll be impressed that you knew enough to ask!

Now think about your ending. Plan how you will get your laptop off the stage. Practice your exit. You wouldn't go on vacation without knowing how you were going to get home . . . don't go onstage without knowing how you're going to get off again. How will you finish your presentation? It's nearly always appropriate to make a little bow with your head, acknowledging the (wildly enthusiastic!) applause.

We're often asked if it's a good idea to rehearse in front of a mirror. We advise against it. The best performances are the ones where you've transformed your *self-consciousness* into *connection with the listener*. Watching yourself in a mirror forms a habit of watching yourself as you speak, and can add to self-consciousness. Ideally your focus is on the audience, not on how you look.

Try to rehearse in front of a small group of trusted people who can give you feedback on what you're doing well, along with a *few* recommendations of what you could do to take your performance to the next level. Or practice in front of your kids. Kids are very direct—and if you can hold their attention, you can hold anyone's attention.

Get feedback from a qualified coach, from someone who is encouraging and nurturing, or from someone you trust. But a word of caution—be very specific about the kind of feedback that you ask for from your rehearsal audience. If you're less than twenty-four hours away from the performance, anything that causes you to radically rethink your presentation can be fatal, even if it's a great idea. A theater director never gives an actor a note to change something one day before the opening night. The doubt and uncertainty that it produces can sabotage your entire performance. Two to three days before the performance is not the time to start working on fundamental issues of personal style. If you say, "Umm," a lot, and you've been doing it for thirty years, you're not going to fix it in the two days before the performance—and focusing on it will only frighten you and put you off your stride. Major changes should be worked on with a coach in a studio setting, long before you enter a high-stakes situation. The choreographer doesn't alter the choreography right before the prima ballerina goes onstage.

If you have fundamental alterations to make, make them ahead of time or leave them alone.

Twenty-four hours before you go onstage, you need *supportive feedback only*. What are you doing that is working well? Be specific when you ask—otherwise, people are all too happy to give you a long laundry list of what is wrong with you, and it's too late to fix it anyway. If you're sharing your content with someone (long before the rehearsal process begins!) you might ask, "Is it clear?" "Does it seem relevant?" "Is it the right length?" During delivery rehearsal, you can ask them, "Is it dynamic enough?" "Am I bringing enough juice to the presentation?" "Am I in the right state?"

The only exception to this is if someone points out to you at the last minute that there is a gross inaccuracy in your data, or a potential legal problem with what you're saying, or if your opening will be horribly insulting to the chairman of the board. In that case, make the last-minute changes with gratitude!

The key to doing a good rehearsal is to practice getting yourself into the right state. If you need the final performance to be confident and steely, or warm and supportive, don't practice your talk when you're dull, bored, and tired. You'll just be reinforcing a negative state. Which leads us, inevitably, to the section on . . .

# Part Three

STATE

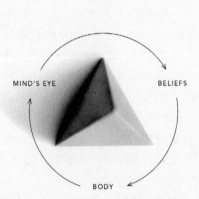

STATE

MIND'S EYE

BELIEFS

BODY

**Y**OUR STATE SPEAKS louder than your words.

Your state is the way you feel. It is the condition you are in—psychologically, physically, and emotionally—at the moment you step into the spotlight or open the conference room door. State is the most important part of communication—and yet it is almost universally overlooked. Your state determines not only your ability to communicate, but also your ability to lead, bond, and respond to what is happening around you.

In Parts I and II, we gave you tactical methods designed to instantly transform your ability to communicate. Part Three is about making a deeper investment. This is the ongoing practice of developing your inner game. These techniques create long-term shifts that will allow you to build your own personal brand in a sustainable way. When it's show time, and you're under stress, tired, or angry, *you must be able to readjust your state.* Mastering your state builds character. It puts you in the driver's seat so that you're having your emotions, instead of your emotions having you.

Actors, tightrope walkers, football players, martial artists, and prima ballerinas all know how to bring themselves to a state of readiness that promotes peak performance. And they do it six days a week. (Everyone gets a day off!)

If you're a tightrope walker, you can't afford to have a bad day. The ballerina who has to spin around three times, leap through the air, and land in her partner's arms can't decide on her seventy-eighth performance of *Swan Lake* that she "just doesn't feel like it." She'll break an ankle. And yet, these human beings have the same genetic makeup that you do. On any given Tuesday, they are affected by the same things that affect you: Weather. Traffic. Money. Family. Health. News. Taxes. How you slept the night before. The trouble is that all of these things, although they powerfully influence your state, are outside of your circle of control. If you have to wait to perform until all of these aspects line up perfectly, you'll never achieve anything.

We all know people who have everything in the world going for them, yet are absolutely miserable. We also know people who have very little, who may be barely able to survive, but who are radiantly happy. What is their secret?

There are three core things that consistently affect your state *and* that you can control on a consistent basis.[1] They are your **body,** your **mind's eye,** and your **beliefs.**

In the next few chapters, we'll walk you through the ways that you can shift your body, mind's eye, and beliefs in ways that pull you forward, instead of holding you back. On the audio download, we'll take you through a preparation method for putting yourself into a peak performance state.

# 7

# BODY

THE FASTEST WAY to build the emotion of confidence is to change what you're doing with your body. By body, we mean specifically the way you: (1) move; (2) stand; (3) breathe; (4) use your facial muscles; and (5) gesture with your hands.

There are physical patterns that produce different emotions in your body. If you want to influence the way you feel, you need to understand these patterns. These are like levers that give you access to certain emotions. You can shift your state by using different combinations of these levers.

We have ways of standing and breathing that correspond to different emotions. For example, if you are breathing quick, shallow breaths, with your chest collapsed in and your eyes darting around, it is *physically impossible to feel happy*. We only breathe in this way if we are under threat, so the neurotransmitters of happiness simply don't flow under this condition.

The great secret to the brain is that the mind-body connection works both ways. If we're frightened, our body will automatically make us breathe in short, shallow pants. But if we breathe in shallow pants, collapse our shoulders, and use our facial muscles to show an expression of fear, we can also create the sensation of fear.[1] Move and breathe the way you do when you're scared, and your brain will assume fear. We now know that the brain fires off the same chemical reaction, whether the threat is real or imagined.[2]

When you change your body, you change your emotions as well. Doubt it? Try it for yourself.

Breathe in short, shallow pants. Pace back and forth. Chew the inside of your lip. Make your torso concave as you slump your shoulders. Dart your eyes around quickly. Twist your hands together. Do this for sixty seconds. How do you feel?

On the other hand, if you move and breathe the way you do when you feel confident, passionate, and determined, your brain associates that movement with a corresponding emotion, and it will obediently supply *that* chemical reaction. Try this: Stand up. Lift your shoulders and your head. Look up. Put a big smile on your face. Punch both arms up into the air. Feel any different?

Constantin Stanislavsky used this fact to develop a system that later evolved into "method" acting, a technique used by many successful actors today. The emotions generated this way look real—because they are.[3] Unfortunately, if you leave it up to your body in a high-stakes situation, your body will default to a poor state. Once again, we are hardwired to mess it up.

When you're at risk, your body naturally goes into patterns that it uses under threat. While that worked beautifully when we were fighting off saber-toothed tigers, we need the exact *opposite* response when facing a crowd. You need to retake the steering wheel of your body, and do what athletes, actors, and high performers have always done—manage your body first, *before* you try to perform. To do this, you just run the pattern backward.

First, identify what emotion you *need* to be experiencing. This is almost always the same emotion that you want your audience to be feeling. The audience takes on the emotion of the speaker. For example, if you're congratulating a team, you need to feel proud. If you can't feel it, they won't feel it.

Second, identify the pattern in your own body, breath, and face that signifies this feeling. Do the things you do when you're feeling confident or triumphant. Walk, stand, and move the way you do when you actually feel those things. (Hint: this is not about *faking* it, just behaving **"as if."** Walk **as if** you felt confident.) There may be a variety of things that you do when you feel proud, but one thing's for sure: they don't include short, shallow breaths, a clenched jaw, and clutching white-knuckled hands in front of your body. Those patterns are universally associated with fear.

When you feel a sense of victory, the arms go up. The eyes go up, the head comes up, the face smiles, you jump up and down. This is true in every culture. To re-create the sensation of victory, just do these movements—the feeling follows.

What all professional performers have in common is this: they know how to prepare. For more than twenty years, Peter has been interviewing top athletes, martial artists, actors, ballerinas, and models. Without fail, they all confess to employing some kind of **performance preparation pattern.**

Watch a tennis pro. One second he might be screaming madly at the referee. The next second, it's time to serve again, and he starts his routine. He bounces the tennis ball once, twice, three times in a certain way—and he's completely focused again, back in state. The bouncing of the ball has nothing to do with the serve; it's his preparation pattern. A ballerina about to make her entrance might always dip her toe three times in the resin and touch her right earlobe, just before she leaps out onstage. A top model who has to turn on the glamour for the camera (even though she's been out partying until four a.m. the night before) might take a breath, flick her hair, and lick her lips in a certain way. Suddenly, the lights come up and she's gorgeous. The hair flick and lick of the lips act as her preparation pattern. Many film actors, just before an important audition, will often jump up and down and laugh like maniacs. They do this because it produces *instant joy and confidence.* Brain research shows that it creates an elevated level of serotonin in the brain. The resulting shine in the eyes and on the face gives them a powerful edge. Joyful energy is universally attractive to other human beings—even casting directors![4]

You, too, employ patterns, whether or not you're aware of them. Almost everyone has a pattern that they use to go to sleep. You might plump the pillow in a certain way, turn out the light, then turn over once. Always a certain pattern, always the same way. Try going to sleep without it once and you'll see how powerful patterns can be.

The problem is that we are rarely aware of the patterns we use, and we fail to make conscious choices about them. Instead of developing positive patterns that help snap us into a performance state, we often default to negative patterns.

Imagine that you're backstage before a high-powered event, and you're nervous. What are you doing? If you're pacing back and forth, shoulders slumped, rubbing your hands together, muttering under your breath as you try to recall your opening, you're defaulting to negative patterns that are destroying your state. The messages your brain is receiving are all ones that will create an amygdala hijack—and before you know it, you'll be standing onstage with your eyes unfocused and your mind blank, trying to remember what you're doing up there.

Once you know how *you* move, breathe, stand, and smile when you're experiencing emotions of joy, confidence, and generosity, you can produce that emotion on demand by reproducing that pattern in your body, breath, and face.[5] If you're about to enter a high-stakes situation, or walk onto a stage, try the following. These are physical triggers that will consistently stimulate a positive emotional response from the brain:

1. **Posture.** Lift your head and your sternum, as if you were being pulled up by a string.
2. **Breathe.** Take long, slow, deliberate breaths that fill your belly with air.
3. **Face.** Find any excuse to put a smile on your face. Laugh. Lift your eyebrows and widen your eyes.
4. **Movement.** Move through the room (if the situation allows), walking the way you walk when you feel confident, strong, and generous.
5. **Gesture.** Use your arms and your hands as you do when you want to share something. Re-create the movements associated with the feeling you want to generate. This can be as simple as opening up your chest and extending your arms for a moment. For example, to feel joy, confidence, victory, lift your arms and hands up over your head, with a huge smile on your face, and you will feel close to the way you do after your team scores. If you want to feel generosity, use your hands the way you do when you're giving a gift—generally with open palms, moving toward the person in front of you.

To assist you with this process, you'll find an audio exercise in the download package (go to www.standanddelivergroup.com) that will put you into an ideal performance state. The exercise is called "Performance Preparation."

On the soundtrack, you will learn to evoke memories of moments when you felt particularly powerful, and layer these emotions to bring you into a peak state. The way that you stand, move, and breathe when in this state will become your personal **performance preparation pattern.**

# 8

# THE MIND'S EYE

S O FAR WE'VE discussed the ways in which your body impacts your state. What else determines the way you feel?

You can only have a feeling about something if you're paying attention to it. There are an infinite number of things in the world around you to which you might choose to pay attention at any given moment. So, it's not the things that are going on in the world around you. What determines how you feel are the things on which you *choose to focus.* Think of this as the **mind's eye.**

You can focus the mind's eye anywhere you choose. Most of the time, however, we don't bother to choose. We just let the mind's eye wander around. In this default setting, the brain will choose its focus primarily based on fear. Why? It's for much the same reason that you're predisposed to fail in a stressful situation through an amygdala hijack. We are built to look for danger. Your brain is not designed to automatically think happy, positive thoughts. Your brain is designed to keep you alive. And for tens of thousands of years, the human brain has done a great job by looking for trouble.

We think of negativity as being a bad thing. But this tendency to search for the problem is actually the sign of a healthy brain. Imagine yourself back in time 100,000 years ago, living in a cave. You might walk to the edge of the cave and look out, scanning the environment. Your brain wouldn't be noticing the flowers, the herd of gazelles, or the lovely sunset. You would be asking, "Is there anything out here that can hurt me?" And if you saw something with stripes and long teeth, hiding behind a rock, you would ignore the sunset and the flowers and hurry back inside the cave. That's how we survived.

We focus the mind's eye through the questions we ask.[1] When you ask a question, the brain immediately sets out to answer it. Imagine your brain pulling out long file drawers, looking for the answer to a question. The question you ask determines the file drawer in which the brain will search. And if you ask enough times, your brain will *always* come up with an answer.

The trouble is, when facing an audience, most people ask questions that cause them to focus on their fear, rather than their objective. Imagine walking onto a large stage, getting ready to speak to a hundred people—all your best friends, closest family members, and biggest fans are out there. But in the third row is *that guy* with the goatee, red pen, and clipboard. You remember him. As you peek out from behind the curtain, where does the mind's eye focus? On the hundred people waiting to applaud you, or on the one guy with his head down, marking his clipboard? You know the answer. Your mind's eye will not only focus on him, it will zoom in so closely that you can count the blocked pores in his nose. And in the process you forget about everyone else.

When you're standing in front of group of people, you reveal yourself. Nothing feels more threatening than facing a mass of human beings, staring at you in the dark. Your genetic memory tells you to cover your core and narrow the target, like a Roman centurion, with his sword and shield. You can't run, and you can't fight. The closest you can get is to assume the "fig leaf" position, or adjust your cuffs. Anything to get your arms in front of you for protection!

Think about a typical question you might ask yourself as you get ready to enter: "Will they ask me hard questions?" The brain, primed to lean toward the negative, searches for an answer. Brain says, "YES!" You start to get nervous. You're panicky, starting to sweat. "Am I prepared enough?" Brain searching . . . searching . . . answer is "NO!" Now you're really losing it. Defaulting to negative patterns, frowning slightly, pacing up and down, taking short, shallow breaths.

"Will they like me?" Brain says . . . "NO!" Welcome to your amygdala hijack.

Questions like "What's missing?" "Will I forget what to say?" "Will I know the answers?" and "Will they find out I'm not as smart as they think I am?" may seem like intelligent questions to ask yourself. But they're actually sabotage questions. The answers to these questions can only produce a negative state.

So what's the answer? *Ask a different question.* The way you control the focus of the brain is by changing the internal questions that you ask.

Imagine a downhill skier, about to perform a risky run in front of television cameras. What will happen to her if she looks down and says, "Will it hurt if I fall and destroy my kneecap?" How fast do you think she would ski, and how well do you think she would perform, asking herself that question? No, a professional skier would ask herself this question, and this question only: "How do I shave a few microseconds off my time and look incredibly sexy while I'm doing it?!"

It's a question with a **presupposition.** A presupposition is an implicit assumption about the world, as revealed in a statement whose truth is taken for granted. For example, the question "What's great about this opportunity?" contains the presupposition that there is, in fact, something great in the opportunity that you haven't noticed yet. What you want are questions that have this kind of **powerful presupposition** in them. This will drive the brain to produce a better answer, and produce a feeling of exhilaration rather than terror.

Examples of powerful questions that have presuppositions in them are: "What's the best part of this presentation?" "What am I most passionate about in this material?" "What's the most powerful way I can impact this audience?" "How can I give them a gift?" "How can I best inspire them?" "How can I make a difference?" "What's the most exciting part of this event?" "How do I know they want to hear from me?"

This is not—repeat NOT—positive thinking. Positive thinking is trying to hypnotize yourself into a different mind-set. It's a bit like a bald man looking in the mirror and muttering, "I DO have hair, I DO have hair."

Asking the right questions before you go on is a very powerful way to manage your state. You're directing the capacity of your brain to search in the right file drawers. You are programming it purposefully, so that it will come up with answers that pull you forward, rather than hold you back.

The architecture of a good question is very specific. It contains a presupposition that forces you to think of new possibilities. Not "Will I succeed?" but "How will I succeed?" Not "Will they ask me tough questions?" but "How can I use Q&A to build their trust?" The first question will get a negative answer. The second question *presupposes excitement,* so that's what your brain will search for.

Be persistent with your brain. Once you get an answer, ask again. Repeat the process. Keep flooding the brain with more and more references until you are in an ideal state to perform. Not "Is it interesting?" but "What is the most compelling part?" "What else is compelling?" And "What else?" Note that there *is* a time to ask the tough questions, and explore everything that could go wrong in your talk. That time is one to four weeks before the event. Ten minutes before you go out, you cannot be asking yourself, "Will it hurt if I fall?" It's too late to do any further preparation. You must turn your attention to your state, and ask yourself performance-enhancing questions only.

# 9

# BELIEFS

F YOU'VE FELT fear when facing an audience in the past, chances are that it was your beliefs, and not the audience itself, that tied your stomach in knots. Your beliefs about yourself as a speaker will determine how you show up.

Human beings don't just assemble facts. We constantly interpret the facts to tell a story, and make sense of what's happening around us. That's how we learn. Beliefs create the meaning you bring to the things that happen. You wear your beliefs like glasses; you view everything through them. And here's the thing about beliefs: *they are always true for you.* Whether or not anyone else would agree is irrelevant.

For example, if you believe that you couldn't hold an audience's attention because you are too new, too old, too young, a woman, a man, an introvert, etc. . . . then that will be true for you. There are no superficial "tricks" that you can put on like a costume to cover anxiety. The problem is that the core source of fear remains. That core is formed from your negative beliefs.

If you perceive that you are in danger of being judged, attacked, or ridiculed, that perception is all that counts. As we discussed earlier, the receptors in your brain respond the same way, whether or not the attack is real. If you close your eyes and imagine biting into a lemon, you will salivate. Whether or not it's really happening, the brain sends the same signal, and the identical biochemical reaction fires off. If you're walking into a room full of PhDs and your fundamental belief is that *you're not really smart enough to speak on this subject,* then you will unconsciously look for all the ways to confirm that belief. When you get in front of the audience and deliver a boring speech, and the audience becomes disinterested, it will confirm what you believed all along. On the other hand, if you believe that *you have a unique perspective on this situation, and this is an opportunity for you to provide insight,* then everything from the way you enter the room, to the way you connect with the group, to the sound of your voice will be very different.

Your beliefs determine how you interpret the things that happen in your life.

Facts are the things that happen. Beliefs are the stories we tell about those facts. With one set of facts, you can tell many different stories.

## PETER

I was once called in to work with the senior vice president of a bank. Jeff was very bright, and highly valued by his boss. But every time he gave a quarterly presentation to the board, he completely fell apart. We worked on his narrative, his delivery, and his slides before I finally got to the core of the issue; I asked him what negative beliefs were holding him back. After some uncomfortable soul searching, Jeff finally admitted the problem.

"I'm a blue-collar worker," he said. "And they all know it. I came from the streets—I was a cop before I came here. Because I didn't go to an Ivy League school, didn't even study business, and never worked my way up through the halls of other financial institutions, they all know that I don't have the background for the job. I just got lucky [limiting belief]."

I asked him what kind of cop he was.

"Sergeant. Narcotics squad."

"Were you good?"

"One of the best."

"What qualities make a good cop?"

"You must have 360-degree vision at all times," Jeff said. "You need a commanding voice that will stop people in their tracks. You have to trust your instincts, and move on them without second-guessing. You have to be able to look people in the eyes, persuade them, and influence them in a split second. You have to be spontaneous, able to think on your feet."

"How many of these skills apply to your job now?" I asked him.

Jeff thought for minute.

"All of 'em," he said.

"So what's really true?"

"My life in the police force was perfect training for my job today," Jeff said triumphantly [new belief]. He went on to achieve great success.

---

You can't change the facts. But you can choose your beliefs about what the facts mean.

We all tell ourselves stories, all the time. We have to. It's the way our brains work—if we were to actually process every scrap of data that we are taking in from our senses, we would go insane. One of the brain's main functions is to selectively repress most of the data that we perceive. We label things, so that we can catalog, handle, and dismiss most of the bewildering data we're constantly receiving.[1]

If you stand up in front of an audience and have a bad experience, you will tell yourself a story about it. The danger is the belief that comes out of that story. Is there any chance that you created a belief at that moment that has kept you from returning to the spotlight? Something like, "I've never been good at this, and I never will be?"

This matters because your beliefs, by way of your biology, will *determine your emotional state.* Cellular biologist Bruce Lipton, PhD, put it this way in his award-winning book *The Biology of Belief*: "Your beliefs act like filters on a camera, changing how you see the world. And your biology adapts to those beliefs. When we truly recognize that our beliefs are that powerful, we hold the key to freedom. While we cannot readily change the codes of our genetic blueprints, we can change our minds." [2]

You can't always control events in the world around you. But you **can control your belief.** And controlling the belief will change your physical state.

Peak performance expert Anthony Robbins says that a belief is like a stool; it is held up by legs. We call these legs "references." If you want to believe that *people are going to judge you,* you can look for and find many references, or legs, to support that belief. If, on the other hand, you choose to believe that *people are eager to learn and you have something valuable to offer them,* you can find an equal number of references to support that belief.

Here's how beliefs are constructed: Imagine that a little girl is bitten by a dog when she's five years old. She goes home, turns on the TV, and sees another dog, growling and looking ferocious. Looking out the window, she sees a boy being chased by yet another dog. Now she's got three legs for the stool. She adds the top, and her belief becomes *DOGS ARE DANGEROUS.*

Over the next thirty years, she will look for and find hundreds of additional references that will reinforce her existing belief. If you bring a toy poodle into her home, she will scream and insist that you take the dog outside. "Dogs are dangerous," she'll say. "Get it away from me." All of your insistence that the dog is harmless will count for nothing. Her belief has references, and rational explanations have no force against the power of her conviction.

There are two distinct types of beliefs: positive beliefs that pull us forward, and negative beliefs that hold us back. A negative belief might be, "Because I'm an introvert, I can never be compelling in front of a large group of people." An example of a positive belief might be, "Because I'm an introvert, I bring more emotional depth and sensitivity to the topic." A negative belief is, "Speaking is torturous." A positive belief is, "Speaking is an opportunity." What are the beliefs that are holding you back? These are the beliefs preventing you from achieving the state you need for peak performance.

Sometimes you might be holding a negative belief not just about yourself, but about the topic you've been asked to address.

## PETER

I once worked with Jacques, a CFO of a major European asset-management firm who was hyperintelligent but utterly lacked presence. He came across as meek and dry. When he spoke in front of a group, his whole body seemed to be saying, "I'm sorry for wasting your time."

It turns out that Jacques's lack of presence was a symptom of a deeper belief. In the course of a single conversation, we were able to uncover a basic assumption that was dulling Jacques's presence.

"I'm an accountant, not a speaker," Jacques said. "Numbers are boring."

Sure, it's easy enough to find supporting evidence for this belief—the stereotype of the joyless number cruncher is everywhere. But I tried to get Jacques to see numbers from another perspective.

"What would you have to believe about numbers for you to speak passionately about them?" I asked.

Jacques paused. "They'd have to be interesting."

So we started to brainstorm about what numbers represented to the firm: profits, bonuses, security. They were a marker of performance. They conveyed the health of the company. They were tremendously appealing, actually . . . interesting.

You could see Jacques come to life as he continued to draw connections and shift beliefs.

His next presentation to the board was inspired—he showed up with purpose and spoke with conviction. Everyone in the room remarked on the change. Jacques had captivated the room with his presence. And the difference was that he had changed his belief from "numbers are boring" to "numbers are the one thing that everyone wants to know about."

---

At the airport, they ask whether you packed your own bags. It's a good question when exploring your beliefs. Did you pack your own bags? Or are you still carrying around old baggage that was packed by your parents, your siblings, or your third-grade teacher? Chances are, many of those stories were put into place when you were too young to decide for yourself. Have they become outdated?

Generally you develop beliefs based on the things that happened to you without your consent or control. You could look at the setbacks, problems, and tragedies in your life, and justifiably prove that you were victimized by events. On the other hand, there are people who look at the adversities in their life, and tell a story of how the problems they encountered drew out their strengths and made them who they are today. Many people who survived extreme hardship report that they wouldn't have changed a thing. They say it was the difficulties they encountered that shaped their character. You can't control the bad things that happen to you. But you can control the way you interpret those things.

Imagine two people presenting in front of a board of decision makers. They both fail spectacularly. Person A interprets that experience this way: "I'm just not good at this." Belief created? *I'm a failure.* The next time he's offered a chance to speak, he'll refuse. Person B thinks about it this way: "That was so painful that I'm going to make sure I *never* fail like that again." The pain impels her to get some training and become an expert speaker. She goes on to great success.

Which type are you? If you're being held back in your career or your personal life, it may be because something bad happened to you—and you want to ensure that it never happens again. Whether it was the book report in fifth grade that went badly, or the music teacher who put you in the back row and told you just to move your mouth, or a flubbed presentation at your last job, you created some beliefs around that event. Now it's time to go back and look at those beliefs. Are they holding you back, or driving you forward?

As human beings, we have the unique ability to creatively construct beliefs that are aligned with our intentions. You can stop, examine, and rebuild your beliefs in a way that fortifies your character and your confidence. You can choose beliefs that will propel you forward, rather than hold you back.

Imagine what would happen if you became intentional about the process. *What if you started with the end in mind, and then created the beliefs that would drive you forward?*

What do you want to do in your life? And what are the beliefs you need to hold in order to accomplish your goals?

True confidence doesn't come from talking yourself into something that isn't true. It comes from transforming negative beliefs that are holding you back into empowering beliefs that drive you forward.

## SHANN

When I was a twenty-six-year-old newspaper reporter, I got a call from Robin Bertolucci, the executive producer of the biggest radio station in San Francisco. She had heard me as a guest on one of the KGO shows.

"You've got attitude," she said. "I want you to try hosting your own talk radio show."

I was terrified. "I could never do that," I told her. "I don't have any experience in radio. I'm not an expert in politics. And I don't have a broadcasting degree, so I'm not qualified." [Spot the negative beliefs?]

Luckily for me, Robin was an expert at developing new talent, and she was able to turn these beliefs around. "Think of it this way," she said. "You can use those things as an asset, instead of a liability. You can say on the air, 'I'm no expert; I just use my common sense.' People will love it. The fact that you're not an expert gives you a fresh perspective." [Spot the positive belief?]

I took her word for it, and accepted the new belief. The result? Ten years of my own radio show—and a whole new career.

---

Your beliefs create your reality. If you want a clue about your own negative beliefs, look at your New Year's resolution list. What are the things that go on the list, year after year, that you never accomplish? If you're consistently not following through on your good intentions, it may be because there's a belief in place that is keeping you from it. If you resolve every year to exercise more, and never get around to it, you are probably holding the belief that *it will be more painful to exercise than to avoid exercise.* On the other hand, if you went to your doctor and she told you that you would be dead in six months unless you went jogging every day, you'd probably lace up your sneakers in a hurry. You won't take action until you change the belief. Once the belief is strong enough, the motivation is easy.

Luckily, it's possible to change the beliefs that are holding you back. How do you do it? Well, words can change the world, from the microscopic to the macrocosmic level. This is true inside your head as well as in the outside world. And the process is the same.

In the content section, you learned a procedure designed to influence another person by giving them an emotional—as well as intellectual—experience. You defined your outcome, and clarified it in terms of what they would need to know and feel. You found the relevance, and clarified your point.

To exert influence over yourself—i.e., to shift a belief—the exact same procedure applies. To begin, as always, you must define your outcome. First, you must **identify the belief that is holding you back.** Imagine yourself standing on a stage in front of an audience, performing at your peak. What's stopping you from achieving that? Do you believe that you are not smart enough, not young enough, the wrong race, the wrong size, the wrong temperament? Write down the negative belief that takes up the most space in your brain.

A note before we proceed: this is not a *bad* belief. This belief was created by the part of your mind whose job it is to keep you alive. You created that story to fill some need. Perhaps it was to avoid getting yourself into frightening situations where you felt threatened. If your belief is "I am a poor speaker," then you have a perfect excuse to keep from ever finding your voice. If you have a belief that drawing attention to yourself is bad form, then you'll do anything to avoid the spotlight. But now you have a different need—you need to step forward and speak out. You need to be heard. You need to dramatically raise your level of influence on the people around you.

Here's a list of some common negative beliefs that we encounter in our work, and how they can be converted into positive beliefs that will pull you forward:

1. "Because I'm a woman [young person, black, Asian, etc.], they don't want to hear from me," vs. "Because I'm a woman [young person, black, Asian, etc.] I have a unique voice and a valuable perspective."
2. "Because I'm too old, they won't respect what I have to say," vs. "Because I have maturity, I bring much-needed experience and wisdom to this topic."

3. "Because I already sent them the data, I don't need to give a presentation," vs. "The facts won't speak for themselves; this is a chance for me to bring meaning."

4. "I don't have time to prepare," vs. "I don't have time NOT to prepare."

5. "Because English isn't my first language, I won't sound intelligent when I speak," vs. "Because English isn't my first language, and I must choose my words carefully, I am concise and clear—which audiences love!"

6. "I'm just a numbers guy, and numbers are boring," vs. "Numbers are sexy . . . numbers tell the story!" (For more info on sexy numbers, see p. 57.)

What's the negative belief that's holding you back? And how could you transform it into a positive belief that would pull you forward?

Behavior is how belief walks into the world. At the heart of your ability to engage with people are the beliefs that you hold about your role as a leader. If you have negative beliefs holding you back, the tough task of a leader is roll up your sleeves and clean house. Remember that your beliefs are a choice. Align your beliefs with your intentions.

## Part Four

---

# HIGH-STAKES
# SITUATIONS

F YOU'RE JUST chatting with Charlie over coffee, then feel free to wing it. But there are other times, when the pressure is on and emotions are running hot. We call these "high-stakes situations." In these environments, you have something at stake: an important account or an important customer. It might be your personal reputation at risk, or the reputation of your entire company. You *must be at your best in these moments,* or you may lose something that you value. These are the times when you need a strategy. This section of the book is designed to give you that strategy.

In **Courageous Conversations,** we give you the techniques to succeed in difficult one-on-one conversations. In **Crisis Communication,** we offer a tried-and-tested structure that will help you step into an assured leadership role in the moments after disaster strikes. Often at these moments you will have to convey your message through one or more of the various technologies available to us these days: e-mail, phone conference, video conference, or PowerPoint. So we've included a chapter called **Using Technology** to help you master that as well.

# 10

# COURAGEOUS CONVERSATIONS

HIGH-PERFORMING TEAMS AND individuals don't have fewer problems than anyone else. *But they are more willing to talk about the problems they have.*

It's generally the conversations that you're not having that are costing you dearly. You know the ones we're talking about. Just the very thought of having *that* discussion makes your heart sink and your stomach lurch. You'll do almost anything to avoid having these conversations. You'll take a different path to the water cooler, handle the problem yourself when it's not really your job, or continue earning less than you know you deserve.

We call these **courageous conversations** because they take guts. It requires courage to ask someone to do something different on your behalf. But the truth is that these so-called courageous conversations are where the really juicy stuff can be found. It's the points of disagreement and conflict that harbor the greatest potential. Resolving these issues is the fastest, most powerful way to create transformation in your life/career/relationship. And of course, if you choose not to deal with the issue, it doesn't go away, does it? It just continues to fester until it ends up poisoning the whole relationship/family/organization.

## PUT THE FISH ON THE TABLE

At the International Institute for Management Development (IMD) in Switzerland, they sum up this idea with the phrase "Put the fish on the table." This is a quote from Dr. George Kohlrieser, professor of leadership at IMD and author of the book *Hostage at the Table,* whose work in this field has been foundational for this section. In Italy, the fish sellers stack the fish up into a huge, high pile on the table. When Kohlrieser asked why, he was told, "If you leave a fish under the table, it starts to rot and smell." [1]

The principle is the same when it comes to dealing with those courageous conversations. You have to **put the fish on the table** and clean it out to get a good fish dinner. If you leave it under the table, it rots, festers, and ultimately becomes poisonous.

What's the fish that you need to put on the table at work? At home? In your community?

You avoid these conversations at your own risk. It is difficult to estimate the cost of this avoidance. When the space shuttle *Challenger* went up, there were engineers inside the organization who knew that the O-rings could fail—and that if they failed, the whole launch system could explode. [2] And yet that knowledge was not shared within the organization of NASA as a whole. The same thing is happening every day, in teams and organizations across the world. Are you willing to speak up—and listen—when a difficult issue needs to be discussed?

# PETER

I was once called in to coach the CEO of a Fortune 100 pharmaceutical company who was preparing for a keynote speech. Before I was allowed to meet the boss, I was cross-examined by an army of anxious underlings:

"What are you going to do with him?" one of them asked.

"You know," whispered another one, "he mumbles."

"He mumbles?" I said.

"We can barely understand what he's saying," they said.

"Has anyone ever told him that?" I asked.

"Oh no," they said. "We would never tell him that."

Sure enough, when I was brought in to hear the CEO rehearse his talk, it was all but unintelligible.

I tried some roundabout ways to get him to enunciate.

"Try extending your vowels," I said, drawing on an old acting exercise. But the CEO, a big, imposing man, soon grew impatient.

He stopped in the middle of a run-through, folded his arms in front of him, and said, "This isn't working for me. I'm uncomfortable."

This was clearly the moment to put the fish on the table.

"Listen," I said. "We've been together for twenty minutes, and I don't understand half of what you're saying. You can be comfortable, or you can be understood. But you can't be both."

The underlings watched and winced.

The CEO let his arms drop . . . and then he smiled.

"I like this guy," he said. "Let's get to work."

It was only by naming the obvious and uncomfortable fact that we were able to move into productive territory.

Your courage and willingness to talk about the difficult issues will often bring you closer to someone, and create a higher level of trust.

You will know if you need to put a fish on the table if the following things happen: (1) You go home and tell your spouse all about it—but don't mention it to the person who is actually involved; (2) You keep revisiting the problem in your mind, and repeating things you'd like to say; (3) You're developing physical symptoms in your stomach or your throat every time you're in the same room with a particular person. So take a deep breath, and read on to acquire some tools that will make you brave enough to charge into your next courageous conversation head-on!

The first thing that needs to be addressed is the **belief** that you're holding about dialogue. Many of us have been taught that it is better to keep quiet, and avoid difficult issues. *If you can't say something nice, it's better to say nothing at all,* right?

Chances are, if you're avoiding the conversation, it's because you're holding some variation on the following beliefs:

1. If I bring it up, we'll get into a fight.
2. I will lose my temper, or she will.
3. It will just make everything worse.
4. She doesn't really want to know the truth.
5. She won't listen to me anyway.
6. She doesn't care.
7. She's only out for herself.
8. It's better to have an easy life.

Try this story on for size, instead: *Courageous conversations are a chance to strengthen the bond between you and the other person* (positive belief). It may sound strange, but it's true. Just as a broken bone heals back stronger in the broken places, a relationship can be strengthened by a frank discussion, if it's handled properly.

The most important goal in any courageous conversation is to **keep the bond.** The bond is the most valuable thing you have. Without a bond, you cannot influence the other person. With a bond, they will walk through fire for you. If you win your point but destroy the bond in the process, what have you really achieved? You get to be right, at the expense of a valuable relationship.

To illustrate the importance of bonding in high-stakes situations, we look to Dr. Kohlrieser's work as a hostage negotiator. This is the starkest possible example of results-driven communication: if you don't communicate persuasively, someone is going to die. When negotiating with a hostage taker, Kohlrieser says, you don't have to like them, or respect them. But to accomplish your goal, which is to get everyone out alive, you must create and maintain a bond.

Imagine that you are negotiating with a hostage taker who has a gun pointed at the head of a hostage. He says, "I'm going to shoot everyone in ten seconds."

You say, "Please don't."

"Why shouldn't I?"

"Because I'd like to see how I can help you."

"How can you help? I'm going to shoot."

"What about your children?"

(pause)

"How did you know I have children?"

Is this a good conversation? You might think not. But from the perspective of a hostage negotiator, it is an excellent dialogue, because he hasn't fired the gun. You're on the way to accomplishing your objective, which is to get everyone out alive. During those thirty seconds, no one has died. You've established your concern for his needs, and he is actually talking to you. So far so good.

A bond is created and maintained by your awareness of someone else's needs. Just as you do with an audience, when you begin by thinking about their needs (see Chapter One), so you focus in on the needs of your listener in a one-on-one conversation. Perceiving and meeting the needs of a person is the only authentic way to influence them.

You don't have to know someone over a long period of time to form a bond and meet their needs. It can be done with a complete stranger, in a matter of moments. This was beautifully illustrated in a 1992 town hall–style debate between then President George H. W. Bush and then candidate Bill Clinton.

An audience member asks the candidates how the recession has affected them each personally, and if it hasn't, how they can expect to find a cure for the "economic problems of the common people" if they have "no experience in what's ailing them."

Bush answers first, and proceeds to annihilate any potential bond that might have existed between himself and the questioner.

He immediately jumps to abstractions and generalities—talking about the national debt and interest rates—and then subtly criticizes the audience member's question and adopts a defensive posture. He backs progressively away from her as he answers, and his eyes lose contact with hers and wander around the room.

Clinton, by contrast, builds a bond with his listener from the start.

"Tell me how it's affected you again," he says, as he walks nearer to her.

He maintains eye contact, and speaks softly and clearly as he transitions to answering her question. He cites statistics and talks policy—just like Bush—but he personalizes his answer, using concrete details. ("When a factory closes, I know the people who ran it. When the businesses go bankrupt, I know them.")

Clinton concludes by returning the focus to "you" ("this decision you're about to make . . .") and a providing series of clear, specific goals.

This short exchange is a master class in speaking to a listener's needs and building trust in the space of a minute.

---

**MASTER TIP:** The only way to influence someone is to speak to his needs.

---

Unless you have cash to bribe someone, or the power to frighten him, you must meet his needs in order to change his behavior.

And yes, if you have the authority, you could coerce him. That worked in medieval times, and it's still going on in some unfortunate organizations and families. But you won't achieve lasting results. He'll only stay influenced as long as you're standing over him. The second your command-and-control grip over him weakens, he's going to rebel. Now, this doesn't mean that you automatically give in and give the other person his way. We're working here for you to achieve *your* outcome, not to earn a position as a doormat.

But consider the following example from *Getting to Yes: Negotiating Agreement Without Giving In,* by Roger Fisher and William Ury: . . . *two men [are] quarreling in a library. One wants the window open and the other wants it closed. They bicker back and forth about how much to leave it open: a crack, halfway, three quarters of the way. No solution satisfies them both.*

*Enter the librarian. She asks one why he wants the window open: "To get some fresh air." She asks the other why he wants it closed: "To avoid the draft." After thinking a minute, she opens wide a window in the next room, bringing in fresh air without a draft.*[3]

Without a full and complete understanding of the needs of your listener, you will not accomplish your objective. Once you understand exactly what he needs, you may be able to skillfully meet those needs in a way that enables him to help you in return.

When the bond is starting to break, regardless of who is right or wrong, your first order of business is to repair the bond. Only then can you start to solve the problem. Often we're addressing the behavior, when the real problem is that the bond has been broken. If the bond is there, the conversation will go more smoothly. You're allowed to make mistakes, and recover. If the bond is broken, no mistakes are allowed. The first time you trip up, it's all over. If the bond is compromised, that's the first issue that needs to be addressed.

## BLOCKS TO DIALOGUE

Now that you've decided to put the fish on the table, you need a strategy that will enable you to go into a loaded situation and resolve it successfully. Instead of just *trying to get your point across,* consider having a **dialogue.** Think of dialogue as "two minds working together to find a higher truth."

Sounds easy, right? So why don't we conduct good dialogues all the time?

In order to master any new technique, it's important to examine the problems that get in our way first. Let's look at the three biggest mistakes that people make. We call these **blocks to dialogue.** You'll notice a similarity to the top three problems that show up in a formal setting, when a speaker is giving a presentation.

1. **PEOPLE TALK TOO MUCH,** and they do this in the following ways:
   - **Overdetailing.** They give you way too much information. You ask for an update, and you get a history of the project.
   - **Self-absorbed.** They're not listening to you, and not paying attention to the cues you're giving. You're edging away, desperate to escape. They don't notice—and just keep talking.
   - **Dominating.** They try to control you with a relentless stream of words that makes it impossible to respond—as though they're trying to pound you into submission. (*Note:* Mysterious but true—nine times out of ten, these types will have bad breath!)
2. **WHAT THEY'RE SAYING IS NOT RELEVANT TO YOU.** They're not addressing your needs. We have an exercise that we do in our trainings, called **autobiographical listening.** In this exercise, people stand in a circle. The object of the game is to make the conversation *all about you.* Player 1 might start out: "I just came back from Hawaii. We had a great time sailing." Player 2: "Sailing—you sail?

We have a sailboat in Sausalito. We take it out every weekend." Player 3: "Weekends? My weekends are mostly spent in L.A., because my kids are down there." Player 4: "L.A.? I went to UCLA!" You get the picture—there is no real dialogue occurring here. Each person is simply using the other people as prompts to stimulate their own personal monologue. Sound familiar? It's shocking how much this happens in real life!

3. **THERE IS NO POINT.** You may have had a conversation, but as you leave, you wonder why you bothered—because nothing has changed. There is no positive outcome.

Imagine you're having a courageous conversation with Anthony, a direct report. He's been showing up late to meetings. You say, "Anthony, I'd like to talk to you about the fact that you've come in late to the last three meetings. Is that okay?" Here are some of the responses you may hear from Anthony, if he's intent on blocking the dialogue. These were adapted from Dr. Kohlrieser's book *Hostage at the Table*. Learn to identify these strategies in yourself as well as others. Notice which ones you tend to use yourself!

- **Passivity:** Anthony stays silent, and simply raises an eyebrow.
- **Negating:** "I wasn't late to the meeting on Tuesday."
- **Discounting:** "I was only five minutes late—what's the big deal?"
- **Redefinition:** "I'm glad you brought that up, because I've been wanting to talk to you about the fact that we have too many meetings in this department."
- **Overly emotional:** "How dare you say that I've been late, when I've worked overtime every day this week!"
- **Overly rational:** "Given the fact that none of the systems in this department work properly, I would say that we need to re-examine the decision-making processes we have in place, particularly as it relates to collective scheduling."

- **Overly general:** "This company has always had a time problem anyway."
- **Overly personal:** "You always pick on the small things— you never appreciate my contribution."
- **Lack of honesty:** "I was late because I was helping a colleague who had an issue at home. She asked me not to say anything."

## BRIDGES TO DIALOGUE

So now that we know what gets in our way, how do you overcome the **blocks to dialogue?** We call the following techniques **bridges to dialogue.** They will help you overcome the blocks, and create a connection.

**Define your outcome,** just as you would in a formal presentation (see p. 37). What do you want to achieve by the end of this conversation? If you are not crystal clear on this point, you may get drawn into the conflict and find yourself just arguing and trying to win. (We've all been there!) If you've ever lost your temper in an argument and said something that you bitterly regretted later, you know that you can become the victim of an amygdala hijack from anger just as easily as from stage fright. The same process applies; in times of emotional stress, the body's instinct is to throw control to the amygdala, which will pump blood into your fight-or-flight muscles at the expense of your thinking brain.

Defining your outcome, and then focusing on it, can help you avoid this disaster. Phrase it this way: "By the end of this call/conversation, he will. . . ." For example: "By the end of this conversation, Anthony will commit to showing up to meetings on time." This is one of the most powerful tools going, and yet *people rarely use it*. If you take thirty seconds before your next phone call to formulate your objective clearly in your head before you pick up the receiver, your chances of achieving your outcome soar. Visualize the conversation going smoothly—use your mind's eye to see the experience you want to have.

**Separate the person from the problem.**[4] If you label the person, even in your own mind, you cannot solve the problem. Example: If Anthony comes late to every meeting and you label Anthony as an irresponsible, rebellious so-and-so, then he is simply a bad employee, and there is no solution to the problem except to fire him. On the other hand, if you separate the person from the problem, you can see that the problem is not Anthony, but his behavior—he is coming late to meetings.

You sit down with Anthony, tell him you need to talk to him about his attendance at meetings and investigate with curiosity to see what is going on with him. It may well be that you discover that Anthony came from another company where meetings always started ten minutes late, and he simply didn't understand that it was a problem. Because you were putting off having the courageous conversation, he didn't know it bothered you. Actually, he's perfectly willing to come in on time. Problem solved—and you've retained a good employee.

**Stop after four sentences.** Brain research shows that most people can only hold full attention in a dialogue for three or four sentences. After that, attention drops off dramatically. Not sure whether this applies to you? Try this at home: check your partner's face after the tenth straight sentence of your monologue. Is she looking at you? Or out the window? Hmm . . .

---

**MASTER TIP:** As a rule, never talk for more than four sentences without stopping and getting a response from the other person.

---

**ASK QUESTIONS.** Whoever asks the questions drives the dialogue. For some strange reason, most of us have the idea that the way to talk someone around to agreeing with us is to drown him with a ceaseless stream of argument. It doesn't work. For one thing, he will turn off after four sentences, as explained above. For another, the simple fact that he's sitting there looking at you doesn't mean that he's listening to anything you say. Face it, most of us are just watching the other person's face to identify the moment when his lips stop moving—so that we know it's our turn to talk! The person who asks the questions in a conversation has his hand on the tiller. That person controls the direction of the dialogue. *Let it be you.*

**REWARD CONCESSIONS.** This one comes from lion taming. A lion tamer working in the ring with a lion is constantly looking for and rewarding small concessions. If the lion tamer cracks his whips and the lion stops, that's a concession. It needs to be rewarded. The tamer does this by physically taking a step back. He essentially says, "Thank you," to the lion by giving him more physical space. If the lion stops after the tamer cracks his whip, and the tamer continues to move forward, the lion would take that as a sign of aggression, and attack. Hopefully your life won't be at risk in these difficult conversations—but the same principle applies. There are various ways that you can do this:

1. *Verbal response* like: "Good," "Thank you," "I understand," "Great," "I get it," "I appreciate that," "That makes sense," "I see."
2. *Semiverbal:* Make affirming noises in the pauses, like "Mm-hmmm," or "Mmm."
3. *Nonverbal:* Smile, move back a little to give them more space, nod. (*Note:* careful with the nodding—it can imply agreement.)

This principle works beautifully in tandem with the previous two: **Don't monologue** and **ask questions.** You can avoid monologues, ask questions, and reward concessions, all at once. First, *open with a question that he can say yes to*: "I'd like to talk to you about our meetings. Is that all right?" Obviously, the only appropriate response there is a "Yes." You've now asked a question, and had a positive response. Good first interaction! You're off and running.

Contrast that to the way you think the conversation might go if you started it this way: "I'd like to talk to you about your rude behavior in coming late to meetings." Bang! Can you hear the doors of his mind slamming shut as he bolts himself inside, prepared to defend against your attack?

Want to talk to your boss about bringing in a new training program? Avoid: "Can we talk about why we don't have any training here?" Instead, try, "I'd like to talk with you about how we could raise the skill level of the team. Is that all right?" If you're talking to your teenager about drugs, don't say, "I want to talk about making sure you're not hanging out with those losers from down the street." Try this instead: "I'd like to talk to you about how we're going to help you succeed in school next year. Is that all right with you?" Of course it's all right! What else can he say? Enter with a focus on the desired outcome. Look for questions they can answer with "Yes."

"Anthony, I'd like to talk to you about our meetings. Is that all right?"

Presumably, Anthony says yes.

Saying yes is a concession. You've got your first agreement! Acknowledge it. It gets you into the dialogue right away.

"That's great. Thank you."

Then you proceed to clarify your point in small sections. End each section with a question, which circles back to the listener. This removes the temptation to launch into a monologue, keeps the other person engaged, and keeps you in the driver's seat of the conversation. In the meantime, you're rewarding every concession you get. This builds a staircase of small successful interaction agreements. This process builds a bond—which is what you're after.


**DEMONSTRATE COMMITMENT.** "I'm committed to finding a solution to this and doing whatever we need to do. How about you?"

**CHANGE THE CLIMATE.** If you get stuck, try these questions:

1. "What do you understand my point to be?"
2. "Is there a seed of truth in what I'm saying?"
3. "What is it that you're committed to doing?"

**USE THE SILENCE.** Rushing to fill a pause indicates insecurity; leaving a silence signals authority. The change that you want to achieve happens in the silence. Simply wait and allow the silence to be there—get comfortable being *uncomfortable* in those moments when no one is saying anything at all.

## Dealing with Anger

Often in a courageous conversation, one of the parties may be angry. This is a difficult thing to face, because once again, your amygdalae will kick in and try to protect you. You may begin to lose your own temper, as your brain prepares you for a fight. A cautionary note on violence—if the angry person in front of you shows any signs of moving toward physical violence, pick up the signs and get out of the situation immediately.

But if you feel that it's physically safe to do so, the solution to the problem, just as in hostage negotiation, is to **create a bond** with the other person.

Sounds odd, right? When you're facing someone who is angry, the last thing in the world that you may feel like doing is connecting with that person. But in fact, that's the only way that you're going to cope with him successfully. You're not going to be able to talk him out of his feelings, or explain why it is that he shouldn't be feeling as he does. You're going to have to defuse him. And to do that, you're going to have to listen.

Think of it as lancing a boil, and then leaping out of the way as all of the stored-up puss comes pouring out. Listen carefully to what he's saying, without trying to block or stop him. Ask questions that help you understand the problem fully, and demonstrate genuine empathy. Name and identify what he's going through, without trying to fix it—yet—and without trying to minimize it. If you minimize, dismiss, or negate the problem, it will only add fuel to the fire. *Note:* when you acknowledge the problem, you're not admitting fault or taking responsibility. You're simply demonstrating that you heard what he said, accurately and with compassion.

Once you have heard what he said, and understand how he feels, you have a platform from which you can rebuild the relationship. That platform is based on a common understanding—a bond—based on a commitment to do what you can to help. You can't help him if you haven't accepted what he said.

If you're a problem solver, a fixer, or a consultant by trade, you will automatically try to fix the problem *before* you've listened to the whole thing. No sooner will he begin to state the problem than you will have a solution. And your solution will be so good that you can't wait to talk about it. This is where the conversation starts to go wrong. Before you get to the solution (no matter how good it is!) the other person needs to *vent.* You need to let him vent, and demonstrate that you heard him accurately, and with concern. This is a necessary stage of the process. To do this, you **listen, ask questions,** and **paraphrase.** We don't mean *parrot phrase:* you don't repeat his exact words back to him. This is obvious and obnoxious, and will only infuriate him further.

To paraphrase, you summarize what you've just heard in a some kind of brief, clear statement that demonstrates understanding: "Okay, let me see if I understand what you're saying. The shipment arrived two weeks late, you're behind on your own orders, and now it sounds like you're in trouble with your boss. Is that right?" When you paraphrase, listen to the modality that he's in: visual, auditory, feeling/ sensing, or numbers/logic. (For more on modalities, see p. 98.) Listen and match his modality. If he's in **feeling/sensing** mode, he might say, "I'm *uncomfortable* with this; we *felt* that we could trust you." Your response might be, "I understand that you're *angry and confused.* We need to figure out how to *get back on track.*"

He'll tell you how he likes to talk. Listen. Be careful to name and identify his anger at the correct pitch of intensity. If he's furious, and you say, "It sounds like you're feeling a little annoyed," you will make the problem even worse. "Annoyed?!" he'll say. "Annoyed?! I'm not annoyed—I'm absolutely outraged!" And you'll have to start all over again.

The moment that you're looking for here is when the angry person in front of you sighs with relief, and says, "Yes. That's right." NOW you can begin to solve the problem. Your attentive, nonintrusive listening has created a bond between you and the angry person in front of you. He feels heard, and understood. And although you have not yet dealt with the technical aspects of his problem, you have accomplished your major objective—to defuse his anger, and form a bond. Now you can have a meaningful, solution-seeking conversation.

It's not easy to hold your ground in the face of a furious torrent of words. Nothing in our biochemistry teaches us to take anger, listen to it, and work with it. In fact, our very biology dictates against it. Once again, you will start to feel the warnings signs of your amygdalae starting to take over. You will feel the irresistible impulse to say, "Hang on, that's not right. That's not accurate. We never promised that . . ." Remember that you are teaching yourself a new skill, one you didn't have before. *If it was easy, everyone would do it.* No matter how crazy his words, how unjust or how inaccurate, there is absolutely no point in objecting until he has finished having his say.

---

**MASTER TIP:** Don't offer a solution until he's completely finished venting about the problem.

---

# 11

# CRISIS COMMUNICATION

C RISES HAPPEN.

When things fall apart, you find out what people are made of. It's a chance for leaders to step forward and become a secure base to the people around them. When it's done well, heroes are made. When it's done poorly, organizations collapse.

You don't have to be under siege in a muddy trench to provide insight where there's confusion, offer security where there's fear, or demonstrate honesty in the face of suspicion. That opportunity has a way of knocking on your door almost every day.

We were in the middle of a training with the CEO and top executives of a Fortune 500 financial company when they took a brief break and returned, white-faced.

They had just been informed that the share prices of their company had plummeted. Most of the people in that room had just seen their personal net worth cut in half. When these men left the training room, they were going to be pounded not only with questions from the press, but anxious queries from employees, wanting to know if their jobs were safe. The temptation each of them faced when they returned was simply to lock his office door, and refuse to comment. We encouraged them to communicate instead.

When in doubt, always overcommunicate. In the absence of any information, people will jump to the most negative conclusion. Your silence is a blank screen onto which they will project their worst fears. To ensure that their message would be effective, we gave them a **crisis communication formula.** This formula is effective because it is loosely based on the pyramid of human needs, as laid out by Abraham Maslow, the founder of humanistic psychology. Maslow's idea was that you must fill people's most basic level of need before you can move on to satisfying more complex needs. Sure, people want to learn, grow, and make a contribution to society; but if they're hungry, they need to eat before they can think about anything else. During a time of crisis or great change, people's fears rush to the surface. That's the time when their needs are most acute. So in this formula you meet the listener's needs for security, connection, and contribution—in that order.

A side note: if you are a senior executive or anybody who has responsibility for a large organization, don't relegate this job entirely to your PR department or to the person who handled your executive communication. It's important for you to be in there with your sleeves rolled up, involved with the development of the message itself. Don't wait around for the speech to hit your desk, only to find yourself disappointed that it's inadequate—and there's no time left to fix it before the press come pounding at your door. After all, you're the one who has to deliver the message—you should be involved in its creation. Earlier, we said that there's nothing like the ring of authenticity. It starts right here.

Here is the formula we taught them that day. We heard from some of them later that it was the most valuable tool they had to take them through that difficult time. Put it in your pocket, against the day that you might need it.

1. **HERE'S WHAT WE KNOW FOR SURE.** The first thing that people need, at the base level, is certainty. You can't move on to the higher-level needs until you deal with this one. Be honest with them about the things of which you are absolutely sure. Even if all you know for sure is that the sun will come up tomorrow, the certainty will calm hysteria. This process roots us back in the things we can count on. Because our survival-primed brains have a naturally negative orientation, we tend to *stack*. What else could go wrong? And what else? And what else? This is how panic and hysteria spreads. For example, you might say: "Here's what we know for sure. Our stock has taken a hit. We have seen this kind of dip many times before, and we have always rebounded. Our assets are solid. We have cash in the bank, unwavering commitments from our clients, and the pipeline is still robust." If they're wondering about a main issue and you don't address it, the wondering will only get louder.

   Don't fudge this section, or make claims that you can't back up! Everyone will be watching you with the sharpened eyes of fear, and they will catch any glimmer of uncertainty or falseness. Only say the things you know to be absolutely true, or your credibility will be destroyed.

2. **HERE'S WHAT WE DON'T KNOW.** "We don't know how long this crisis is going to last." Again, be honest. Hearing you speak with authenticity will calm them down. If you insist that everything is just fine, without acknowledging the reality, everyone will dismiss you as a liar, and your credibility will be permanently damaged. Think of yourself as a doctor. You don't have to make a list of all the terrifying possibilities; that's not helpful to the patient. Simply draw a ring around one or two of the main concerns in the situation, admitting that there's no way to be sure of them.

3. **HERE'S WHAT I THINK.** This is the section in which you have a real opportunity to step up as a leader. You are in a privileged position; you have insider knowledge that others don't have. Presumably,

you have insight, or you wouldn't be in a leadership position. This is where you can move forward into the vacuum that is created in any crisis, and hold the space. You're allowed to tell us your opinion. People want to know what you *believe*. "My gut reaction is that things will get better, and that it will take about nine months."

4. **HERE'S WHAT YOU CAN DO.** People need to contribute; they need to feel that they're making a difference. There's nothing worse, in a dangerous situation, than having to sit by and be idle. Nobody wants to be passive; the act of having a job makes you feel instrumental in your own destiny and helps to quell panic. The future is based on the actions of the present; what happens will be dependent on how well everyone pulls together. "I need you to work harder and faster than you've ever worked before. We need to show that when things get tough, this team responds by raising our performance."

5. **HERE'S WHAT YOU CAN COUNT ON FROM ME.** Make a commitment. Be sure that it's one on which you can follow through. "I'll continue to meet with you every week, and give you updates on plans as they evolve. I will continue to lobby the board. I will push hard, and support every single one of you." Ensure that you become a **secure base** for the people who look up to you. Making and keeping commitments is one of the main functions of a leader—it creates an environment of trust.

6. **HERE'S WHY IT'S WORTHWHILE.** People need hope. It's your job as a leader to *create meaning* out of the facts, and communicate that meaning to the people who are looking to you for guidance. What's the reason for the suffering? How will the struggle make you stronger in the long run? What are the potential benefits of winning this battle? Note that this is very different from telling them that there's light at the end of the tunnel. Avoid at all costs shellacking a tough situation with false optimism. People want the truth; they want authenticity. Remember the example of the speech Winston Churchill gave in 1940 when he became prime

minister? He began, "I have nothing to offer but blood, toil, tears and sweat."[1] No false optimism there! But he ended on this note: "At this time I feel entitled to claim the aid of all, and I say, 'come then, let us go forward together with our united strength.'" People want to feel part of something bigger than themselves. Give them a sense of *greater purpose*.

# TWO CASE STUDIES IN CRISIS COMMUNICATION

In April 2010, an oil rig contracted by British Petroleum (BP) exploded off the Louisiana coast, killing eleven workers, injuring seventeen others, and starting a massive oil spill in the Gulf of Mexico. BP's handling of the crisis was a case study in poor communication. Instead of immediate transparency and full disclosure, BP downplayed the extent of the damage—the company's first statements about the amount of oil leaking from the well were substantially lower than other experts' measurements, and BP initially refused to let independent scientists measure the spill rate. And instead of accepting full responsibility for the disaster, BP sought to cast blame on its subcontractors.

The company's CEO at the time, Tony Hayward, did little to bolster its image. He wore pin-striped suits, offering a vivid contrast with the grimy coveralls of the Gulf workers whose lives had been affected by the spill, and he took time off in the middle of the crisis to attend a yacht race in England. When he told a reporter he was eager to get through the crisis because "I'd like my life back," his self-focused comment quickly eclipsed his formal statements of apology.

By contrast, juice maker Odwalla's handling of a crisis in 1996 revealed the value of swift action, transparency, and clear communication. After a link was discovered between several cases of the *E. coli* bacteria and Odwalla's fresh apple juice, the company acted immediately and was able to convey an image of honesty, sympathy, and responsibility. CEO Stephen Williamson ordered an immediate recall of products from 4,600 retail outlets and placed ads in local papers to share information about the recall with consumers. Within forty-eight hours, the company had set up a crisis-related Web site to give reporters and consumers access to information (even though, in those early days of the Web, Odwalla did not have a corporate or promotional Web site).

The company offered to pay medical expenses for anyone affected by the contamination and, within five weeks of the recall, Odwalla had implemented a new pasteurization process to avoid future disasters.

"We had no crisis-management procedure in place, so I followed our vision statement and our core values of honesty, integrity, and sustainability," Williamson said in a 2001 interview with Fast Company. "Odwalla has been scarred forever by the mistake that we made in 1996. We don't try to hide that scar. We don't cover it up. We keep it in plain sight to remind us of the tragedy that we must avoid at all costs."

# 12

# USING TECHNOLOGY

I N A HIGH-STAKES situation, you need everyone to stand together. You cannot afford to be boring when buy-in counts. And yet so many of our communication technologies create environments in which it is difficult to keep people engaged! Take the audio conference, for example: how many times have you suffered through an audio conference so boring that you put yourself on mute and started your e-mail?

You're not alone!

We're surrounded by a mind-boggling array of recently developed communication technologies: e-mail, instant messaging, audio conference. We've all struggled through poorly conducted examples of these media, and we've all paid the price.

So, how can we use these new technologies in ways that are more successful, engaging, and productive? Which medium should you choose for any given situation, and how can you use it to your advantage as a better substitute for face-to-face communication?

When you are communicating using technology, just as in any other form of communication, the *human connection is the only thing that really matters.* Without human connection, there is no bond, no engagement, no moving of the listener from point A to point B.

But technology on its own won't create a bond, just as a musical instrument won't play itself. You have to learn to play the medium so that it projects *you* through the space and wires. We need to use the technology in a way that keeps the human connection bright and alive, rather than letting it become deadened and gray. If you don't use the technology skillfully, it will deaden the connection by default. So the question becomes, how do we bond, while using the technology?

The goal is to do everything you can to humanize and personalize the medium. Think in terms of trying to **warm** the medium you are using. Why is it important to warm it up? Because if you are using a medium to try to impact someone, you need to use every human influence you have. The further you get from the warmth of direct, face-to-face communication, the harder you have to work at re-creating that intimacy.

Face-to-face communication is what we call a "warm" medium. When you speak to someone who is in the same room, you have the advantage of using your body, your face, and your eyes, as well as your voice. Human beings have been doing this for hundreds of thousands of years. This is the environment where bonding is the easiest.

Put a camera between you for a video conference, or turn the lights down in a slide presentation, and you lose a degree of physical connection with your audience. This "cools" the communication down. Take away the face, eyes, and body, and you're left with a phone call, or audio conference. This chills everything down another notch, forcing you to rely solely on your voice to convey meaning.

The "coldest" medium is e-mail, in which you have nothing but the written word. E-mail is the most commonly used medium of communication, but can also be the most dangerous, as anyone knows who has tried to tell a joke or be sarcastic in an e-mail—and had it go badly wrong! As the medium strips you of your human tools, in increasing degrees of "coolness," you have to work that much harder to reach across the gap created by the electronic distance.

## E-MAIL

More than two million e-mails are sent every second.[1] You may feel like most of them end up in your in-box. Guess what—every correspondent you have feels the same! Ever get an e-mail from someone, and feel your heart sink as soon as you see the name? You just know it's going to be long, confusing, and need more mental bandwidth than you've got to spare.

*Don't be that person.* You are building your reputation conversation by conversation, and e-mail by e-mail. Make your e-mails the ones that the sender looks forward to opening—because they are brief, easy to read, and crystal clear.

Use e-mail for what it can do well, which is deal with facts. To ask or answer a question, make a single, uninterrupted point, or send data, use e-mail—don't phone or leave a voice mail message. People don't want to sit through a half-hour meeting to receive information that you could have sent them in a five-minute e-mail. And they don't want to listen to a ninety-second voice mail, full of complicated facts that they then have to write down! Do the heavy lifting for them— organize and write your thoughts down in a way that's easy to read. Here are some suggestions to improve your e-mails:

1. **GIVE THE READER A WAY IN.** Because an e-mail should be brief, you don't have time to go through the classic elements of a ramp. But the opening sentence should still be about relevance. Make it immediately clear to the reader why she should care about what she's about to read. "Suzanne, you did a nice job of pointing out the need for training in our organization at the last meeting. I appreciate your suggestions. Below you'll find my response."

2. **BEWARE OF I-ITIS.** This is the disease where all your sentences start with "I." Have a quick look through your in-box, and check out how many of your e-mails (the ones you send as well as the ones you receive!) start with the word "I." You'll be amazed! The cure for I-itis is proper application of the I:You ratio. (For more on the I:You ratio, see p. 54.) Your reader wants to know what's in it for him. Talk about his favorite subject—himself. Open with the word "You." Consider the following example of I-itis: "**I** have some indicators here that **I've** put together regarding team performance. **I** think they're doing well, and **I'd** like you to take a look at these. **I** think you'll agree that **my** conclusions are justified."

And note how differently this e-mail would read if you apply a positive I:You ratio: "Since you're concerned about how the team is performing, here are a few indicators that might reassure you."

Here's another example. Contrast the following: "I want to talk to you about three things I would like you to improve: (1) delegate more to the team; (2) be more proactive in senior meetings; and (3) be more aggressive out in the field."

Or this: "Alex, you told me last week that you're interested in becoming a managing director here. You know that I believe you have the skills to accomplish this. There are three things holding you back at the moment, that I think you could easily shift: (1) delegate more; (2) participate more in senior meetings; (3) be more aggressive in the field." A side note: ideally, a management conversation like this would happen face-to-face, or at least on the phone. But the reality of today's global environment is that sometimes you just can't talk. It's *got* to be done on e-mail. So it becomes even more important than you are intentional and conscious about the way your e-mails are coming across.

3. **PUT YOUR E-MAILS ON A DIET.** Most e-mails are *obese*. They are way too long. The greatest courtesy you can show your reader is to use her time well; it is incredibly disrespectful to ask her to wade through long, rambling e-mails that she will have to read two or

three times before she gets the point. Write your e-mail, and then go back and cut it in half. When you're writing to a senior person, the rule is: the more senior the person, the shorter the e-mail. (*Note:* most people do exactly the opposite!) The higher in the organization you go, the less time they have to listen. If you write a three-paragraph e-mail to a senior manager, you run the risk that it won't be read through to the end. Sad, but true. *Brevity is power.*

4. **LIMIT YOURSELF TO ONE SUBJECT PER E-MAIL.** This makes it easier for the reader to respond to and file.

5. **INCLUDE ALL THE NECESSARY INFORMATION IN THE E-MAIL,** so your reader doesn't have to scroll down to figure out what you're talking about. An e-mail that says, "It's at three," in the in-box of someone who receives two hundred e-mails a day is no use at all. "The Ramsey meeting is at three in the conference room," is what he wants to know. Don't make your reader work harder than he needs to.

6. **DO THE "FRONT PAGE TEST" BEFORE YOU HIT SEND.** This means that you should never, never write anything in an e-mail that you wouldn't be happy to see on the front page of *The New York Times,* with your name on it. It might feel like e-mails are casual, transitory, private things—and so it might feel safe to fire off the odd dirty joke or crack about your boss to your coworker. Nothing could be further from the truth. Consider every e-mail you write to be permanent, infinitely replicable, and easy to send all over the globe in a second—because it is. And someone in your organization may well be reading everything you write. About a third of big companies in the United States and Britain hire employees to read and analyze outbound e-mail to guard against legal, financial, or regulatory risk.[2]

7. **USE *ITALICS* OR BOLD** to create cadence, rhythm, or emphasis in your sentences. This makes it easier for the reader to understand the nuance of what you're saying, in the absence of your voice. Note the difference in the following two sentences:

- If you want to capture everyone's attention, think about their needs before the meeting.
- If you want to capture everyone's attention, think about their needs *before* the meeting.

Try to write the way you speak—conversationally, stressing opera- tive words to make your meaning clear. Be intentional about the emo- tional effect you're creating. In the absence of your eyes, face, and voice, the reader is grasping for any indication of tone. Any small in- dicator will be magnified—be careful. Never use all caps in an e-mail or text—it's like shouting. Exclamation marks can be used to heat up the emotional tone of an e-mail, which is quite cold by nature. Note the difference in emotional feel between the following:

- Nice job.
- Nice job!!

8. **CONSIDER NOT SENDING IT AT ALL.** Do you *really* need to send this e-mail? Everyone in an organization is already staggering un- der the weight of their in-box. The most courteous thing you can do for someone is to resist the impulse to automatically copy him on things that have nothing to do with him.

9. **WHAT ABOUT THANK-YOU E-MAILS?** Busy people tend to hate hav- ing their in-boxes cluttered up with extraneous e-mails, and some people consider thank-yous to fall into that category. *However,* this is very much a matter of personal preference, and it's worth having a brief conversation in order to find out. There are people who think it's incredibly rude not to send a thank-you at the end of an interaction. If you get it wrong, you'll be constantly damag- ing your relationship with that person, like sandpaper on a deli- cate surface. It's the kind of minor detail that a boss may not feel is worth going into battle over. But she may be gritting her teeth ev- ery time you get it wrong. So, ask!

10. **ADDING "NRN" ("NO REPLY NECESSARY")** to an e-mail is another matter of personal preference. Again, be judicious. Some people love this, considering it to be a great way to limit their workload. Others feel that it's arrogant and obnoxious, and shuts down the channels of communication. Check in with the other person (especially if it's your boss!) and find out how they feel about it.

11. **HOW ABOUT EMOTICONS** and the cute little abbreviations like LOL, etc.? If you're in a formal organizational environment, *proceed with extreme caution.* Generally emoticons are not considered good form among senior leaders, and from a cost-benefit angle, it's hardly worthwhile. If you use an emoticon in an e-mail to someone who despises them, you will damage your own brand with her. Is it really worth it, just for the sake of adding a smiley face? We suggest that you save the emoticons for your friends and family.

12. **REGARDING EMOTIONS IN GENERAL:** If you're involved in an e-mail exchange and emotions start to run hot, it's generally best to try to get off the e-mail and pick up the phone. But sometimes, the cool temperature of an e-mail can be a useful tool—especially if you're likely to lose your temper in a face-to-face confrontation! It provides time to reflect, and a way for you to get your point across in a calm and orderly way. You can even add a ramp framed around meeting the reader's interest. For example:

> *Dear Carlos,*
> *As you know, Padma needs a final decision from us on how we are going to handle this new account by the end of the day. I imagine that you're as eager as I am to demonstrate our ability to collaborate and do what's best for the team, despite our disagreement at the meeting today. I think we both agree on the goal, even if we favor different means of getting there. Below, I've outlined three ways we might move forward together. I'd love to get your input on this.*
> *Best,*
> *Miyako*

## PHONE

Before you make a phone call, take thirty seconds to clarify your outcome. What do you want to happen during the course of the conversation? Why should they care? What's your message, in one sentence? This is particularly important if you're trying to repair the bond with someone if things have gotten confusing or emotional.

Human beings are naturally designed to read each other's physical cues—the body speaks first. On the phone, because you can't see the other person, it's hard to tell how they're reacting to you. To compensate for this lack, ask questions that confirm understanding. Pause to find out if they're still with you. Our experience is **that you shouldn't go for more than seven minutes** in an audio conference without stopping to check in with the participants. You can say, "Let me pause here and see if there are any questions," or "How does that sound so far?" or "What are your thoughts on this, Lucia?" or "Is what I'm saying consistent with what you need to know?" or "How does this sound so far?"

On the phone, your voice is the only thing you've got. The good news is that your voice can be a powerful tool. The bad news is that on the phone we have a tendency to depress our volume and level of passion. When we listen to a speaker for an extended period of time over the phone, just as in a presentation, the primary problem we encounter is **monotone.**

Boredom comes from sameness. If you drone on and on, your listeners will fall asleep. When you're on the phone, it's even more important to bring color and vibrancy to your voice—or, as we say, cultivate **vocal variety.** (For a review on creating vocal variety, see p. 109.) To check your own vocal variety on the phone, relisten to the message each time you leave a voice mail. In radio, we call this an "air check," and it's the best way to find out how your voice is interacting with the technology. How does your voice sound? Are you flat or vibrant? Monotonous or varied? Are you conveying warmth and personal presence through the line?

Presence comes from energy. Since the tendency on the phone is to flatten out, the solution is to use more energy—without shouting. John Erlendson, the owner of JE Talent in San Francisco and a well-known voice-over teacher, describes this as "imploding" your voice. To do this you create resistance at the front of the mouth, and imagine focusing your voice on the head of a pin—like *Horton Hears a Who!*

It's important to be in a performance state on a phone call, just as when you're speaking in front of a live audience. But it's more difficult. Onstage, your adrenaline will charge you up. On the phone, we tend to get lazy and complacent because we talk on the phone so frequently.

Think about creating an *active vitality* in your eyes, lips, and cheeks as you speak. The aim here is not to be theatrical, but to animate your voice to the level where it is easy for the listener to absorb your ideas. Rarely does someone come off a call and say, "I wish she hadn't been so animated!"

If the call is important, move to the edge of your chair and sit up straight. Keeping your chest from collapsing inward will improve the quality of your voice. If the call is critical, stand up! Research shows that your brain works better from the standing position. If you're tired, standing or sitting up straight will give you a welcome energy surge.

---

**MASTER TIP:** Speak with a slight smile on your face. The listener can hear it.

---

Try this: Go back and read the preceding paragraph with drooping facial muscles, slumped shoulders, and a collapsed chest. No, really. *Try it.* Now sit up straight, pull your shoulders back, put a grin on your face, and read it again. Hear the difference? It changes your voice, and your listener will register the difference every time. It gives your voice a quality of aliveness and vitality. If you want to hold people's attention, you're going to have to dig deep and find that energetic level that will make it a pleasure to listen to you.

A phone call involves the interaction of your voice and phone technology. So *use good technology*. Get off the speakerphone—it gives your voice an echoing, distant quality and makes you difficult to understand. Instead, invest in a good-quality handset or a headset. Speak into the mouthpiece, and keep it relatively close to your mouth. Call someone you trust, and ask them how you sound. Try to create a sense of warmth and intimacy. Newscasters are trained to imagine that they're speaking into someone's ear, instead of shouting into a crowd.

Avoid monologues. Say three or four sentences and then pause to ask a question. **You lose the listener's focus after four sentences.** On the phone you need to keep your sentences short and move your ideas forward faster, or your listeners will get bored. Don't repeat yourself.

## SHANN

On the radio, our jobs depended on our ratings—and the ratings were calculated every quarter hour. If you got boring, the listener would simply change to another station. Imagine that your listener is sitting there with a dial in his hand, ready to tune you out if you lose his attention—and that your job depends on keeping him engaged!"

## AUDIO CONFERENCING

It's not enough to be able to communicate well with just one person on the phone—these days, you need to be able to function well while communicating with an entire group of people whom you can't see. During phone conferences, participants tend to phone in and then put their phones on mute, listening with half an ear while they tend to their e-mails and other tasks. Everyone can hear what's being said, but no one has the responsibility to respond. This creates an environment where the levels of energy and engagement are so low that it's difficult to get anything accomplished—resulting in endlessly long confer-ences that drain enthusiasm and soak up huge amounts of time. Imag-ine how good it would be for your reputation to be known as the person who conducts phone conferences that are so clear, interesting, and brief that everyone looks forward to being involved!

In order to conduct a successful audio conference, someone needs to be in charge of hosting the call, or it will turn into a chat session and waste everyone's time. If you've called the meeting, then take charge. You've got to move at a good pace, create presence through the medium, and remove the quality of anonymity that keeps participants on mute. If you can prepare an agenda and send it out in advance so that people know what's coming, terrific. But we know that in the real world, people are often in meetings back to back, with no time to look ahead to the next one. So, we just learn to build the airplane in midair. Here's how:

**FRAME THE MEETING.** What are you doing? Is it a creative meeting to generate ideas, or a fact-finding mission? Are you exploring dif-ferent opinions, solving a problem, making a decision, airing things out, bringing people closer, clearing the air, pursuing the truth, or defining a strategy? Get clear on your outcome. What are you committed to achieving by the end of this meeting?

**CREATE A ROAD MAP.** "We have one hour. In the first fifteen minutes I'll present the findings, and then each of you will have five min-utes to share your ideas as well. That leaves fifteen minutes at the end for us to have a discussion and make a decision as a group."

**ASSIGN ROLES.** People tend to get passive in an audio conference. So use their names, and give them a job. "We're going to hear from Bashir about his results. Jo Lin, I'd like you to be ready to step in with feedback after he's finished. Anne Marie, please chime in with any relevant R&D along the way, and we'll ask Ingmar to summarize for us at the end."

**WATCH OUT FOR DEAD AIR.** This is radio terminology for the most dreaded of all occurrences—that crackling moment of unintentional silence when absolutely nothing is being said. You get a lot of dead air during a conference call, mostly because everyone has his mute button on. A question will be asked, or explosive statement made, and instead of a lively response, as you would have in a roomful of people, there will be a numb, frozen silence.

*Dead air kills energy and rapport.* If you've just stepped up with a new idea, and it is met with a long, cold pause, you will assume that everyone thinks you're an idiot. Result? You secretly swear never to risk contributing again.

Why is dead air so harmful?

Human beings naturally rely on a series of acknowledgments from the other person—*encouragement cues* confirming that the listener has understood the point so far, and wants to hear more. When you're face-to-face with someone, these cues may be offered subtly by the movement of his head, body language, the expression on his face, or the look in his eyes. This creates a feedback loop that allows the speaker to track the experience of the listener. But on the phone, the only encouragement cues you can give or receive are verbal: "Mmm-hmm . . . Yes . . . Right." And if everyone is on mute, you won't even get those little markers of agreement. Our brains tend to leap to the most negative explanation, and we interpret the silence as discouragement or disapproval.

**SET UP THE RULES OF ENGAGEMENT.** During conversations with everyone, ask the group to stay off the mute button and participate. Ask a lot of questions, and insist on getting responses from the group. Pause and invite these check-ins: "How does that sound so far?" "Lucia, what are your thoughts on the proposal?" "Let me pause here and see how this sounds to you."

Make the conference interactive. If you speak for too long without pausing to check in, you run the risk that the listener has disengaged. Maybe they're daydreaming; maybe they've lost interest in what you're saying. But they're not in the dialogue. They've gone invisible, and you have to make them visible again. Think of it like dancing with someone in the dark—you have to keep reconnecting with them, to find out where they are.

If you're giving a presentation during an audio conference, apply all of the universal principles of High Performance Communication—but compress them. Do a ramp—but do it in three sentences, rather than taking three minutes. When you come to your Points of Discovery, spend four minutes instead of fifteen. Keep it brief.

**EIGHTEEN MINUTES IS THE MAGIC NUMBER.** Don't talk for longer than that! Research shows that adult learners can stay tuned in to a lecture for no more than eighteen minutes before there's a significant drop-off in attention. After eighteen minutes, make a shift. Tell a story, show a video, create a discussion, give them a break, ask someone else to speak, or engage in open dialogue with the group.

If it's your job to facilitate the meeting, make it easy to generate ideas. Think of the dialogue as a ball that you're holding—pitch that ball so that everyone gets a chance to catch and throw. Pass the ball around.

**HAVE A LIST OF GREAT QUESTIONS READY.** This will stimulate thinking and dialogue. There are two types of questions: **point questions,** which cover the topic, and **double click questions,** which go deeper. A point question might be, "Let's look at this in terms of how it will affect us financially." "How will this affect us in terms of innovation?" A double click question invites you to go deeper into a topic. "Say more about that." "How does this relate to what we said earlier?" "What makes you say that?" "How do we know this to be true?" "What implications does this have for us?" Also have a list of everyone's names in front of you, so that you can ask questions to specific participants, and check that everyone is staying engaged.

As facilitator, you direct who gets the question. People often want to contribute, but may not feel that their ideas are welcome. A good facilitator will ask their opinion and demonstrate genuine interest in the answer. Like a radio talk show host interviewing a guest for the benefit of the listeners, you ask the questions for the benefit of the other attendees.

When asking a question, always call the person's name out first, and then throw in another comment before you hit him with the question. This gives him a critical few seconds to refocus his attention and prepare his response. For example, you might say, "Fritz, this is your region, you've got a lot of experience here. What do you think?" Avoid abruptly saying, "What do you think, Fritz?" with his name at the end of the question. This runs the risk of taking Fritz off guard and making him stumble. Professional soccer players kick the ball right to the feet of a teammate, to make it as easy as possible. Do the same—when you ask a question, kick the ball to his feet. Always make your teammates look good.

Sometimes there's one person who tends to talk over everyone else. You know this guy—once he gets started, he's nearly impossible to stop, and no one else can get a word in edgewise. Ideally, this should be handled at the management level—this person's boss needs to have a courageous conversation with him.

Failing that, here are a few suggestions: the most effective way to initially stop the flood of talk is to say his name. You may have to say it more than once, raising your volume each time, until you get his attention and he stops talking: "Frank . . . Frank . . . FRANK!" Once he has responded, then you need to ask him a question. You can just say, "Can I ask you a question?" He'll say yes . . . and in those few seconds, you will have thought up a question to ask. The content of the question is not the most important thing; what matters is that asking the question disrupts Frank's pattern, and brings his awareness back to the group. The question also returns control of the interaction to you as facilitator. You could also ask a question like, "Can we hear from some others in the meeting about their thoughts on this topic?" Or say, "Let's get some input here from some other members of the team."

A skillful facilitator summarizes the findings and looks for patterns to reflect back to the group. "What I'm hearing in terms of themes are . . ." "What I'm noticing is . . ." "What I'm experiencing here is . . ." The meeting needs to be captured, ideally by someone other than the facilitator, so that you have a record of what happened and what was said.

For an example of how this works, imagine that we're eavesdropping on an audio conference hosted by Jasmin, the manager of a global team that sells technology. Her team is spread all over the world, and she has to bring them together. Her challenge is that people are not collaborating, and not talking to each other enough.

Here's one way to run the meeting:

"Welcome, everyone. I want to talk to you about something that I think is very important to all of us." She carries on for over twenty-five minutes, running through ideas including why it's important for them to collaborate, why working in silos is not a good idea, how they're not leveraging their talent or market position. At the end of her monologue, she asks if there are any questions. There's a nineteen-second pause. No one speaks. Jasmin says, "Well, if there are no questions, let's get an update on the finances. Birgit?" More silence . . . "Birgit? . . . Are you there? . . ." Finally, with a click, Birgit speaks up, sounding flustered. "I'm sorry, I was on mute." (It's obvious that she hasn't been paying attention.) "Could you repeat the question, please?" Sound familiar?

Here's a more powerful way for Jasmin to run the meeting. "Each and every one of you has the opportunity to be part of a major push forward as we take back the market in the next six months. But to do that, we need to share our best ideas as a team. In today's conversation, I've asked each of you to come to this meeting with prepared requests and recommendations. Areas where you need help from others, and areas in which you can offer help. We'll hear from everyone, region by region, starting with you, Jack. In the last fifteen minutes we'll put together a plan for a way forward. How does that sound to you?" She gets a chorus of response. Nothing fancy, just people saying, "Good," "Fine," "Yes . . ." and she's off and running.

Jasmin could also add face contact to her meeting. But only if she knew how to use . . .

## CAMERA AND VIDEO CONFERENCING

Using video can be a powerful way to connect with people, particularly in a global environment. As organizations become increasingly aware of the carbon costs of flying employees from place to place, video technology has become standard equipment in the workplace. It's not just movie stars who need to be able to transmit their presence through a camera anymore! The ability to use the medium well is now essential for anyone working on a global team.

Video can be helpful when you need to make a message more personal—make an apology, inspire, congratulate, or show that you care. Video offers you a powerful additional tool, which is your eyes. Your eyes reveal more about you than you know. Making a video says, "I care enough about you to reach out, and allow you to see me face-to-face." You become more transparent. If your intention is clear, it will come through your eyes.

The great thing about working with a video camera is that the camera will do most of the work for you. Just allow the feeling to come through your eyes, and the camera will do the rest of the work for you.

**PICTURE THE VIEWER.** Because you are talking to a glass lens in camera work, the tendency is to come across with a "flat" expression. Your expression is robbed of the warmth and movement it would naturally display when you talk to a real person. People who make their living in front of a camera remedy this by *imagining someone on the other side of the lens.* Then they talk to that person. Choose a specific person to put inside the lens—someone who is eager to hear what you have to say. It can be someone who is actually in the audience, or a member of your own family. Choose someone who brings out a feeling of warmth in you.

**BE YOUR OWN DIRECTOR.** Set up the lighting so that you look your best. Overhead lighting will cast shadows down on your face, making you look evil. Not good for your brand! A light directly behind you will create a halo effect. A room that is too dark will make it difficult for people to see you. Get hold of a gooseneck desktop lamp, and experiment with angling it so that the light in your video image is clear and warm.

**ADJUST THE CAMERA HEIGHT.** If you're shooting video off your computer, be aware that the lens is below you, creating an unflattering camera angle. If possible, play with stacking books underneath the camera to adjust the level to the point where you look best. Try to correct the level of the camera so that it is at your eye level. This will create the sensation that you are speaking directly to someone, rather than talking down at someone, with the lens looking up your nostrils.

**PAY ATTENTION TO WHAT YOU WEAR.** White will catch too much light. Solid, bright colors are the best. Avoid busy patterns—they create a zig-zag "moiré" effect in the eye of the camera. If you have long hair, pull it back so that your face can be seen. Remove flashy jewelry and long, dangling earrings—these things will catch the light and distract the eye of the viewer.

**AVOID EXCESS MOVEMENT.** You're doing a close-up, and any movement will be magnified. Cultivate "soft movements" with your hands, face, and body; avoid jerky, abrupt motion. Tics like playing with your hair, pulling on your ears, touching your nose, etc., on camera lower your status and make you look twitchy. Stillness conveys authority.

**LOOK DIRECTLY INTO THE LENS WHEN YOU SPEAK.** This is the most important thing about using a camera, particularly if you're working off a laptop. Because of the location of the camera lens on most laptops, if you are looking at your screen, the viewer won't see your eyes. In a video conference, look into the lens when you're talking, and then drop your eyes to your screen to watch his face as he speaks. It may feel strange at first—but it will create a greater sense of intimacy.

And then there's that favorite tool of speakers today . . .

## POWERPOINT

As anyone knows who has sat through endless slide presentations in a darkened room, PowerPoint can be mind-numbingly dull! It's ironic, isn't it? Many organizations decide that their team members need more "face time." They fly the members of the team into the same city, and put them up in a hotel, at great expense. Then the members are all herded into a room, where the first thing they do is turn off the lights, so no faces can be seen. A huge screen comes down, and the speaker takes his position at the edge of the stage, usually partially hidden behind a podium. As the presentation begins, what happens? Too often, the speaker begins to read his slides, turning his back on the audience. Since anyone with a second-grade education can read faster than the speaker can talk, this results in a cascade of slides so boring that the audience grabs desperately for any caffeine or sugar available to keep them awake.

And then we wonder why people feel alienated and disengaged in meetings.

Is this human connection? Is this quality face time? Not really.

If you have a choice, the most powerful way to connect with an audience is to face them using the full range of your facial and body expression—with the lights turned up. But understanding that presentation programs like PowerPoint are here to stay, these techniques will help you use them successfully:

Stand so that from the audience's point of view, you are to the **left** of the screen. Because their eyes move from left to right when reading, whatever is on the left-hand side has visual prominence. *You* are the most important part of the presentation, not the slides.

When you're using slides, construct your narrative first, and then match the slides to it. The slides should support the narrative—not the other way around.

You need to **ramp** a slide; make them curious about the slide before it appears. You can do this in one of the following ways:

1. Ask a rhetorical question. "So, what does this look like, region by region?" *(Cue slide of map.)*
2. Give an introduction that links it to the previous material. "So we've looked at the past, and we've looked at the present. Now let's take a look at the future." *(Cue slide of future.)*
3. Give it a context. "Many of you may have been wondering about the architecture of the new building. Will it fit into the style and history of the campus? Well, you don't need to wonder anymore, because here it is." *(Cue slide of building.)*

**Slides are not for prose.** Don't put a lot of text on a slide. Use slides to show visually interesting pictures, graphs, pie charts, or a few bullet points to support what you're saying. Keep it simple and brief. The most powerful slide is a white slide with one picture, graph, word, or phrase. *Don't read slides out loud to your audience*—they can read faster than you can talk. Instead, use the slide as a springboard for your ideas. The text can provide a framework, a blueprint of the big picture. Then you fill in the details with the words that you speak. The important principle is that each slide is a link in your narrative—a visual illustration of the story that you're telling.

**Direct the audience's focus.** Speak directly to the audience, and then turn and send your audience's attention to the screen (using the open hand gesture) at the appropriate juncture. Your audience will look where you do. Tell them where to look, particularly if it's a complex slide. If the slide shows four financial quarters, for example, say "Notice what happens from Q2 to Q3." If there is something that you want them to see and reflect on, then pause for a moment. *Don't let your slide deck hijack your presentation.* You're still the center of the exchange. To hold the room, you must retake the focus between slides. At the end of the presentation, hit the "B" button on the keyboard, and turn the lights back on. Deliver your dessert face-to-face, using your eyes to reconnect with individuals in the audience.

All of these new technologies act as magnifiers, allowing you to send your message out to increasing numbers of people, over longer distances than ever before. But remember that your message still connects to **one person at a time.**

## SHANN

KGO Radio is what they call a "flamethrower station"; 50,000 watts of power means that at night, when there is less interference, the signal travels all the way from Canada to Mexico. That means that at times I might have anywhere up to 1 million listeners.

But I was trained very specifically to foster the sensation of intimacy by speaking to one person at a time. People *listen* one person a time. Especially at night, each person tends to be alone with the radio. And that's the way you need to address them. That's the way you create the bond.

# FINDING YOUR VOICE AND MAKING IT HEARD

*To thine own self be true.*

—*HAMLET*, ACT I, SCENE 3

FINDING OUT WHO you are is a lifelong process—because you're always changing. But unless you know what you're willing to fight for, then it's difficult to know what you want to say. You may not want to change the world, or wrap yourself in a flag; but you *must know what you're passionate about.* It could be your kids' school, or creating a great neighborhood community, or opening a new library. In those moments when your voice counts, your sense of conviction will come from having found those things that drive you—and make you *want* to speak out.

**Part Five** gives you a three-part strategy to accomplish this by first **creating a personal vision.** Then you will look at the important people in your organization (or personal life) and you will set up a **relationship dashboard** to keep them front of mind. Finally, you'll learn techniques that will allow you to **collaborate and innovate** with others.

You are the artist of your own life; you craft your own reality, day to day, conversation by conversation. When you know what you stand for, you know what you want to create. And then you will find your voice—and make it heard.

# 13

# CREATING A PERSONAL VISION

*All things are created twice. There's a mental or first creation,*
*and a physical or second creation to all things.*

—STEPHEN COVEY[1]

REAT LEADERS CREATE a shared vision. Great speeches are driven by the need to bring that vision alive. Before the words, before the slides, you need the ability to go to the source of your own inspiration. Create a vision, by starting with your own life.

Most of us live in reaction to the things happening around us. We get pushed down the path of life by the demands of people and events, rushing from one urgent situation to another. We're constantly putting out fires and responding to the requirement of the moment. If you've ever fallen into the trap of being yanked through life by your to-do list, you recognize this feeling. And at the end of a day—even a successful day, when you've checked off most of the items on your list—it's easy to feel empty.

Now imagine getting to the end of your life—and looking back with that same feeling. We can get confused by the activity trap, hypnotized into thinking that staying busy will give our lives meaning.

But there's a big difference between success and fulfillment. The system will drive you toward success at any cost, and yet it's entirely possible to do well at work and still feel unfulfilled. "Great," you might end up thinking. "Now that I'm successful, why do I feel so empty?" Roman philosopher Seneca the Younger put it this way: "If you have no port of call, no wind is a good wind." [2]

It's your job to make sure that you're fulfilled in your life. In order to do this, it's critical to be articulate about your own values. We want to invite you to get off the merry-go-round for a minute, and take a look at what matters most to you. If communication is the way in which we create change, and manifest our deepest hopes and dreams, it's important to identify what those hopes and dreams are. If you were to start up a new company tomorrow, one of the first things you would ask yourself is what the vision of the organization would be. Where are you going, and how do you want to get there? How do you want to be perceived by the people who use your services? What kind of reputation do you want to have? You wouldn't dream of embarking on a business venture without doing this kind of clarification first. If it's good enough for a start-up venture, it's good enough for your life.

What is the vision that you have for your life? Where are you going, and more important, why? Without a deep sense of purpose about what you really want and why you want it, you run the risk that your communication becomes just another tool to get you through the day. Why is it worth spending time on your own vision? Well, if you don't have a personal vision, someone else will surely come up with a vision for you. You'll get pushed and pulled around by the needs of others and things *will* get decided—just not by you. So take control! The tool we use for this purpose is called a **vision statement.**

A vision statement is not a list of goals, or things to do. It's not about how much money you make, what kind of house you own, or which job you have.[3] It is a statement about the qualities of character by which you commit to live. This process is often taken for granted, because we just adopt a vague list of "good character" qualities from our families, communities, or churches. Rarely do people stop and decide in an intentional way how they want to craft their own character. This is essential in communication, because often it's not *what you say* but *how you say it* that comes through the loudest. And that comes from your character. Once created, your personal vision statement becomes a North Star by which you can guide yourself and make decisions.

The following exercise is designed to help you clarify a vision for yourself. It's designed to be experiential. To do it, you're going to need a quiet space, some uninterrupted time, paper, and a good pen. You can do it on your computer if you like, but new brain research tells us that the personal discovery process goes deeper when you write with paper and pen. As you write during this exercise, we're going to ask you to use **automatic writing;** write without stopping, without taking the pen off the paper, and without evaluating or critiquing your own words. Capture as much information as you can possibly download from your brain. You can go back and fix the writing later, but don't edit while you write. Be unrestrained! Allow the thoughts to flow freely, like water in a river.

The audio download accompanying this book (go to www.standand delivergroup.com) will walk you through this process in a way that will stimulate your imagination and the power of your subconscious. If possible, turn on the download now and complete the exercise.

## STEPPING INTO YOUR FUTURE

The words you hear on the audio go something like this: Step into your future. Depending on how old you are now, imagine yourself ten, twenty, or thirty years from now, ready to retire. You are looking back at a life and a career full not only of success, but of personal fulfillment.

You've accomplished many of the goals you set out to achieve. But more important, there is a deep sense of satisfaction that you have lived a life in line with your character, your values, and the person you intended to be. Imagine looking back from the rocking chair at a life of contribution, during which you have made a real difference for your family, your colleagues, and your community.

You're now at the end of your career, and you've had such an amazing impact on the people around you that they're throwing you a retirement dinner. Imagine that you're walking into a beautiful restaurant, filled with tables covered with white tablecloths and set for a three-course meal. As you walk in, you see people with whom you spent time over the past thirty or forty years, in a variety of jobs. Friends, colleagues, bosses, direct reports—the room is filled with them, all dressed in their best, smiling and waving at you.

As the salad is served and the meal begins, someone in the middle of the room stands up and clinks a glass. You look up and see someone you've always looked up to and respected. It could be your past or current boss, your father, or a mentor. He or she says, "You've impacted all of us in the room, in one way or another. I would like to open with a toast." Now, write the toast you'd ideally like to hear; the words that would confirm that you lived the life you wanted to live. Remember, don't be reasonable. This isn't what you think they *will* say but what you would *like* them to say. Be generous with yourself. Give yourself permission to dream. (After each section, we have included some prompts to stimulate the imagination if you need them. Use them as suggestive guides, or ignore them, as you choose.)

What kind of behaviors did he see in you? When did you have courage, while others backed off? What new initiatives did you conceive, what new ideas did you propose? How did you take a stand when other people sat down? Where were you innovative? What does this person say about the way you handled yourself during times of transition? How did you set a new standard? Keep the pen going, and let the ideas flow out of it. What would surprise you? Breathe into the scene, step into it, as if you were really there. What did he discover about himself? How did you help him? In what different ways did you become a model?

**PROMPTS:** *"What I remember most about you is . . . When things got difficult, we could always count on you to . . . Even though I saw you struggle at times, what you always demonstrated was . . . When I think about how you impacted the people here, what I remember most is . . . The one thing that always distinguished you was . . ."*

Stay in the scene. The first toast is over, and there was a massive round of applause. Now the main course is being served. Another person stands up and raises a glass. This is a friend, a colleague, a partner, or a spouse: someone who worked side by side with you for many years, and knows you well. Write the toast that would bring a huge smile to your face.

**PROMPTS:** *"I also want to say something about you, and how you've always been there for me . . . When I needed help, you . . . What you did that always surprised me was . . . What I remember most is . . . What I learned from you was . . . You always . . . You changed my life many times by . . . I'll never forget the time you . . . I saw you struggle, and I saw how you conducted yourself. What impressed me the most was . . .")*

Now dessert has been served, and the guests are drinking cognac and coffee. The evening is drawing to a close, when suddenly someone rushes into the middle of the dining room. You look up. It's someone whom you had hoped would be there, but had given up on because he or she lives so far away. You look up to see that standing in front of you is your son, your daughter, your niece or nephew—someone who looked up to you as a child. A waiter hands him or her a glass; he or she raises it.

"Mom [or Dad], I know I said I couldn't make it, but I wouldn't have missed this for the world. Before the evening is over, I'd like to say a few words about the impact you've had on my life." Write the toast. What would you hear that would make you think it had all been worthwhile?

**PROMPTS:** *"No matter where I go, I'll always remember . . . While I was growing up, what I remember most about you . . . You taught me a lot of things, but what I learned most by watching you was . . . We had our rough times, but the thing you did that kept us together was . . . You never ceased to surprise me, especially when you . . . The thing I learned from you, that I taught my own kids was . . . )*

## YOUR PERSONAL VISION STATEMENT

Congratulations—you've just stepped into an imagined future for yourself. The images, feelings, and language you summoned to do this exercise give you a vivid picture of what's important to you. This is useful information. While it may seem that you were just writing toasts, what you've actually done is capture the *values that you consider essential to your own life fulfillment.* Whatever you wrote in those toasts reflects your highest aspirations for the future. Notice that very few of those values have to do with a big house, a new boat, or meeting your sales targets.

Qualities of character are the things that last; these toasts represent your aspirations. You already have everything you need to achieve this, starting now. It's a way of being that requires no preparation, and no purchase of special equipment. The next step is to distill this information into a more usable form.

First, go back through the toasts and circle anything that looks like a value. If someone said, "You were always the one I could turn to," that means you value *loyalty.* If someone else said, "You were willing to think creatively," you value *innovation.* Notice which themes and patterns occur over and over again. Jot them down. These are your **values.**

Now you're ready to write your **personal vision statement.** This is a simple paragraph, or list, that crystallizes the way in which you aspire to live your life, in order to walk your personal values into the world. Use sentences that begin with phrases like "I am committed to . . ." and "I will seek . . ." Define roles in your life, and look for an inspiration vision for each. "As a father I will . . ." "As a husband I will . . ." "As a boss I will . . ." What do you stand for? What do you believe in? What drives you? What fulfills you? What gives you a sense of purpose?

For inspiration, here are two classic examples. The first is Mahatma Gandhi's "Resolution":

> *I shall not fear anyone on Earth.*
> *I shall fear only God.*
> *I shall not bear ill will toward anyone.*
> *I shall not submit to injustice from anyone.*
> *I shall conquer untruth by truth.*
> *And in resisting untruth, I shall put up with all suffering.*[4]

And here is Benjamin Franklin:

1. **Chastity:** *Rarely use venery but for health or offspring, never to dullness, weakness, or the injury of your own or another's peace or reputation.*
2. **Cleanliness:** *Tolerate no uncleanliness in body, clothes, or habitation.*
3. **Frugality:** *Make no expense but to do good to others or yourself; (i.e., waste nothing.)*

4. **Industry:** *Lose no time; be always employed in something useful; cut off all unnecessary actions.*

5. **Justice:** *Wrong none by doing injuries, or omitting the benefits that are your duty.*

6. **Moderation:** *Avoid extremes; forbear resenting injuries so much as you think they deserve.*

7. **Order:** *Let all your things have their places; let each part of your business have its time.*

8. **Resolution:** *Resolve to perform what you ought; perform without fail what you resolve.*

9. **Silence:** *Speak not but what may benefit others or yourself; avoid trifling conversation.*

10. **Sincerity:** *Use no hurtful deceit; think innocently and justly, and, if you speak, speak accordingly.*

11. **Temperance:** *Eat not to dullness; drink not to elevation.*

12. **Tranquility:** *Be not disturbed at trifles, or at accidents common or unavoidable.*[5]

Here are some more examples, from ordinary people. Michelle is a manager who works in a factory:

*I'm committed to consistently bringing out the best in people. As a manager I will bring a quality of generosity, kindness, and insight to my work. I will challenge fixed ideas in the status quo, but constantly strive to be a team player. I will do what's best for the group. I will keep my promises and commitments. I will always give people the benefit of the doubt and seek forgiveness myself. I will hold no grudges. I will be forward-thinking, constantly searching for new ideas. I will do what's best for the company, but I will look out for my people first. I will think of my team as members of my extended family. I will lead by example, never asking my team to do anything I'm not willing to do myself. I'll go the extra mile, seeking to create fairness and value in other people's lives. I will be thoughtful, deliberate, and intentional about the words I choose when I communicate with people, seeking always to leave some-one feeling better when I walk away than they did before.*

Your vision statement might be quite brief. Aiko is a consultant:

*I will seek to have fun, bringing joy, playfulness, and a sense of humor to all my relationships. I will remind myself and the people around me that it is a choice to be happy. I will commit to being kindhearted. I will always look for the lighter side of things.*

## GETTING PRACTICAL

Okay, so now you have a personal vision statement. What do you *do* with it?

Like a compass, your vision statement is a guide that will always help you determine whether or not you're on course. In order to correct your course, you need some way of measuring where you are. Look first at where you're spending the most precious nonrenewable resource you have—your time.

Start by writing down between five and seven roles that you play in your life. For example: employee, boss, husband, father, church member, brother, son. Now imagine that you have 100 points total to allocate to these roles. Quickly estimate and write down the number of points—out of 100—that you are spending on each role at the moment. (Hint: if the final total is over 100, that's interesting, too. It shows you that you're not being realistic about your work-life balance. You're overcommitted.) Now go back and reread your vision statement. Does your point allocation line up with the values that you discovered to be important to you? (And if it's over 100—how do you need to rebalance your time so that you're not so overextended?) If you really want to jolt yourself into action, think yourself ten years into the future. Then think fifteen years . . . twenty years. If nothing changes, and you continue spending your time the way you're spending it right now, how will those retirement dinner toasts sound? Will you hear what you dream of hearing?

For most people who do this exercise, the result is astonishing, and usually painful. The vast majority of folks have it exactly backward. They are spending the *least* amount of time and energy on the roles and relationships that are actually the *most* important to their personal values and the way they want to live their life.

So here's the important question: **What would your point allocation need to be if you were living in a way that was consistent with your own personal values and vision statement?** Write down those roles, along with the point allocation that you would need to live the life you want to live. Now pick three key people per role, with whom you need to relate successfully, to accomplish the goals that you have for your life. We'll explore ways to develop successful communication strategies with those people in the next chapter.

Why is this important? Because it's no use having a lot of personal values that simply sit on the shelf in a binder. You have to put your values to work in a practical way, using them to guide your communication choices. In order to help you do that, we've created something called the **relationship dashboard,** detailed in the following chapter.

# 14

# RELATIONSHIP DASHBOARD

*Keep your friends close, but your enemies closer.*

MICHAEL CORLEONE, *THE GODFATHER: PART TWO*

WHATEVER YOU DO to make a living, you're *in the relationship business.* Your success in any organization (including a family) is the sum total of the interactions that you have every day—in person, over the phone, by e-mail, letter, fax, or text. Your ability to manage these relationships strategically requires a tool for keeping everyone in sight. Most of us manage these relationships by default. We react when we see an e-mail or phone message, or when a problem arises. You might say that we have an urgency addiction—we only take care of our relationships when the blinking light draws our attention to an emergency.

In each area of your life, there are certain key people with whom you must engage successfully. You cannot afford to overlook those relationships. You can only achieve your goals in collaboration with others, whether it's at work or at home. It's essential that you understand what your outcomes are for each key relationship, and that you make a plan to achieve those outcomes over time. This includes managing relationships with people who are your enemies, as well as your allies!

But most of us are so busy and have so many people with whom we need to interact that we simply get overwhelmed. If you're in sales, for example, you automatically pay a lot of attention to your customers. But what about your direct reports? What about the colleagues whose help you might need on the next project? How about the guy who's trying to get your job? How do you get the timing right when handling multiple communications in a complex organization? Without a way to keep track, you run the risk of overlooking a key relationship—and creating a blind spot that may cost you dearly in the long run.

If you have a high-stakes situation or project that requires careful planning, it's essential that you go beyond tasks, and think about communication. You need to manage the experiences of the people who matter. You do this by following these steps:

1. Set a clear objective.
2. Identify their need.
3. Define the content, timing, and medium of the messages they need to hear.

A good car has a dashboard that lets you know when the oil gets low, so that you can prevent a breakdown. We have developed something that we call the **relationship dashboard.** Like the dashboard on a car, it is a method that allows you to manage your relationships *before* things go wrong, without relying on memory or emergency.

A relationship dashboard gives you a way to put the important people first, and keep them in sight over time. Think of it as a strategic relationship management kit. You can develop an overarching relationship dashboard that contains all your roles and contacts, or you can create a separate one dedicated to a particular project or role. It can be customized in any way you like, to suit your needs. An Excel spreadsheet works admirably for the purpose, or we've supplied one in your download packet.

Let's work through the process of drawing up a relationship dashboard for a guy named Emil. Emil is navigating through the political landscape of a recent merger in his company. His boss, Marco, has given him six months to demonstrate that his team is relevant to the new organization. Emil has four direct reports, three of whom are located in other countries. They're all nervous, unsure of whether they will still have a job in six months. Some of them may be looking elsewhere for work. Then there's Alejandro, a colleague in the organization who wants Emil's job. Alejandro continually goes behind Emil's back, and tries to poison Emil's relationship with his boss. Emil needs a relationship dashboard that will help him survive the next six months with his career and his team intact. Each of the following steps is slotted into the spreadsheet on the following page.

1. **DEFINE THE OVERALL OUTCOME.** This is the big purpose of the relationship dashboard. For Emil, it's to ensure the survival of his team and organization through the course of the merger.

2. **DEFINE KEY PEOPLE YOU NEED TO INFLUENCE.** To do this, list the major roles you play, and then list each of the people with whom you need to communicate in that role. As an EMPLOYEE, Emil needs to communicate with his boss, Marco. As a MANAGER, Emil needs to keep in touch with his direct reports, Kristina, Hafiz, Laurent, and Bruno. As a COLLEAGUE, Emil needs to keep his eye on Alejandro, who's after his job.

3. **IDENTIFY THE NEEDS OF EACH PERSON.** Emil defines the needs of his boss, Marco, as follows: Marco needs to feel secure that the division can be profitable (*certainty*), and to look good to his own boss (*status*). Emil goes on to define the needs of each person on

# Emil's Relationship Dashboard

| EMPLOYEE | Needs | Outcome | Communication Strategy January |
|---|---|---|---|
| Marco (Boss) | Certainty, preserve reputation with his boss, division can be profitable. | Supports our business, advises through the transition, and requests ongoing budget to continue our work for the next three years. | Meet to present plan, budget, and goals. |

| MANAGER | Needs | Outcome | Communication Strategy January |
|---|---|---|---|
| Kristina | Security, risk reduction, connection, clarity. | Recommits to the team and agrees to head the new division immediately and grow the business 10 percent. | Meet to provide incentive to stay with team and discuss strategy. |
| Hafiz | Challenge, growth, status. | Identifies new markets and prepares a strategy for next year. | Conference to explore possible markets. |
| Laurent | Peer approval, contribution, money. | Creates a portfolio of marketing materials that create greater visibility for the team. | Meet to hear his ideas and select specific approach, discuss bonus. |
| Bruno | Novelty, change, connection, contribution. | Lets go of his pet project in research and agrees to put his energy into refining existing products. | Meet to discuss long-term possibilities for research into new product line. |

| COLLEAGUE | Needs | Outcome | Communication Strategy January |
|---|---|---|---|
| Alejandro | To win, status, peer approval. | Agrees to speak directly to me instead of going to my boss. | Conversation to discuss ways to feature Alejandro's contributions in the new product line. |

the dashboard. His direct report Laurent, for example, wants to be accepted by the group and acknowledged for his ideas. Emil can offer him the chance to be featured at the team meeting. Bruno the IT guy, on the other hand, is smart and easily bored. What he needs to keep him engaged is novelty. Emil will keep Bruno interested by offering him new development projects.

4. **CLARIFY THE OUTCOME YOU'RE COMMITTED TO ACHIEVING WITH EACH PERSON.** An outcome for someone in your own family might be as simple as, "We'll be close again." In business, it might be, "I'll win back this client's trust." With your boss, it might be, "Gain a promotion by the end of the year." Emil's outcome for his boss could be, "To gain Marco's moral and financial support for the work we're doing in product development."

5. **PLAN A SERIES OF INTERACTIONS OVER A GIVEN PERIOD OF TIME.** The plan should include:

- **Content** of the message—what does she need to know? Emil's direct report, Kristina, is a single parent, and her major need is *risk reduction*. His messages to her need to provide her with maximum reassurance and keep her engaged. Emil decides to ask Kristina to copresent at the team meeting with him, to raise her profile and feeling of inclusion.
- **Timing** of the message—frequency and date. Since Kristina is feeling shaky, Emil decides that he needs to talk to her every week. IT guy Bruno, on the other hand, would prefer to be left alone. Emil only needs to talk to Bruno once a month.
- **Communication medium**—e-mail, phone call, face-to-face, presentation, or video conference? Emil will have a special face-to-face meeting with Kristina right away, to provide maximum personal contact. Then he'll move to a series of weekly e-mails, finishing up with the team meeting where they will copresent.

You might be thinking at this point, "I don't have time to plan!" We say, "You don't have time, because you don't have a plan." You're being run by the demands of the moment.

Your own personal relationship dashboard will help you climb out from under your to-do list, and become intentional about your communication strategy in an increasingly complex environment. The small investment of time it takes to think about *what people's needs are,* and *how, where, when,* and *in what form* you're going to address those needs, has huge payoffs. Not only will mastering this technology bring you immediate results, but it will help you stay close to the most important part of any organization—the people. Your relationships are precious. Take care of them.

# 15

## COLLABORATION AND INNOVATION

I MAGINE THIS: YOU'VE been asked to find a creative new solution to a problem at work. For the last three months, you've done exhaustive research, putting your heart and soul into the process. Finally, you put together a forty-five-minute presentation to the team, demonstrating your ideas. You deliver your presentation, making it as clear and compelling as possible. As you finish, you hear this: "Nice presentation . . . I like a lot of the thinking. It's clear that you've worked hard, and some of these ideas are pretty good. . . ." You can hear the next word coming . . .

**BUT!**

This tiny three-letter word that we use so often, so unconsciously, is responsible for destroying much of the creativity in the world today. We create ideas through language; we kill them the same way. "But" is a block to dialogue. It is a way of negating and canceling out what the other person has just said. Now, don't get us wrong, we think critical thinking is a good skill. As we've already discussed, the brain is inherently designed to look for danger; it will zoom in on what's wrong, or out of place. The problem, once again, is that this brain skill has become overused.

The word "but" is a way to hold off someone else's ideas. You're dismissing their concepts, and preparing to advance your own. People try to gain credibility by putting down someone else's idea. Our default reaction is to be negative, and to squash a new idea instead of encouraging it. We have all become expert at standing at the gates of our own creative process, killing new ideas as fast as they emerge.

At so-called "brainstorming" meetings we often strangle one idea after another, until there's only one left standing. Then we take a break, and shred that last one while standing around the coffee machine. The cost of this process is massive. The end result is an environment in which no one is willing to come forward with their thoughts, because it's not worth the risk of being humiliated. True innovation ceases. How often have you heard someone say, "Can I play devil's advocate for a minute?" We already have enough devil's advocates in the world to make a new hell. How about becoming an advocate for creativity instead?

Advocating for creativity and fostering creative ability in others are crucial skills for a leader to possess. Traditionally, we have tended to think of creativity as the exclusive territory of artists. Not true. Creativity is a muscle; you can develop it, and make it stronger. And like a muscle, it will atrophy without use.

If you require the ability to constantly innovate, reinvent, and react to changing conditions, moment by moment, on a daily basis, your competitive advantage depends on developing new ideas. You can't afford to kill the creative spirit in a team. You need a method that enables you to rapidly generate ideas. And it wouldn't hurt to add more enthusiasm and energy in your meetings, as well. But how?

## YES, AND . . .

There are patterns to creating new ideas, just as there are patterns to killing them. Those patterns are rooted in the language that we use. To develop the technology, we turn to the experts in creativity: artists.

What artists know is that you cannot create and critique at the same time. There needs to be a period of time during which all ideas are welcomed and encouraged. The opposite of "Yes, but . . . ," is "Yes, AND." You grab someone else's idea, celebrate it, and add on to it, no matter how crazy it sounds.

**"Yes, and . . . ,"** is at the heart of what theatrical improvisers do—it's the secret to how they create an entire comedy sketch without a script. The shorthand they use to refer to this is "Accept all offers." The world-famous design and innovation company IDEO, which handles accounts for Pepsi-Cola, Apple, Samsung, and Procter & Gamble, uses a similar process, through "rapid prototyping."

In the theater, a professional director generally has a five-week period in which to put a play together. The process is nearly always the same: first, the actors sit down together and read the play. Frequently, the director will say, "Okay—let's put the scene on its feet. Follow your instincts. Try *anything*." Maybe an actor comes out and tries his lines standing on a chair. Maybe he wears a cape. Maybe he speaks with an accent, or walks with a limp. Are these elements likely to make it into the final production? Probably not. But if the director immediately says, "No, cut that, it's that's ridiculous!" then the actor will quickly retreat into conventional behavior. Only if the director continues to encourage will the actor continue to come up with new ideas, confident in the knowledge that the creativity really is acceptable and welcomed. And *then* the good ideas start to flow. Actors start reaching down and pulling out gold. The reason this works is that an environment of safety is where great ideas show up.

Imagine the creative urge as a small, shy creature that pokes its head cautiously out of its burrow. If met with criticism, it will instantly withdraw. Creativity thrives only if it is met with warmth and enthusiasm. Learn to fan the flames of another's creativity.

## THE INNOVATION LADDER

Many organizations use a "brainstorming" process in which everyone writes ideas on yellow sticky notes, and puts them up on a board. This method is better than your typical "Yes, but . . ." However, it fails in one important respect: *the ideas are isolated.* They're not building on one another, and thus failing to capitalize on the real brain trust that is available.

Powerful ideas emerge when you stand on the shoulders of the idea you've just heard. "Yes, and . . . ," accomplishes this. This is a linguistic structure that forces the brain to accept the idea you've just heard, and build onto it.

The process may take you down avenues you've never contemplated before. If you're the leader of a group trying to come up with a creative solution to the problem, your role in the process is crucial. Start by asking a powerful question. The thought processes are determined by the questions we ask. By default, the question we usually ask is, "What's wrong with this idea?" Change the question. Ask, "What's great about this idea?" "How can we build on it?" "What else is possible?" Questions stimulate creativity. The questions that you ask as a leader will determine the focus of the group.

---

**MASTER TIP:** To stimulate creativity, ask better questions.

---

The point here is to institute a process of creativity that gets everyone excited about contributing. At the end of a meeting like that, participants will walk out feeling refreshed and enlivened, having stretched their creative muscles.

Set up the rules of engagement. Explain that for the next fifteen minutes, everyone is to say only, "Yes, and . . . ," instead of, "Yes, but . . ." All offers will be accepted—every idea treated like a great one. Try saying to the team, "I want to hear some dumb ideas!" Sound strange? If you say, "I want to hear only good ideas," stand back and watch the silence. *Asking for dumb ideas creates the safety that allows good ideas to emerge.* Encourage participants to grab each idea and build onto it.

Get everyone up on his feet. Standing around a flip chart is a natural way to make this work—capture the ideas as they emerge. Research shows that your brain works better standing up than sitting down, and the energy levels will be higher. Use your face, your body, and your eyes to encourage. Add words. "Yes!" "Great!" "I like it!" "What else can we do?" As a leader, everyone is watching you. You can kill the flow of creativity with one grimace or eye-roll. This will feel incredibly unnatural and uncomfortable, *because it is.* By nature, we are hardwired to criticize, not encourage.

To create a breakthrough, you have to step out of your comfort zone. Creativity is not about being comfortable. It's about creating a concentrated, highly energized environment that heats up the imagination until it boils, and produces something new. You can't use ordinary methods if you want to create extraordinary results. After the fifteen minutes are over, call a halt. *Now* you can bring out the critical part of the brain. Scratch off all the ideas that are ridiculous. Sort through the ones that remain. Look out for the one diamond that emerges!

To summarize, here's the process of building an innovation ladder:

1. Write the problem on a flip chart. "How do we create a better mousetrap?"
2. Assign one person to capture ideas as they emerge.
3. Get everyone on his feet. Explain that for the next fifteen minutes, you are going to rapidly generate as many ideas as possible, building on top of the previous idea like a spiral staircase.

Each phrase must begin with the phrase "Yes, and . . ." There should be no silence! No blocking, critiquing, or "Yes, but . . ." Interrupting and jumping in is fine, as long as it's enthusiastic.

4. The atmosphere should be energetic. Congratulate and celebrate your coworkers with your face, body, and eyes. They did something scary by coming forward; as a leader, you need to make them feel good about their contributions.

5. At the end of the fifteen minutes, apply critical skills. Sift and sort. Discard the crazy ideas; keep the diamond.

6. Note that you accomplish two objectives here:
   - You've come up with a great new idea.
   - You've created an environment where people are excited about contributing. More fertile ground for next time!

## WATCHING YOUR PROCESS

This process also comes into play in less formal settings, as you engage in conversations during the course of the day. Start to pay attention to how often you hear, or say, "Yes, but . . ." How often are you blocking the ideas of others? How often are they blocking yours? You're probably not even conscious of how often this happens. Become curious about the reasons behind your own blocking. What's at stake here?

Many of us tend to block the ideas of others because new ideas can be frightening. **Risk reduction** is a powerful driver. The moment you stop saying, "Yes, but . . . ," things can get scary. It takes a certain amount of emotional discipline to stay open, and truly listen without blocking. But you may find that it improves not only the quality of your ideas, but also the closeness of your relationships. Try to keep from imposing your negativity on others. If you can hold your own ideas in abeyance, you remain much more open to change. As a leader, it's your responsibility to demonstrate the ability to stay open.

Try this with your family. What could you do together this weekend that you've never done before? Kids will love the process, although it's not natural for them—the default reaction for everyone is to be automatically negative about someone else's ideas. Initiate the process during the main course, and by dessert you could have an entire new game plan for family time. The only rule is that you must say, "Yes, and . . . ," instead of, "Yes, but . . . ," After you've generated twenty-five crazy ideas, go back and sift through for the one or two diamonds.

If you can do it with your family at home, you can do it with your team at work. Set a goal of creating an environment that makes people say, "I love being on that guy's team."

# CONCLUSION: PRESENCE

*Some people walk into a room and light it up. Some people walk out of a room and light it up.*

—ANTHONY ROBBINS[1]

S **PRESENCE** SOMETHING you were born with, or something that you can cultivate? After twenty years of coaching tens of thousands of people, we are convinced that presence is something available to each and every one of us. Presence is energy. It is the full, uncompromising energy that comes pouring through when a person is passionately committed to what she is saying or doing.

A baby can have presence. Watch a baby trying to walk, and you will see presence at its best. Every cell in his body is totally focused on his outcome. There is no doubt, no fear, no limiting belief. After falling down two or three times, the baby doesn't say, "Well, I guess I'm just not a walker." He keeps going. He is completely absorbed in his pursuit of the goal, and we watch him with complete attention.

Nothing is more fascinating than watching a human being completely immersed in a task that he considers worthwhile—especially when it's difficult. The harder the task, the more presence a person has when he is committed to it. And the more compelling he is to watch.

So, if we have natural presence as babies, how do we lose it? You kill presence with the massive amount of energy that you expend covering up who you really are. Most of us spend most of our time **trying to look good** and avoid mistakes. Because we are frightened in a presentation situation, we protect ourselves by putting on "armor." Your natural vitality is being sapped by the weight of the armor that you're holding up, trying to keep your true self from being seen. It requires a lot of excess energy to hide. *Armor is heavy.*

Developing presence is a process of subtraction, not addition. You don't need to add anything. What you must do is take away the thing that is veiling your authentic self. Presence has to do with pulling back the curtains and peeling off the armor. It takes courage to be vulnerable in front of a group of people. But your authentic self is the well from which your leadership presence will spring. Allow the audience to really see you, without trying to hide or defend.

Nothing will kill presence faster than a **halfhearted attempt.** If you go out there without a clear commitment, or with puny, selfish goals ("looking good," or "just getting through the speech") then your presence will be puny, because your purpose is puny. Presence = purpose + energy.

You can also kill presence by being **preoccupied with your fear.** Fear is a real emotion that everyone experiences. Pushing your fear down and covering it up will only waste your energy and drop your presence. You need to be present with your fear. One way to do this is the ancient Buddhist meditation practice of tonglen, as taught by Buddhist nun Pema Chödrön.

To practice tonglen, you breathe in whatever you are feeling, with the intention of breathing it right into your heart. You pause for a moment, to feel connected with all the people all over the world who are feeling the exact same thing, at this very moment. Then you breathe out relief, for yourself and for everyone else who is suffering. Tonglen reverses our usual habit of avoiding suffering and seeking pleasure. By turning toward your fear and breathing it in, then releasing it, you embrace your demons—and they vanish. Your poison becomes your own medicine.

So, we've talked about ways that we diminish our own presence.

Now, how do we actively go about the process of cultivating presence?

1. **CHANGE YOUR STATE.** The process of cultivating presence begins before you walk into the room. Start by preparing your body. Become intentional about the way you stand. Lift your chest and solar plexus, and open up the curtains in front of your face. Stand as if you could dilate your own pupils, and let presence flood out of your eyes.

2. **DEFINE YOUR OUTCOME** in terms of a contribution: what are you giving people with this speech or presentation? Aim your mind's eye at possibility. Ask yourself questions that create energy, passion, and drive. Make a passionate commitment of energy to your goal.

3. **FIND THE RELEVANCE.** This time, you're thinking about why this matters to *you*. Why is this the right thing to do? Identify the fundamental beliefs you have about yourself that reinforce your actions. Think about your greater purpose. Power comes to those who serve. Connect with the part of yourself that is serving a larger purpose, for the larger community, and watch your presence grow. As George Bernard Shaw said, "This is the true joy in life, the being used for a purpose recognized by yourself as a mighty one . . . I am of the opinion that my life belongs to the whole community and as long as I live it is my privilege to do for it whatever I can. It is a sort of splendid torch which I have got hold of for the moment, and I want to make it burn as brightly as possible before handing it on to future generations."

## PUTTING IT ALL TOGETHER

How often do we stop and realize what an honor it is that other people have taken time out of their day and come to us, by phone or in person, because they want to hear from us? The Masai tribe believes that words are like food—they should be offered with the intention to nourish.

We agree.

The listener wants you to speak. They have come for something. They are hungry. They're hoping that you can give them something that they didn't have before they came in.

How can we create narratives that will feed one another?

Once we shift from thinking, "Do I have the right words?" to, "How do I provide an experience that will nurture my listener?" then the words and the slides become about creating that experience. Not, "How will I be judged," but "How can I best serve their needs?"

No matter where you are in an organization, whether you are the secretary or the CEO, you've got to serve someone. The secretary answers to the CEO—but the CEO answers to the board, and the board answers to the shareholders. We are all in service.

Being in service to someone else solves your biggest problem—your self-consciousness. Get rid of your self-consciousness and everything else—your hands, eyes, body, voice, content, ideas, and delivery—all fall into line, in a magical, virtuous spiral that will take you to levels of peak performance that you never imagined possible.

When you stop worrying about *what they think of you,* and concern yourself with *what you can bring to them,* then any tendency you might have toward inauthenticity, charlatanism, or spin will drop away.

What a delight, to wake up every morning and realize that you've got this hidden power, through your words. You have this gift to give. You can make a difference in people's lives, all day long, simply by speaking to them.

You cannot *not communicate.* Everything you say and do sends a message. There is no neutral. We are constantly affecting people.

How often do we stop and ask what that effect is?

We rarely pause to ask the question, "Have I left this person feeling uplifted, warmed, enlightened? Or have I left them confused, angry, and frustrated?" You don't have to be some sort of saint when you communicate. You simply have to be intentional and aware.

Begin to ask the question, "What is my intention for this meeting? What is the experience that I want them to have?"

To become intentional about your impact on others not only shifts the quality of your conversations—it begins to alter the path in front of you. Communicating in this way shifts your own destiny. Imagine five years from now—what would it be like, to see the way in which those thousands of conversations have inexorably taken your life in a new direction? Even the slightest change in your approach impacts everyone around you. How many tens of thousands of lives will you touch in the next decade, each conversation rippling through lives and cascading through communities? What differences would you see after fifteen years? A whole career? A lifetime?

When you do something for the greater good, rather than just for yourself, it brings about a different way of being. It comes with a built-in generosity of ideas, a surge of spirit and empathy. At that moment, you're able to tap into the thing that makes us uniquely human. You can see—and share—things that are not yet knowable, that can just barely be imagined.

The gap between what *is* and what *might be,* is often bridged by your words. This is, literally, the meaning of the word **inspire**—to breathe life into another human being. This is what it's all about.

In our normal day-to-day routine, we are generally completely unconscious when we speak to each other. We just go on automatic pilot. Consider the possibility that *each word is a way of touching another person.* Speak to another person with the intention of creating something that wasn't there before.

Martha Graham, one of the best-known teachers and choreographers of modern dance, said it this way: "There is a vitality, a life force, an energy, a quickening that is translated through you into action, and because there is only one of you in all of time, this expression is unique. And if you block it, it will never exist through any other medium and it will be lost."

The words that you were born to say will remain unspoken if you don't summon the courage to speak them.

Show up in the world. Be generous with your voice. Share what you have to say. Give your gift; the world is waiting to receive it.

# ACKNOWLEDGMENTS

THERE'S AN OLD saying in Texas: "If you see a turtle sitting on a fence post, you know he didn't get up there by himself."

We'd like to offer our deepest appreciation to all the folks who helped put us up on the fence post. We couldn't have done it without them.

You learn from the people you hang out with.

We're fortunate to have learned from some of the very best—our colleagues at Stand & Deliver. We'd like to thank the incredibly talented theater directors, actors, and performers who have joined the faculty, bringing their expertise and inspiration. They have all been instrumental in helping us to explore human communication in ways that bring humor, drama, heart, and emotion to the process. They include (in alphabetical order) Rich Cox, Nike Doukas, Janice Erlendson, William Hall, Alexandria Hilton, Dan Klein, Jeff Raz, Richard Seyd, Melissa Smith, Deb Sussel, Robert Weinapple, and the invaluable support of assistant Cassondra Prince.

To Peter Borland, who saw the vision, said yes, and gave us the opportunity to make it real. But more than that—when it really mattered, he rolled up his sleeves, put his hands in the dough, and pounded the book into shape. From the bread to the baker—thank you! It would never have happened without you.

To Nick Simonds, who patiently helped us get the whole thing into shape.

To Bonnie Nadell, who worked with us from the beginning, made it all possible, and held our hands the whole way.

To Sarah Gershman, Rob Baedeker, and Rachel Finkelstein, our wonderful research assistants, who tracked down all those tricky quotes and statistics, and worked like fiends to get it all done in time.

To Dr. George Kohlrieser, who has been a mentor. Without his guidance and inspiration this book would not be possible.

Peter says: It's often said we teach what we most need to learn. To my family, Marcia, Lucas, and Tyler, who have never faltered in their love and support—thank you for your patience! I dedicate this book to the memory of my father, Howard Meyers, who early on instilled in me the value of the spoken word as the greatest gift we have.

Shann says: To my darling husband, Rich, who did everything but put me on his back and carry me cross-country during this project— and if I had asked, would have done that as well. Where have you been all my life? I love you. To my family—Taid, Ceris, Elen, Joli, and Benjamin—you were all brilliant. Thanks for all the support— and for being understanding about all the deadline stress! And thank you to my parents, Ann and Don Nix. I learned the great pleasures of inspirational communication across their dinner table.

# APPENDIX 1:
# Further Assessment

You've already examined your communication from the inside out. Now we're going to take a look from the outside in. A self-assessment is your opinion of yourself. But when you're communicating, the only thing that really counts is *other people's experience of you.* To find out what that is, make five copies of the communication feedback form on page 261. (You can also download fresh forms at www.standanddelivery group.com.) Hand them out to at least five people you know. Ask them to complete the questions. Keep the forms anonymous, so that they can be completely honest. They don't have to add up the numbers for you—you'll do that later.

Now take the following steps:

1. When you get the forms back, add up the numbers. Plot the dot from each person separately, on the performance grid from page 24. Look for clusters or patterns, which will show you how you're being received. For example, you may think you have great content, but lack in delivery. When your team hands back their sheets, you may be shocked to discover that they think your delivery is quite strong, but your content is

just okay. Do an analysis. What are you seeing? Where are the patterns? Are there gaps between how you perceive yourself and how other people perceive you? In the end, it's not what you say, it's what people remember.

2. If you're *really* serious about improving your performance, hand out five copies of the communication feedback form to customers, five to colleagues, and five to family members. This is a fascinating snapshot of your communication in the real world, and it might surprise you! It might turn out that you're great at communicating to your team at work, but you get home and just grunt at your family. Or maybe you're giving everything to your customers, and not much to your co-workers. Are you showing up differently with different people? Are there patterns? Are you giving your best to some people and taking others for granted? If the answer is yes, consider the cost!

(For instructions, please refer to pages 25–28.)

# Communication Feedback Form

| CONTENT |
|---|

PLEASE RESPOND TO THE FOLLOWING WITH:

5 = *almost always true*
4 = *usually true*
3 = *sometimes true*
2 = *usually not true*
1 = *almost never true*

| | |
|---|---|
| | He/she brings insightful analysis and relevant detail to presentations and supports ideas with evidence and examples to illustrate key points. |
| | He/she speaks to my emotional needs, as well as my intellectual concerns. |
| | He/she uses stories and vivid imagery to help me feel and see what is being described. |
| | He/she creates powerful closings that come full circle—reinforcing the key point and leaving me feeling satisfied. |
| | He/she creates a strong opening by talking about what I care about. He/she rarely opens by talking about him/herself. |
| | His/her talks resemble an engaging story more than a presentation of information. |
| | He/she typically opens a conversation or presentation with a central theme, which is reinforced throughout. |
| | He/she organizes ideas in an integrated and sequential flow with ideas building upon each other, making it easier for me to understand. |
| | He/she uses brevity, and never goes on too long. I leave presentations knowing exactly what he/she was saying. |
| | There is a clear purpose and objective when he/she speaks. I am consistently moved to new insight, decision, or action by his/her words. |
| | His/her language is fresh, active, and easy to understand. He/she rarely uses vague or confusing jargon, acronyms, or clichés. |
| | **< CONTENT** TOTAL SCORE |

## DELIVERY

PLEASE RESPOND TO THE FOLLOWING WITH:

5 = *almost always true*

4 = *usually true*

3 = *sometimes true*

2 = *usually not true*

1 = *almost never true*

| | |
|---|---|
| | He/she is responsive to what is happening in the moment and adjusts as needed. |
| | He/she uses gestures comfortably in front of a group and rarely looks awkward using his/her hands. |
| | He/she is a skilled listener. In conversations and meetings, I feel he/she cares about my point of view. |
| | He/she can display a range of emotions that are appropriate and helpful for the situation. |
| | He/she begins by gaining rapport with me. He/she starts a conversation or presentation by creating common ground (shared interests with me) before jumping into his/her own agenda. |
| | He/she maintains eye contact while speaking in group or team settings. He/she looks me in the eye when we talk one-on-one. |
| | His/her language and tone are conversational. |
| | He/she uses slides, handouts, or media only to support his/her presentation, and does not let the slides take over. |
| | When speaking, he/she varies the tempo, pitch, and volume to enliven his/her content with dynamics and variety. |
| | **< DELIVERY** TOTAL SCORE |

# APPENDIX 2:
# Ramps and Desserts

Here are some classic examples of ramps and desserts:

1. Franklin Delano Roosevelt, "The Four Freedoms"

   *Mr. President, Mr. Speaker, members of the 77th Congress:*
   *I address you, the members of this new Congress, at a moment unprecedented in the history of the union. I use the word "unprecedented" because at no previous time has American security been as seriously threatened from without as it is today.*

   *http://www.americanrhetoric.com/speeches/fdrthefourfreedoms.htm*

2. Bill Cosby, "Address at the NAACP on the 50th Anniversary of *Brown v. Board of Education*"

   *Ladies and gentlemen, I really have to ask you to seriously consider what you've heard, and now this is the end of the evening so to speak. I heard a prize fight manager say to his fellow who was losing badly, "David, listen to me. It's not what's he's doing to you. It's what you're not doing."*

*Ladies and gentlemen, these people set—they opened the doors, they gave us the right, and today, ladies and gentlemen, in our cities and public schools we have 50% drop out. In our own neighborhood, we have men in prison. No longer is a person embarrassed because they're pregnant without a husband. No longer is a boy considered an embarrassment if he tries to run away from being the father of the unmarried child.*

http://www.americanrhetoric.com/speeches/billcosby
poundcakespeech.htm

## 3. Lou Gehrig's "Farewell to Yankee Fans"

*Fans, for the past two weeks you have been reading about a bad break I got. Yet today I consider myself the luckiest man on the face of the earth. I have been in ballparks for seventeen years and have never received anything but kindness and encouragement from you fans.*

*Look at these grand men. Which of you wouldn't consider it the highlight of his career to associate with them for even one day?*

http://www.historyplace.com/speeches/gehrig.htm

## 4. Lyndon B. Johnson, "We Shall Overcome"

*I speak tonight for the dignity of man and the destiny of Democracy. I urge every member of both parties, Americans of all religions and of all colors, from every section of this country, to join me in that cause.*

*At times, history and fate meet at a single time in a single place to shape a turning point in man's unending search for freedom. So it was at Lexington and Concord. So it was a century ago at Appomattox. So it was last week in Selma, Alabama. There, long suffering men and women peacefully protested the denial of their rights as Americans. Many of them were brutally assaulted. One good man—a man of God—was killed.*

http://www.historyplace.com/speeches/johnson.htm

5. Michelle Obama, "2008 Democratic National Convention Keynote Address"

*And as I tuck that little girl in—as I tuck that little girl in and her little sister into bed at night, you see, I—I think about how one day, they'll have families of their own and how one day, they—and your sons and daughters—will tell their own children about what we did together in this election. They'll tell them—they'll tell them how this time, we listened to our hopes instead of our fears; how this time—how this time, we decided to stop doubting and to start dreaming; how this time, in this great country—where a girl from the South Side of Chicago can go to college and law school, and the son of a single mother from Hawaii can go all the way to the White House—that we committed ourselves— we committed ourselves to building the world as it should be.*

*So tonight, in honor of my father's memory and my daughters' future, out of gratitude for those whose triumphs we mark this week and those whose everyday sacrifices have brought us to this moment, let us devote ourselves to finishing their work; let us work together to fulfill their hopes; and let's stand together to elect Barack Obama President of the United States of America.*

*http://www.americanhetoric.com/speeches/convention2008/*
*michelleobama2008dnc.htm*

6. Steve Jobs's commencement speech to Stanford in 2005

*When I was young, there was an amazing publication called the* Whole Earth Catalog, *which was one of the bibles of my generation. It was created by a fellow named Stewart Brand not far from here in Menlo Park, and he brought it to life with his poetic touch. This was in the late sixties, before personal computers and desktop publishing, so it was all made with typewriters, scissors, and Polaroid cameras. It was sort of like Google in paperback form thirty-five years before Google came along. I was idealistic, overflowing with neat tools and great notions.*

*Stewart and his team put out several issues of the* Whole Earth Catalog, *and then when it had run its course, they put out a final issue. It was the mid-seventies and I was your age. On the back cover of their final issue was a photograph of an early morning country road, the kind you might find yourself hitchhiking on if you were so adventurous. Beneath were the words, "Stay hungry, stay foolish." It was their farewell message as they signed off. "Stay hungry, stay foolish." And I have always wished that for myself, and now, as you graduate to begin anew, I wish that for you. Stay hungry, stay foolish.*

*http://www.freerepublic.com/focus/chat/1422863/posts*

# NOTES

## INTRODUCTION

1. Daniel Goleman, *Emotional Intelligence: Why It Can Matter More Than IQ for Character, Health and Lifelong Achievement* (New York: Bantam Books, 1995).
2. "Employees Most Frustrated by Lack of Communication in the Workplace, Opinion Research Corporation Study Finds," Business Wire, November 7, 2007, accessed at http://www.allbusiness.com/labor-employment/labor-sector-performance-labor-force/5307054-1.html.
3. Denise Thornby, "Beginning the Journey to Skilled Communication," *American Association of Critical-Care Nurses Advanced Critical Care* 17, no. 3 (July–September 2006): 266–71.
4. Penny Wells, Glenn A. Greenberg, and John Cusolito, "*Teens Today* Study Highlights Poor Communication As One Reason for Wide 'Reality Gap,'" accessed at http://www.sadd.org/teenstoday/teenstodaypdfs/survey.pdf.

## CHAPTER 1: PREPARATION

1. Antonio R. Damasio, *Descartes' Error. Emotion, Reason, and the Human Brain* (New York: HarperCollins, 1994).
2. Alan Weiss, *Million Dollar Consulting: The Professional's Guide to Growing a Practice* (Columbus, OH: McGraw-Hill, 2003), 98.

## CHAPTER 2: ARCHITECTURE

1. Patricia Fripp, "15 Tips for Webinars: How to Add Impact When You Present Online," Fripp THE Executive Speech Coach, September 8, 2009, http://fripp.blogs.com/presentations/2009/01/index.html.
2. Roger Ailes and Jon Kraushar, *You Are the Message: Getting What You Want by Being Who You Are* (New York: Doubleday, 1995).

## CHAPTER 3: TECHNIQUES

1. Daniel L. Schacter, *The Seven Sins of Memory: How the Mind Forgets and Remembers* (Boston: Houghton Mifflin, 2001).
2. Chip Heath and Dan Heath, *Made to Stick: Why Some Ideas Survive and Others Die* (New York: Random House, 2007).
3. Keith Johnstone, *Impro for Storytellers* (New York: Routledge, 1999).
4. Dan Roam, *The Back of the Napkin* (New York: Portfolio Inc., 2008). "Picture This," American Management Association, April 10, 2008, accessed at http://www.amanet.org /training/articles/Picture-This.aspx.
5. Many popular expressions are actually metaphors:

> "I'm dead tired."
>
> "She's the apple of my eye."
>
> "He wore me down."
>
> "I'm heartbroken."
>
> "Strong as an ox."
>
> "Hunka hunka burnin' love."
>
> "An old flame."
>
> "Boiling mad."
>
> "A feverish pace."
>
> "Heated debate."
>
> "A warm reception."
>
> "They were kindling a new romance."

Some famous metaphors include:

> "All the world's a stage,
> And all the men and women merely players;
> They have their exits and their entrances . . ."
>> —William Shakespeare, *As You Like It,* Act 2, Scene 7, from *The Complete Works of William Shakespeare,* first published in 1864.

> "My friend, the swift mule, fleet wild ass of the mountain,
> panther of the wilderness,
> after we joined together and went up into the mountain,
> fought the Bull of Heaven and killed it,
> and overwhelmed Humbaba, who lived in the Cedar Forest,
> now what is this sleep that has seized you?"
>> —*The Epic of Gilgamesh,* trans., N.K. Sanders (Harmondsworth, Middlesex, England: Penguin Books, 1960).

> ". . . rise from the dark and desolate valley of segregation to the sunlit path of racial justice."
>> —Martin Luther King Jr., "I Have a Dream," in Drew D. Hansen, *The Dream: Martin Luther King, Jr., and the Speech that Inspired a Nation* (New York: HarperCollins, 2003), p. 177.

". . . sweltering with the heat of oppression, will be transformed into an oasis of freedom and justice."
>—Martin Luther King Jr., "I Have a Dream," in Hansen, *The Dream*, p. 177.

"rising tides of prosperity and the still waters of peace" versus "gathering clouds and raging storms"
>—Barack Obama's inaugural address. Complete transcript available at *The New York Times*, http://www.nytimes.com/2009/01/20/us/politics/20text-obama.html.

". . . And as hope kindles hope, millions more will find it. By our efforts, we have lit a fire as well—a fire in the minds of men. It warms those who feel its power, it burns those who fight its progress, and one day this untamed fire of freedom will reach the darkest corners of our world."
>—George W. Bush's second inaugural address. Available at National Public Radio, http://www.npr.org/templates/story/story.php?storyId=4460172.

Less famous metaphors can be seen as well:

>"The winds were ocean waves, thrashing against the trees limbs. The gales remained thereafter, only ceasing when the sun went down. Their waves clashed brilliantly with the water beneath, bringing foam and dying leaves to the shore."
>
>"The teacher descended upon the exams, sank his talons into their pages, ripped the answers to shreds, and then, perching in his chair, began to digest."
>—Writesville, http://www.writesville.com/writesville/2006/01/examples_of_met.html.

6. George Orwell, "Politics and the English Language," in *The Complete Works of George Orwell*, http://www.george-orwell.org/Politics_and_the_English_Language/0.html.
7. Thanks to writer/researcher Rob Baedeker, who contributed to this section.
8. Maike Looß, "Types of Learning?: A Pedagogic Hypothesis Put to the Test." Organisation for Economic Co-operation and Development, http://www.oecd.org/dataoecd/42/13/34926352.pdf.
9. Mitsugi Saotome, *The Principles of Aikido*, Boston: Shambhala Publications, 1989; and Rick Higgs, "Aikido, Satyagraha and Nonviolence," East Bay Aikido, http://www.eastbayaikido.com/articles/higgssatyagraha.html.
10. George Lakoff, *Don't Think of an Elephant!: Know Your Values and Frame the Debate: The Essential Guide for Progressives* (Vermont: Chelsea Green, 2004).

## PART TWO: DELIVERY

1. A new behavioral study, commissioned by Lloyds TSB Insurance, reveals that the average attention span is now just five minutes and seven seconds, compared to

more than twelve minutes a decade ago. "'Five-minute-memory' Costs Brits £1.6 Billion," Lloyds TSB Insurance, November 27, 2008, http://www.insurance.lloydstsb .com/personal/general/mediacentre/homehazards_pr.asp.

## CHAPTER 4: VOICE

1. Jack Welch, *JACK: Straight from the Gut,* with John A. Byrne, (New York: Warner Business Books, 2003).
2. George Yule, *The Study of Language,* 3rd ed. (New York: Cambridge University Press, 2006).

## CHAPTER 6: FACE AND EYES

1. Ross W. Buck, Virginia J. Savin, Robert E. Miller, William F. Caul, "Communication of Affect Through Facial Expressions in Humans," *Journal of Personality and Social Psychology* 23, no. 3 (September 1972): 362–71.
2. Tom Scheve, "How Many Muscles Does It Take to Smile?" How Stuff Works, http:// health.howstuffworks.com/mental-health/human-nature/happiness/muscles-smile .html.
3. Rick Waters, "Is This Man Lying?" *The TCU Magazine* (Winter 2008), http://www .magarchive.tcu.edu/articles/2005-01-AC2.asp.
4. Erin Takoner, MS, "Look Me in the Eyes—From Eye Contact to 'Fear Blindness,'" December 23, 2008, http://brainblogger.com/2008/12/23/look-me-in-the-eyes-from-eye-contact-to-fear-blindness/.

## PART THREE: STATE

1. We have drawn heavily on the work of Anthony Robbins, the world's great expert on state and how to control it. For more about Anthony Robbins's methods and teachings, see his works listed in the bibliography.

## CHAPTER 7: BODY

1. John H. Riskind and Carolyn C. Gotay, "Physical Posture: Could It Have Regulatory or Feedback Effects on Motivation and Emotion?" *Motivation and Emotion* 6, no. 3 (1982): 273–98.
2. Ibid.
3. Constantin Stanislavski, *An Actor Prepares,* trans. Elizabeth Reynolds Hapgood (New York: Routledge, 1989).
4. Michael Lewis, a psychology professor at Cardiff University, published a study in the March 2009 issue of *Journal of Cosmetic Dermatology* showing that Botox may lighten people's moods by literally preventing them from frowning. Lewis favors the theory that facial muscles influence brain activity directly, and points to earlier research that suggests such a neurological link.

5. Modern forms of therapy use this facial-feedback loop to create instant results. Laughter therapy, for one, works by consciously engaging the smiling muscles to release endorphins.

## CHAPTER 8: THE MIND'S EYE

1. As detailed by Richard Bandler and John Grinder in their groundbreaking work *Reframing: Neuro-Linguistic Programming and the Transformation of Meaning* (Moab, UT: Real People Press, 1982).

## CHAPTER 9: BELIEFS

1. Tamara L. Watson and Bart L. Krekelberg, "The Relationship Between Saccadic Suppression and Perceptual Stability," *Current Biology* 19, no. 12 (June 23, 2009): 1040–43.
2. Bruce H. Lipton, PhD, *The Biology of Belief: Unleashing the Power of Consciousness, Matter & Miracles* (Carlsbad, CA: Hay House, 2008).

## CHAPTER 10: COURAGEOUS CONVERSATIONS

1. George Kohlrieser, *Hostage at the Table: How Leaders Can Overcome Conflict, Influence Others, and Raise Performance* (San Francisco, CA: Jossey Bass, 2006).
2. Diane Vaughan, *The Challenger Launch Decision: Risky Technology, Culture, and Deviance at NASA* (Chicago: University of Chicago Press, 1996); "Engineering Ethics: The Space Shuttle Challenger Disaster," Department of Philosophy and Department of Mechanical Engineering, Texas A&M University, http://ethics.tamu.edu/ethics/shuttle/shuttle1.htm (accessed October 26, 2009); and Kurt Hoover and Wallace T. Fowler, "Studies in Ethics, Safety, and Liability for Engineers: Space Shuttle Challenger," The University of Texas at Austin and Texas Space Grant Consortium, http://www.tsgc.utexas.edu/archive/general/ethics/shuttle.html (accessed October 26, 2009).
3. Roger Fisher and William Ury, *Getting to Yes: Negotiating Agreement Without Giving In* (New York, Penguin Books, 1991).
4. Ibid. This principle, again, is drawn from Fisher and Ury's *Getting to Yes,* and it's an important one.

## CHAPTER 11: CRISIS COMMUNICATION

1. Winston Churchill, first speech as prime minister to House of Commons, May 13, 1940:

> "I have nothing to offer but blood, toil, tears and sweat. We have before us an ordeal of the most grievous kind. We have before us many, many long months of struggle and of suffering. You ask, what is our policy? I can say: It is to wage war, by sea, land and air, with all our might and with all the strength that God can give us; to wage war against a monstrous tyranny,

never surpassed in the dark, lamentable catalogue of human crime. That is our policy. You ask, what is our aim? I can answer in one word: It is victory, victory at all costs, victory in spite of all terror, victory, however long and hard the road may be; for without victory, there is no survival. Let that be realised; no survival for the British Empire, no survival for all that the British Empire has stood for, no survival for the urge and impulse of the ages, that mankind will move forward towards its goal. But I take up my task with buoyancy and hope. I feel sure that our cause will not be suffered to fail among men. At this time I feel entitled to claim the aid of all, and I say, "come then, let us go forward together with our united strength."

## CHAPTER 12: USING TECHNOLOGY

1. Technology market research firm The Radicati Group estimates the number of e-mails sent per day (in 2008) to be around 210 billion. 183 billion messages per day means more than 2 million e-mails are sent every second; about 70 to 72 percent of them might be spam and viruses. The genuine e-mails are sent by about 1.3 billion users. "You've Got Mail—A Ton of It," *Miami Herald,* August 9, 2008.
2. Reuters, "Companies Read Employee E-mail," June 2, 2006.

## CHAPTER 13: CREATING A PERSONAL VISION

1. Stephen R. Covey, *The 7 Habits of Highly Effective People: Powerful Lessons in Personal Change* (New York: Simon & Schuster, 1989).
2. Seneca the Younger, *Epistulae Morales.*
3. For our work on personal vision we have drawn heavily on the work of Stephen Covey. For more of his work, see his books listed in the bibliography.
4. Gandhi, Mahatma, *The Collected Works of Mahatma Gandhi* (New Delhi: Publications Division, Ministry of Information and Broadcasting, Government of India, 1994).
5. Benjamin Franklin, *The Autobiography of Benjamin Franklin* (Stilwell, KS: Digireads.com Publishing, 2005).

## CONCLUSION: PRESENCE

1. Adapted from a Yiddish proverb: "Some people are electrifying. They light up a room when they leave."

## APPENDIX ONE: FURTHER ASSESSMENT

1. Dr. Frank Luntz, *Words That Work: It's Not What You Say, It's What People Hear* (New York: Hyperion, 2007).

# BIBLIOGRAPHY

Outside of a dog, a book is man's best friend. Inside of a dog, it's too dark to read.

*—Groucho Marx*

Here's a list of books that we've found constructive, inspiring, and influential, from a variety of disciplines. Enjoy!

Ailes, Roger. *You Are the Message: Getting What You Want by Being Who You Are.* With Jon Kraushar. New York: Bantam Doubleday Dell, 1995.

Berry, Cicely. *Voice and the Actor.* New York: Macmillan, 1973.

Booker, Christopher. *The Seven Basic Plots: Why We Tell Stories.* London: Continuum, 2004.

Buckley, Reid. *Strictly Speaking.* New York: McGraw-Hill, 1999.

Chapman, Gary. *The Five Love Languages: How to Express Heartfelt Commitment to Your Mate.* Chicago: Moody Publishers, 2004.

Chekhov, Michael. *To the Actor: On the Technique of Acting.* New York: Harper & Row, 1953.

Chopra, Deepak. *The Seven Spiritual Laws of Success: A Practical Guide to the Fulfillment of Your Dreams.* San Rafael, CA: Amber-Allen, 1994.

Cialdini, Robert B. *Influence: The Psychology of Persuasion.* New York: HarperCollins, 2007.

Collins, Jim. *Good to Great: Why Some Companies Make the Leap . . . and Others Don't.* New York: HarperCollins, 2001.

Covey, Stephen R. *The 7 Habits of Highly Effective People: Powerful Lessons in Personal Change.* New York: Simon & Schuster, 1989.

———. *The 8th Habit: From Effectiveness to Greatness.* New York: Free Press, 2004.

———. *Everyday Greatness: Inspiration for a Meaningful Life.* Nashville: Rutledge Hill Press, 2006.

———. *The Leader in Me: How Schools and Parents Around the World Are Inspiring Greatness, One Child at a Time.* New York: Free Press, 2008.

Csikszentmihalyi, Mihaly. *Flow: The Psychology of Optimal Experience.* New York: Harper & Row, 1990.

Damasio, Antonio R. *Descartes' Error: Emotion, Reason, and the Human Brain.* New York: HarperCollins, 1994.

De Pree, Max. *Leadership Is an Art.* East Lansing, MI: Michigan State University Press, 1987.

Dowis, Richard. *The Lost Art of the Great Speech: How to Write One, How to Deliver It.* New York: American Management Association, 2000.

Egri, Lajos. *The Art of Dramatic Writing: Its Basis in the Creative Interpretation of Human Motives.* New York: Simon & Schuster, 1972.

Fisher, Roger, and William Ury. *Getting to Yes: Negotiating Agreement Without Giving In.* New York: Penguin Books, 1991.

Florida, Richard. *The Rise of the Creative Class: And How It's Transforming Work, Leisure, Community and Everyday Life.* New York: Basic Books, 2002.

Franklin, Benjamin. *The Autobiography of Benjamin Franklin.* Stilwell, KS: Digireads .com Publishing, 2005.

Gallwey, W. Timothy. *The Inner Game of Tennis: The Classic Guide to the Mental Side of Peak Performance.* New York: Random House, 1974.

Gandhi, Mahatma. *The Collected Works of Mahatma Gandhi.* New Delhi: Publications Division, Ministry of Information and Broadcasting, Government of India, 1994.

Gardner, Howard. *Leading Minds: An Anatomy of Leadership.* In collaboration with Emma Lashin. New York: HarperCollins, 1996.

Gilbert, Daniel. *Stumbling on Happiness.* New York: Vintage, 2007.

Goleman, Daniel. *Emotional Intelligence: Why It Can Matter More Than IQ for Character, Health and Lifelong Achievement.* New York: Bantam Books, 1995.

Grabhorn, Lynn. *Excuse Me, Your Life Is Waiting: The Astonishing Power of Feelings.* Charlottesville, VA: Hampton Roads, 2000.

Heath, Chip, and Dan Heath. *Made to Stick: Why Some Ideas Survive and Others Die.* New York: Random House, 2007.

Herrigel, Eugen. *Zen in the Art of Archery.* Translated by R. F. C. Hull. Pantheon, 1953.

Johnstone, Keith. *Impro for Storytellers.* New York: Routledge, 1999.

Kohlrieser, George. *Hostage at the Table: How Leaders Can Overcome Conflict, Influence Others, and Raise Performance.* San Francisco, CA: Jossey–Bass, 2006.

Lakoff, George. *Don't Think of an Elephant!: Know Your Values and Frame the Debate: The Essential Guide for Progressives.* White River Jct., VT: Chelsea Green, 2004.

Lipton, Bruce H., PhD. *The Biology of Belief: Unleashing the Power of Consciousness, Matter & Miracles.* Carlsbad, CA: Hay House, 2008.

Livesey, Peter J. *Learning and Emotion: A Biological Synthesis.* Hillsdale, NJ: Lawrence Erlbaum, 1986.

Luntz, Dr. Frank. *Words That Work: It's Not What You Say, It's What People Hear* New York: Hyperion, 2007.

Mamet, David. *True and False: Heresy and Common Sense for the Actor.* New York: Random House, 1997.

Marcus Aurelius. *Meditations.*

Pine, B. Joseph II, and James H. Gilmore. *The Experience Economy: Work Is Theatre & Every Business a Stage.* Boston: Harvard Business Press, 1999.

Renvoisé, Patrick, and Christophe Morin. *Selling to the Old Brain: How New Discoveries in Brain Research Empower You to Influence Any Audience, Anytime.* San Francisco: SalesBrain, 2003.

Rilke, Rainer Maria. *Letters to a Young Poet.* New York: Random House, 1934.

Robbins, Anthony. *Awaken the Giant Within: How to Take Immediate Control of Your Mental, Emotional, Physical and Financial Destiny!* New York: Simon & Schuster, 1992.

———. *Notes from a Friend: A Quick and Simple Guide to Taking Control of Your Life.* New York: Fireside, 1995.

———. *Unlimited Power: The New Science of Personal Achievement.* New York: Fireside, 1997.

Rosenberg, Marshall B., PhD. *Nonviolent Communication: A Language of Life.* Encinitas, CA: PuddleDancer, 2003.

Saotome, Mitsugi. *The Principles of Aikido.* Boston: Shambhala Publications, 1989.

Schacter, Daniel L. *The Seven Sins of Memory: How the Mind Forgets and Remembers.* Boston: Houghton Mifflin, 2001.

Senge, Peter M. *The Fifth Discipline: The Art and Practice of the Learning Organization.* New York: Doubleday, 1990.

Shipley, David, and Will Schwalbe. *Send: Why People Email So Badly and How to Do It Better.* New York: Knopf, 2008.

Simmons, Annette. *The Story Factor: Inspiration, Influence, and Persuasion Through the Art of Storytelling.* New York: Basic Books, 2006.

Stanislavski, Constantin. *An Actor Prepares.* Translated by Elizabeth Reynolds Hapgood. New York: Routledge, 1989.

Strunk, William, Jr., and E. B. White. *The Elements of Style.* New York: Macmillan, 1959.

Vaughan, Diane. *The Challenger Launch Decision: Risky Technology, Culture, and Deviance at NASA.* Chicago: University of Chicago Press, 1996.

Weiss, Alan. *Million Dollar Consulting: The Professional's Guide to Growing a Practice.* New York: McGraw-Hill: 2003.

Welch, Jack. *JACK: Straight from the Gut.* With John A. Byrne. New York: Warner Business Books, 2003.

Yamashita, Keith, and Sandra Spataro. *Unstuck: A Tool for Yourself, Your Team, and Your World.* New York: Penguin, 2004.

Yule, George. *The Study of Language,* 3rd ed. New York: Cambridge University Press, 2006.

Zander, Rosamund Stone, and Benjamin Zander. *The Art of Possibility: Transforming Professional and Personal Life.* Boston: Harvard Business School Press, 2000.